Tourism and Generation Y

———————————————

Mixed Sources
Product group from well-managed
forests and other controlled sources
www.fsc.org Cert no. SA-COC-1565
© 1996 Forest Stewardship Council

FSC

Tourism and Generation Y

Edited by

Pierre Benckendorff

James Cook University, Australia

Gianna Moscardo

James Cook University, Australia

Donna Pendergast

Griffith University, Australia

www.cabi.org

CABI is a trading name of CAB International

CABI Head Office
Nosworthy Way
Wallingford
Oxfordshire OX10 8DE
UK

CABI North American Office
875 Massachusetts Avenue
7th Floor
Cambridge, MA 02139
USA

Tel: +44 (0)1491 832111
Fax: +44 (0)1491 833508
E-mail: cabi@cabi.org
Website: www.cabi.org

Tel: +1 617 395 4056
Fax: +1 617 354 6875
E-mail: cabi-nao@cabi.org

A catalogue record for this book is available from the British Library, London, UK.

Library of Congress Cataloging-in-Publication Data

Tourism and generation Y / edited by Pierre Benckendorff, Gianna Moscardo, Donna Pendergast.
  p. cm.
  Includes bibliographical references and index.
  ISBN 978-1-84593-601-3 (alk. paper)
1. Tourism.   2. Tourism--Social aspects.   3. Culture and tourism.   I. Benckendorff,
Pierre.   II. Moscardo, Gianna.   III. Pendergast, Donna.

G155.A1T589135 2010
306.4'819--dc22

2009023331

ISBN-13: 978 1 84593 601 3

Typeset by SPi, Pondicherry, India.
Printed and bound in the UK by the MPG Books Group.

The paper used for the text pages in this book is FSC certified. The FSC (Forest Stewardship Council) is an international network to promote responsible management of the world's forests.

Contents

Contributors

Amanda Ayling, *Griffith Business School, Gold Coast Campus, Griffith University, Gold Coast QLD 4222, Australia. a.ayling@griffith.edu.au*

Pierre Benckendorff, *School of Business, James Cook University, Queensland 4810, Australia. pierre.benckendorff@jcu.edu.au*

Sandy Blair, *University of Florida, 325 FLG PO Box 118209, Gainesville, FL 32611, USA. sdblair@hhp.ufl.edu*

Russell Brayley, *School of Recreation, Health and Tourism, George Mason University, 10900 University Blvd, 4E5, Manassas, VA 20110, USA. rbrayley@gmu.edu*

Jeremy Buultjens, *Regional Futures Institute, School of Commerce and Management, Block R, Southern Cross University, Military Drive, Lismore, NSW 2480, Australia. jeremy.buultjens@scu.edu.au*

Grant Cairncross, *School of Tourism & Hospitality, Southern Cross University, Hogbin Drive, Coffs Harbour, NSW 2450, Australia. grant.cairncross@scu.edu.au*

Carl Cater, *Institute of Biological, Environmental & Rural Sciences, Aberystwyth University, Llanbadarn, Aberystwyth, Ceredigion SY23 3AL, UK. cic@aber.ac.uk*

Stephen Charters, *Reims Management School, France, 59 rue Pierre Taittinger, 51100 Reims, France; and Edith Cowan University, Perth, Australia. stephen.charters@reims-ms.fr*

Barbara C. Coleman, *Hull College of Business, Augusta State University, 2500 Walton Way, Augusta, GA 30904–2200, USA. bcoleman@aug.edu*

Joanna Fountain, *Environment, Society and Design Faculty, Lincoln University, PO Box 84, Lincoln, 7647, New Zealand. joanna.fountain@lincoln.ac.nz*

Petra Glover, *The University of Queensland, School of Tourism, GPN 3, Level 4, St Lucia Qld 4072, Australia; and University of East London Business School, 4–6 University Way, London E16 2RD, United Kingdom. p.glover@uel.ac.uk*

Yu-Chin Huang, *Graduate Institute of Sustainable Tourism and Recreation Management, National TaiChung University, 140 Min-Sheng Road, Taichung City 403, Taiwan. ychuang@mail.ntcu.edu.tw*

Hochan Jang, *Korea National Open University, Jongno-Gu, DongSung-Dong 169, Seoul, Korea 110-791. hcjang@knou.ac.kr*

Gayle Jennings, *Griffith Business School, Gold Coast Campus, Griffith University, Gold Coast QLD 4222, Australia. g.jennings@griffith.edu.au*

Young-Sook Lee, *Griffith Business School, Gold Coast Campus, Griffith University, Gold Coast QLD 4222, Australia. young-sook.lee@griffith.edu.au*

Seokho Lee, *Korea National Open University, Jongno-Gu, DongSung-Dong 169, Seoul, Korea 110-791. gaddi@knou.ac.kr*

Marsha D. Loda, *Hull College of Business, Augusta State University, 2500 Walton Way, Augusta, GA 30904-2200, USA. mloda@aug.edu*

Brooke Lunny, *Surf Coast Tourism, PO Box 350, Torquay, Victoria 3228, Australia. blunny@ surfcoast.vic.gov.au*

Gianna Moscardo, *School of Business, James Cook University, Queensland 4810, Australia. gianna.moscardo@jcu.edu.au*

Claudia Ollenburg, *School of Hotel, Resort and Tourism Management, Bond University, Gold Coast, Queensland, 4229, Australia. collenbu@bond.edu.au*

Minkyung Park, *School of Recreation, Health and Tourism, George Mason University, 10900 University Blvd, 4E5, Manassas, VA 20110, USA. mparka@gmu.edu*

Donna Pendergast, *School of Education and Professional Studies, Gold Coast Campus, Griffith University, Queensland 4222, Australia. d.pendergast@griffith.edu.au*

Lori Pennington-Gray, *University of Florida, 325 FLG PO Box 118209, Gainesville, FL 32611, USA. penngray@hhp.ufl.edu*

James F. Petrick, *Department of Recreation, Park and Tourism Sciences, Texas A&M University, 2261 TAMU, College Station, TX77843-2261, USA. jpetrick@tamu.edu*

Scott Richardson, *School of Hospitality & Tourism, Taylor's University College, Level 3, Block C, Leisure Commerce Square, No. 9 Jalan PJS 8/9, 46150 Petaling Jaya, Selangor Darul Ehsan, Malaysia. scott.richardson@taylors.edu.my*

Jeff Wilks, *Tourism Safety, 64 Anchorage Way, Runaway Bay, Queensland 4216, Australia; and School of Public Health and Tropical Medicine, James Cook University, Townsville, Queensland 4810, Australia. jwilks@tourismsafety.com*

About the Editors

Pierre Benckendorff, PhD, is a senior lecturer in Tourism Management and Business in the School of Business, James Cook University, Australia. He has taught and developed undergraduate and postgraduate curricula in introductory tourism management, international tourism, tourism transportation, tourism technologies, tourism analysis, and personal and professional skills in business and marketing communications. His research interests include visitor attraction management, tourist shopping, tourism in built environments, tourism and technology, bibliometric analysis of tourism, tourism and generation Y, and tourism education. He has authored and co-authored a number of academic articles and publications in these areas. Pierre is a 'cusper', born between Generations X and Y. His partner and siblings are members of Generation Y and he is the proud father of the next great generation of youth.

Gianna Moscardo, PhD, is a professor of Business Studies and Associate Dean of Research in the Faculty of Law, Business and the Creative Arts at James Cook University (JCU), Australia. She has authored or co-authored more than 140 refereed international research publications including three research books and four edited books, 60 articles in international academic journals, 34 chapters in edited academic books and 42 refereed papers published in international conference proceedings (including 2 best paper awards). She has published with 42 different co-authors including JCU colleagues, other academics – within Australia and internationally – research students and research staff. Gianna's contribution to tourism as a field of study has been acknowledged by her peers with her election to the International Academy for the Study of Tourism (IAST). She is a member of the editorial boards of the *Journal of Travel Research and Tourism Analysis*. Gianna describes herself as a Gen Yer trapped in the body of a Baby Boomer. She has two Gen Y children and Gen Z grandchildren.

Donna Pendergast, PhD, is Associate Professor and Head of the School of Education and Professional Studies at Griffith University, Gold Coast Campus, Australia. She has published widely in the fields of teacher education, particularly middle school, adolescents, learning and engagement, family and consumer studies, public health, generational theory with a focus on Y generation, and hospitality and tourism education. In 2007, she published the book *The Millennial Adolescent*, which took a socio-cultural look at contemporary school students and their multi-generational teachers. The lens employed for this venture was generational theory. Donna has presented more than 50 school professional-development sessions along with several international keynote addresses on the topic of generational theory applied to a range of contexts. Donna has Silent Generation parents and is an X Gener, married to a Baby Boomer. She has X Generation siblings, four Y Generation nieces and nephews and a Z Generation daughter.

Introduction

Tourism is often described as a contemporary social phenomenon, and as such the relationship between tourism and society is complex and mediated by many variables. The purpose of this book is to explore the concept of generational cohorts and its implications for tourism. In particular, this book focuses on a generational cohort variously referred to as Generation Y, the Y Generation, the Net or Web Generation, the Millennials, Nexters, Thatcher's Children, Generation Next, Echo Boomers or the Digital Generation, and these labels are used interchangeably throughout the book. While there is some dispute over the exact time frame, most definitions used in this book refer to people born between 1977 and 2003 – although some chapters discuss a narrower range within these broad parameters. This generational cohort is now reaching adulthood, creating new opportunities for research exploring their characteristics, values, attitudes and consumption patterns in tourism. This cohort will by 2020 become the leaders, managers and consumers of tourism experiences.

Cohort analysis is based on the notion that generational cohorts share a common and distinctive social character shaped by their experiences through time. This distinctive and unique pattern of values, attitudes and behaviours has important implications for how a generation will respond to, and create change in, a number of public and social arenas. While a focus on generational or cohort effects is not a new theme, what is noteworthy about Generation Y is the widespread discussion of this as a uniquely different generation to those that have gone before. Within the tourism literature, the evidence to support such claims is limited and there is no substantial empirical support for the assumption that this age cohort shares a set of social values and attitudes that is both widespread within the cohort and uniquely different to other cohorts.

Much of the material describing Generation Y and proposing future implications from these descriptions is generated by the mass media, commercial consultants and social survey research companies. This information is, however, limited in that few, if any, methodological details are provided, and often quite contradictory claims are made leading to very disparate conclusions and recommendations. In some countries, the popular media has enthusiastically embraced the concept of generational differences and this has served to reinforce the notion of generational difference in the minds of the general public. In Australia, two high rating television shows – *Packed to the Rafters,* launched in August 2008, and *Talkin' 'Bout Your Generation*, launched in May 2009 – are based around the notion of generational stereotypes. Many Hollywood films also reinforce these generational stereotypes, irrespective of whether they are actually accurate. From a sociological perspective, these observations suggest that generational differences exist simply because people believe they exist – in a sense generational cohorts become a self-perpetuating fabrication. Generational stereotypes have also infiltrated the tourism industry. The 'Asia-Pacific Baby-Boomer Tourism Summit' was recently hosted in Sydney, Australia, and was designed to define and understand the Baby-Boomer generation and to respond to the issues influencing its growth. The Queensland Tourism Industry Council (QTIC), also in Australia, has recently established a project called QTIC-Y to raise the awareness of Generation-Y priorities to the wider tourism industry, government and media. These developments suggest that there is a growing need for an academic voice to provide critical appraisal and research.

Generation Y is emerging as a topic of interest in academic literature but the material that is available in academic publications is almost exclusively based on US populations. In contrast with other age-related market segments (i.e. seniors' tourism), surprisingly little research has been conducted on Generation Y and tourism. The genesis of this book represents an attempt to explore whether generational cohorts such as Generation Y can be identified in a tourism context, and whether they exhibit characteristics that are different to other generations. A great deal of tourism research has focused on cross-cultural differences and their implications for the management of tourism organizations and destinations. While the term 'culture' has many connotations, in some respects it can be argued that cultural differences are akin to generational differences and that these differences are equally important in the management of tourism.

The book includes a range of applied and conceptual chapters. The applied chapters offer a mix of both qualitative and quantitative studies. While there are a number of contributions from Australasia, the book also includes chapters from North America and Asia. These chapters have been arranged into three parts. The first four chapters adopt a holistic approach. The first chapter by Donna Pendergast provides an overview of generational cohorts and discusses some of the unique characteristics that have been associated with Generation Y. The second chapter by Gianna Moscardo and Pierre Benckendorff provides a more critical appraisal of the research, in an attempt to separate Generation-Y myths from the facts. This chapter also presents a framework for understanding and researching generational differences and argues for the need for longitudinal research. Yu-Chin Huang and James Petrick's chapter adopts a market segmentation approach to explore the differences between the Baby Boomers, Gen X and Gen Y. The fourth chapter applies a simple version of the model proposed by Moscardo and Benckendorff in Chapter 2 to a longitudinal data set, in an attempt to systematically analyse the generational characteristics of travellers visiting the Great Barrier Reef in Australia.

Part II of the book examines the behaviour of Gen Y travellers in a range of tourism contexts and niche areas, including wine tourism, adventure tourism and nature-based tourism. The qualitative contribution on wine tourism (Joanna Fountain and Steve Charters) summarizes the experience of 24 Generation-Y participants visiting various wineries in Australasia, and identifies a number of implications based on expectations of cellar-door experiences among this group. In a similar vein, the chapter from Gayle Jennings and colleagues provides some insight into the importance of quality to Generation-Y adventure travellers in Australia. The chapter by Lori Pennington-Gray and Sandy Blair offers a strong empirical contribution using Palmore's cohort analysis to determine whether Generation Y is mainly responsible for the increased participation in nature-based travel in North America. The chapter by Minkyung Park and colleagues on the Net Generation in South Korea is particularly interesting as it represents the only Asian contribution to this book. This chapter begins to address the very clear need for further studies to extend our understanding of Generation Y across a range of ethnic groups, religions and nationalities. The final two chapters of Part II represent strong conceptual contributions from Jeff Wilks and Donna Pendergast, but deal with two quite different issues related to traveller safety. A chapter on beach safety provides a unique perspective on two groups of Y-Generation youth involved in tourism: travellers and those tasked with ensuring their safety. The chapter on personal safety adopts a much broader perspective and discusses external threats such as terrorism and crime, and physical and environmental risks that confront Generation-Y travellers.

The final part of this book examines the role of Generation Y as consumers and producers of tourism experiences. The chapter by Marsha Loda and Barbara Coleman argues convincingly that while Gen Y is the most technologically savvy in history, they still continue to consume traditional media such as television and magazines, which should not be ignored by advertisers. The next two chapters examine Generation Y as employees and producers of tourism experiences. Scott Richardson presents a useful analysis of Generation Y's attitudes and perceptions towards a career in the industry, while Grant Cairncross and Jeremy Buultjens present the results of a series of focus groups and individual interviews with tourism and hospitality managers. The final chapter by Petra Glover attempts to provide a glimpse of the future by presenting an overview of the opportunities and challenges that may arise when the older members of Generation Y are in their 30s and early 40s.

In spite of the work presented in this book, there continues to be a paucity of data on generational differences and their impact on tourism. From a marketing perspective, there is a need to examine not only Generation Y, but also Generation X and the Baby Boomers, who represent substantial market segments. From a human-resource management perspective, there are some serious gaps in our understanding of generational differences and their implications for tourism workplaces. This book seeks to provide a landmark publication discussing the latest developments, trends and research dealing with Generation Y and tourism. It is hoped that this book will stimulate debate and interest around the topic of generational cohorts and tourism. The quest to understand generational characteristics is never ending. As the chapter by Petra Glover illustrates, as each generation passes through different life-cycle stages, there are likely to be new questions that need to be answered. Tourism researchers and scholars are in a unique position to attempt to answer these questions in an objective manner.

Pierre Benckendorff

Gianna Moscardo

Donna Pendergast

1 Getting to Know the Y Generation

Donna Pendergast
Griffith University, Gold Coast, Australia

Introduction

The profile of the tourism industry is characterized by multigenerational visitors and a multigenerational workforce. A major shift in the balance of generational dominance is currently occurring, with the 'Baby Boomer' generation exiting the leadership roles in the workforce and the Y Generation dramatically entering, both in the workforce and as visitors. According to generational theory, each generation brings with them somewhat predictable traits, values and beliefs, along with skills, attributes, capacities, interests, expectations and preferred modus operandi directly attributable to their generational location. For the tourism industry, insights gained through the lens of generational theory has the potential to guide the incentives, the motivators, the leadership models and the overall culture of the profession to better connect with the Y Generation as the most recent members of the tourism workforce and as the current and future visitor market. This chapter sets out to provide some foundations around the concept of generations, discuss the demography and unique character traits of members of the Y Generation by drawing on a renowned generational theorist, and begin to consider this cohort as tourism, consumers. This chapter will thus serve as a platform for the following chapters in the book.

Generational Theory

Concept

The idea of 'generation' and 'generation gap' derived from generational theory is not a new concept (Mannheim, 1952), nor is it uncontested (Donnison, 2007; Huntley, 2006). Furthermore, there is not one accepted or 'true' version of generational theory, there are a number of competing versions available as credible and legitimate for theorizing using this framework. This chapter draws on several of the more popular and internationally renowned theorists in the field, in particular Mannheim (1952), Howe and Strauss (2000) and Huntley (2006). In addition, the work of newcomers Fields *et al.* (2008) will be utilized.

Generational theory seeks to understand and characterize cohorts of people according to their membership of a generation, which is objectively assigned according to the year of birth. It is a dynamic, socio-cultural theoretical framework that employs a broad brush-stroke approach, rather than an individual focus. Hence, it features patterns and propensities across the generational group, rather than individuals. Generations and generational units are informally defined by demographers, the press and media, popular culture, market researchers and by members of the generation themselves (Pendergast, 2007; Fields *et al.*, 2008). While members of the generation are alive, it is known as a living generation, and will continue to evolve and redefine itself, usually within bounds that are broadly predictable from the traits of the generation.

Generational theory is one way of investigating aspects of the tourism industry. Like other demographic lenses, it allows those in the field to consider possibilities utilizing a particular framework. As such, it is burdened by limitations and assumptions, many of which will become evident as this chapter unfolds.

The first of the challenges of adopting a generational perspective is that there is no absolute consensus as to the exact calendar years constituting each generation. The boundaries adopted in this chapter align relatively closely with many generational theorists, with 20–22 years being the typical generational range (see Table 1.1).

Generational theory is originally an American concept, but it is widely applicable to anglophones, that is, those who speak English natively or by adoption and have a cultural background associated with the English language, regardless of ethnic or geographical differences. With the effects of globalization and the permeation of Information and Communications Technologies (ICTs), especially access to the world wide web (WWW), the creep of anglophone influence and the monoculturalization of society means the number of people who can be included in the generational cohorts is increasing dramatically. Many professions with a global reach such as tourism utilize English as the main language for information dissemination, and this reinforces and facilitates the reach and effect of generational patterns and impacts (Fields *et al.*, 2008).

Table 1.1. A summary of living birth generations.

Birth years	Generation name	Age range in 2009
1901–1924	GI	85–108
1925–1942	Silent	67–84
1943–1960	Baby Boomer	49–66
1961–1981	Generation X	28–48
1982–2002	Generation Y	7–27
2003	Generation Z	6 or younger

Generational location, actuality and units

Several decades ago Mannheim (1952) developed the core tenets of generational theory, which remain both current and relevant today, including the concepts of generational location, generation as actuality and generation units. Each of these core tenets will be explained.

Generational location is a passive category based on the chronological span of time for the birth years of a cohort of individuals. This location will affect the potential of the generation. As Mannheim (1952, p.291) explains:

> [B]elonging to the same generations or age group endows the individuals sharing in [it] with a common location in the social and historical process, and thereby limits them to a specific range of potential experiences, predisposing them for a certain characteristic mode of thought and experience, and a characteristic type of historically relevant action.

Generational actuality moves from the passive location designation to consider the way a generation responds to 'social changes and how these responses form the persona of the generation' (Donnison, 2007, p. 4). The basic principle is that a cohort sharing a generational location also shares a set of experiences during their formative years, including a particular set of social and economic conditions. These shared experiences and conditions influence the generation collective in particular ways that in turn shape their thinking, values and beliefs, forming the generational persona. Extending this concept further, members of the same generation experience events while at similar life stages, with those events that occurred during the formative years having a particularly profound impact on the enduring characteristics – traits, values and beliefs – of the generation.

As detailed in Table 1.2, a typical lifespan and the social role associated with the values and belief systems goes through four phases – acquiring, testing, asserting and transferring.

Generation units are the subgroups within the generation timespan, which acknowledges variation within the typically 20–22-year generation location span. For example, Generation Y, the most recent generation completing its

Table 1.2. Four phases in life.

Phase of life	Ages	Social role
Childhood (formative years)	0–20	Growth: being nurtured, acquiring values and belief systems
Young adulthood	21–41	Vitality: testing values
Mid-adulthood	42–62	Power: asserting values, managing institutions
Elderhood	63–83	Leadership: transferring values, leading institutions

Generational location, actuality and units, which are integral components of the theory of generations, point to the idea of inter-generational differences, exemplified by the traits, values and belief systems of the various generations. Traits of generations are used to construct common patterns such as attitudes to work, political behaviours, consumer patterns, qualities in the workplace and family orientation. These traits, values and beliefs are defined by demographers, the press and media, popular culture, market researchers, sociologists and by members of the generation themselves (Howe, 2006; Huntley, 2006; Fields *et al.*, 2008).

birth cycle, is made up of three generation units: Generation Why (born 1982–1985); Millennials (MilGens; born 1985–1999); and iGeneration (born 1999–2002). Members of the Generation Why unit are on the cusp of the X Generation, so share some common traits with that generation, while members of the iGeneration are on the cusp of the Z generation, so are likely to exhibit some of the traits typical of that generation. Millennials are the central band of the Y-Generation cohort, so are likely to exhibit the character traits of that generation most compellingly.

Generation type: idealist, reactive, hero, artist

According to Howe and Strauss (2000), generations follow a repeating cycle, with four generational types typically following in the order of idealist, reactive, hero and artist. When the generational types are tracked across the life cycle, there are characteristics that appear consistently throughout successive generations based on this factor. These are outlined in Table 1.3.

Table 1.3. Characteristics of generational types. (Adapted from Strauss and Howe, 2000.)

Life-cycle type	Idealist (prophet)	Reactive (depressed/ nomad)	Heroic	Artistic (adaptive)
Childhood				
Nurture received	Relaxed	Under-protected	Tightening	Overprotected
Young adulthood				
Style	Reflecting	Competing	Building	Remodelling
Nurture given	Tightening	Overprotective	Relaxed	Under-protective
Mid-adulthood				
Attitude	Judgemental	Exhausted	Energetic	Experimental
Elderhood				
How perceived	Wise, visionary	Persuasive	Busy, confident	Sensitive, flexible
Leadership style	Austere, safe	Pragmatic	Grand, inclusive	Pluralistic
Motto	Truth	Persuasion	Power	Love
Positive attributes	Principled, resolute	Savvy, practical, perceptive	Rational, competent	Caring, open-minded
Negative attributes	Selfish, arrogant, ruthless	Pecuniary, amoral	Overbold, insensitive, unreflective	Indecisive, guilt-ridden

Generations move as a collective through society, passing through the four phases of life, occupying different phases at different times and always maintaining their unique generational characteristics. Each generation acquires values and belief systems principally during the formative or childhood years of each generation. Table 1.4 provides a summary of the typical values and beliefs for selected generations, which also incorporates the features of the generational type.

In summary, generational theory brings together four main elements:

- Repeating trends based on generational type (idealist, reactive, heroic and artistic).
- Recognition that the formative years of childhood, where exposure to a range of factors occurs, determines the fundamental values and belief system of the generation.
- Recognition of the life-cycle stage (childhood, young adulthood, mid-adulthood and elder adulthood (elderhood)), and hence characteristics evident for the generational type at that stage.
- The relevant birth generation with its unique attributes at any given time (e.g. Baby Boomer, Generation X).

Current living generations

In order to gain the full benefit of generational theory, it is important to assemble the various elements together. Table 1.5 outlines the key features of the current major living generations.

Baby Boomers, already identified as an idealist or prophet generation, are entering elderhood. This cohort is regarded as being a 'driven' generation, with clear agendas and purpose. The civil rights movement is an example of the type of energy and direction a prophet generation might have. Members of the Baby-Boomer generation currently dominate many of the leadership positions in the tourism field, both in the private and public domains. Typically, policy makers currently setting and driving agendas are also Baby Boomers. Some of the older Baby Boomers are the grey nomad cohort often cited in the tourism literature. Members of this generation have typically spent their working lives developing and refining their expertise. They have a strong work ethic, believe in authority, are comparatively formal and accept authoritarian leadership and control. They are analytical and work well independently. They are prepared to wait in turn for promotions, which are often based on seniority.

Table 1.4. Differences between selected generations. (From Pendergast, 2009.)

Factors	Baby Boomer	Generation X	Generation Y
Beliefs and values	Work ethic, security	Variety, freedom	Lifestyle, fun
Motivations	Advancement, responsibility	Individuality	Self-discovery, relational
Decision making	Authority, brand loyalty	Experts, information, brand switchers	Friends, little brand loyalty
Earning and spending	Conservative, pay upfront	Credit savvy, confident, investors	Uncertain spenders, short-term wants, credit-dependent
Learning styles	Auditory, content-driven, monologue	Auditory or visual dialogue	Visual, kinaesthetic, multi-sensory
Marketing and communication	Mass	Descriptive, direct	Participative, viral, through friends
Training environment	Classroom style, formal, quiet atmosphere	Round-table style, planned, relaxed ambience	Unstructured, interactive
Management and leadership	Control, authority, analysers	Cooperation, competency, doers	Consensus, creativity, feelers

Table 1.5. Current cyclic location and characteristics of generations.

Generation	Current phase of life	Social role	Stage of cycle
Silent	Elderhood	Leadership: transferring values, leading institutions	Artistic
Baby Boomer	Elderhood	Leadership: transferring values, leading institutions	Idealist
Generation X	Midlife	Power: asserting values, managing institutions	Reactive
Generation Y	Young adulthood	Vitality: testing values	Hero
Generation Z	Childhood	Growth: being nurtured, acquiring values and belief systems	Artistic

The nomad or reactive generation always follows the idealist generation, and is typified as extremely cynical and often depressed. It is a response to the energy and enthusiasm of the previous prophet generation. Generation X is the current living nomad generation, and hence is regarded as pessimistic and depressed. Members of Generation X are in the midlife phase of their life cycle. They are entering the power phase, and frequently can be found in management roles in the workforce. The older of the X Generation are moving into leadership positions. Ironically, this generation is also known as the Baby Bust generation, and there is a proportionately smaller number of Generation X compared to the previous Baby Boomer generation. Members of the X Generation are also typically experts in their fields, but differ from Baby Boomers in that they see cooperative leadership and teams as desirable work practices.

The next in the cycle is the hero generation. Currently, Y Generation members are the hero generation. They are characterized as conventional and committed, with respect for authority and with civic pride. The hero generation usually produces some key influential international leaders. Y-Generation heroes are team-oriented, have a focus on how they feel and experience events and workplaces. They are expert novices – good at learning new things – which has direct consequences for workplace training and professional development models. They are collaborative and interactive, and believe in performance and merit, not seniority, which is often at odds with the values of both the X-Generation and Baby-Boomer managers and leaders with assumed seniority and expertise over Y-Generation members.

The generation following the hero generation is the artists, a generation that is regarded as emotional and indecisive, and at the opposite end of the continuum from the hero generation in terms of leadership and initiative.

All of these elements of generational theory, like other forms of supposition and speculative analytic tools, provide a particular way of reflecting on the past, and if harnessed effectively, of providing possible insights and directions for the future. This chapter now turns to the focus of the book – exploring the Y generation.

Y Generation

Generational theory has much to offer to those wanting a foundational understanding of the young people in our society, who are entering the workforce and who are the new visitors in the tourism market. This cohort is in the young adulthood phase of life, with the social role of vitality and testing of values. Drawing on a wide range of theorists in the field such as Howe and Strauss (2000), Huntley (2006) and Fields *et al.* (2008), it is possible to establish some consistently articulated characteristics of the generation. It is a hero generation, with a focus on brands, friends, fun and digital culture. Members of the Y Generation are confident and relaxed, conservative and the most educated generation ever. They have been sheltered, but have had high expectations placed on them, they are special and safety is paramount. They are impatient and self-focused, yet value teams and collaboration. They are multitaskers who are networked rather than individually focused, hence are strongly influenced by friends and peers. All these characteristics are generated from the interplay between the social and economic context during the formative years of the generation, coupled with the effects of the older generations providing nurturing and care, developing policies and community practices, shaping the character traits of the Y Generation. The effect, as Fields *et al.* (2008, p. 2) note, is that 'Gen Y, as a group, has tremendous influence in our culture, with a powerful impact on the workplace' and they are increasingly portrayed as being a 'cultural phenomenon'. This identification of Generation Y as representing a major generational shift is the product of generational shaping, which is regarded as profound when compared to any previous generation in human history. The reason for this is now explained.

Societal context shaping the Y Generation

Since the early 1980s, we have witnessed a major paradigm shift in society that has aligned with the formative and hence values-acquisition years of our most recent full birth generation – the Y generation (Huntley, 2006). The last 25–30 years have been an era of unprecedented transition from industrial to information-based culture and economy, from print-based to multi-mediated, digital approaches to communication effects of ICTs, globalization and the emergence of the digital native. The simultaneous alignment of Generation Y and The Information Age has had an enormous impact, creating a larger than usual generation gap – or values and character-trait difference – between previous generations and the Y Generation, a gap accentuated by what is now recognized as the most significant shift in our society to date, when compared to similar but smaller shifts occurring with the introduction of the printing press in the 15th century, and before that alphabetic literacy in 4th century (Pendergast,

2007). This is the reason why Y-Generational work is so important. It is critical that the gap between X and Y Generation does not become a chasm, serving to separate the generations in society. This imperative has been identified by the United Nations (2005, p. 2) and is evident in the comment:

> there is a simple but often ignored fact: young people today are different from any of the previous generations of youth. It is essential to ensure that youth interventions are relevant and valid for the current young generation in society and not mired in the realities of times past.

Y Generation is the first generation born into The Information Age, and for this reason members are known as digital natives (Prensky, 2006). Everyone alive today whose birth precedes the Y Generation is known as a digital immigrant. Digital natives are characterized as: operating at twitch speed (not conventional speed); employing random access (not step-by-step); parallel processing (not linear processing); graphics first (not text); play-oriented (not work); connected (not stand-alone). They get more screen time (TV, computer) than fresh air. Consider the following:

- 97% of Australian Y-Generation students have access to computers at home, including 82% of indigenous students.
- 87% of Australian students use a computer at home on a frequent basis.
- 74% of students use the Internet frequently as a tool for finding information and almost 70% for communication.
- Socio-economic background does not have a great effect on use of computers or confidence (Thomson and De Bortoli, 2007).

These young people are members of the Y Generation and their native comfort level with ICTs ensures they connect with the digital world through play, enjoyment and desire, rather than as a necessary requirement of work, as is the case for most Baby-Boomer and Generation-X digital immigrants. A flow-on effect of this digital lifestyle is evident in marketing and communication, with a shift across the generations from mass marketing and communication that appeals and is effective for the Baby Boomer generation, through to direct marketing for Generation X; and then to viral, participative, interactive and networked for Y-Generation members. This means that others' opinions – in particular the opinions of their friends – is highly valued by Generation-Y members. In this case, the meaning of 'friends' also differs for generations, with Baby Boomers and X-Generation members classifying friends in quite different ways. For the Y Generation, a friend is a member of a network and may be relatively unknown to the individual, while for previous generations a friend is more likely to be a person you feel comfortable meeting for coffee. This points to the removal of geographical boundaries for the Y Generation. Digital technology facilitates the end of enclosure based on proximity, making the new neighbourhood of the Y Generation the global digital community. The world is literally the playground for this generation.

This loss of boundaries and enclosure refers also to the sharing of knowledge and information, with access through channels such as the world wide web available to all who have network access and basic search skills. Knowledge is no longer confined to professionals with years of education and the development of detailed knowledge, as was the case prior to era of digital natives. Wikipedia, the free multilingual encyclopedia written collaboratively by volunteers around the world, is often the starting point for Y-Generation natives, along with their X- and Baby Boomer and prior-generation immigrants, to commence gathering information on any topic under investigation. This results in a flattening of the value of expert knowledge, which in past generations was typically acquired over a lifetime and led to the positioning of those individuals as the powerful leaders in society.

The digital character of members of the Y Generation has led to the proliferation of digital tools. For instance, a recent American study of more than 7000 Y-Generation members found that 97% own a computer and 94% own a mobile phone (Reynol and Mastrodicasa, 2007).

In terms of their computer use, the following example demonstrates some typical patterns. The social-networking website Facebook, launched in early 2004, has the following features:

- More than 150 million active users, approximately 45% males and 55% females.
- The largest demographic is the 18–25-year-old group.
- The average user has 100 friends on the site.
- More than 3 billion minutes are spent on Facebook each day (worldwide).
- More than 13 million users update their status at least once each day.
- More than 800 million photos and 5 million videos are uploaded to the site each month.
- More than 20 million active user groups exist on the site. (http://www.facebook.com/press/info.php?statistics)

These statistics corroborate the Y-Generation digital traits of being connected, play-oriented and graphics first explicitly (Fields *et al.*, 2008). In a study of millennial students, McMahon and Pospisil (2005) monitored their use of technology in both education and social settings, characterizing them as having:

- Information connectedness – the need for rapid access to information.
- Multitasking – the ability to manage multiple aspects of their lives at once.
- A focus on immediacy – an intolerance for delays.

Generation Y is also the first generation born into the 'age of terrorism'. As global citizens they have been shaped as a cohort unlike any previous generation in this domain. This is a combination of both timing – the series of terrorism events that has occurred during their formative years has happened when their values and belief systems are being shaped as a collective; and exposure – ICTs have the capacity to expose large numbers of people to almost instant news of terrorism and other events. The most profound of these to date, and now recognized as a marker between Generation X and Generation Y, are the 11 September 2001 terrorist attacks in the USA. In these attacks in New York on the World Trade Centre twin tower landmark buildings, and in Washington, DC, on the Pentagon, using civilian aircraft hijacked by the terrorists, the total number of victims is recorded as

2998, the overwhelming majority of whom were civilians, including nationals from over 80 different countries. Many people across the world watched in shock, horror and amazement as the events unfolded, and were telecast live on their television screens as a spectacular form of infotainment. This medium gives the viewer a sense of being live on site, involved in the action of an event as it unfolds. The sharing of information is and often neither edited nor refined, and often taken from a range of angles, facilitating the viewer to experience the event in a more informed way than many of those actually involved.

It is not surprising that a recent study of teenaged members of the Y Generation (13–17 years old in 2006) conducted by the New Politics Institute (2006) found that these young people are 'particularly concerned with security issues such as crime and terrorism' and they seem to be 'strikingly shaped' by such experiences during their formative years. In creating fear, terrorist events are often of an incredulous nature, such as the indiscriminate and random targeting of civilians including children in public places. This reinforces the difficulty of avoiding terrorist incidents, as one can simply be in the wrong place at the wrong time. Terrorism events and their viral dissemination using digital tools have resulted in a strong safety net being thrown around the Y Generation. With this sheltered background, the management and policing of the 'risk' society (Beck, 1992) is a prevailing characteristic of the generation.

Financially, the generations differ in their behaviours resulting from the societal trends in their community. Y-Generation members are credit-dependent, and often financially dependent on parents and others much later in life than was typical for previous generations. For this reason they have been nicknamed the 'helicopter kids' because they hover about the family home (Salt, 2006). This compares to Baby Boomers who are collectively regarded as being conservative spenders and a generation with a 'pay upfront' approach. This contrasts starkly with the Y Generation, who are uncertain spenders, with short-term wants, who are likely to rely on credit. They also have many more temptations to spend money and the desire and need to constantly update technol-

ogy tools to remain at the edge of their potential dominates many consumer behaviours. The global financial crisis of 2008 is impacting on the Y Generation at a time they are making their entry into the workforce. Predictions of job losses, business closure, credit tightening and house-price slumps mark a shift from an era of stable, robust and confident economic times to a more uncertain financial future.

When these impacts are taken together, there is an emphasis on immediacy, short-term satisfaction, risk, safety and communication for Generation Y. It is therefore not surprising that values for this generation reflect the need for safety and security, and a certain confidence and set of capabilities given their capacities with ICTs. Frequent change and technological progress are the comforting realities for the Y Generation, yet the same environment provides unsettling challenges for those generations before them.

While the key societal events shaping the Y Generation are yet to be confirmed, it is likely to include the following factors that significantly impacted on them during their formative years:

- The digital revolution, such as the Internet, WWW, e-mail, chatlines, blogs, short message service (SMS) and texting (the information age).
- Terrorism, such as the World Trade Center attacks (the age of terrorism).
- Financial uncertainty.

Demography of Y Gen

The features of the Y Generation have been detailed by a number of historians including Neil Howe and William Strauss (2000), whose work has informed much of the thinking in this chapter. Their work has been described as 'brilliant', 'applicable to everyone around the world' and 'enlightening'. It is widely used in marketing and communication fields, in product development, in higher education and in the media as a way of targeting defined populations. It has been used by professions and professional association researchers to predict membership and to develop strategic directions to target, engage and retain selected generations (cf. Brooks,

2006, 2008). Much of the information that follows draws directly or indirectly from their extensive work, and from those who have also used their theoretical perspective as a foundation for their own purposes.

Generation Y is the first generation born into a society that features international interdependence and global engagement. It has the technological capability and personal capacity to participate virtually as global community members and, generally speaking, regards itself as a participant of a global community to an extent unprecedented in generational traits. For this reason, a global perspective is the demographic platform for building a profile of Generation Y (Fields *et al.*, 2008).

In 1982, the first birth year of the millennium generation, the world population was 4,608,724,252, and in 2002, the last of the birth years of the Y Generation, the world population was 6,246,193,906, an increase of 1,638,469, 654 (United States Census Bureau, 2006). In 1982, Australia's population was 15,184,200. In 2002, at the birth end of the Y Generation, it had grown to 19,662,800, an increase of over 4 million (Australian Bureau of Statistics (ABS), 2004). While the difference does not constitute the number of births that also include migration and is impacted upon by a longer life expectancy, clearly there is a large number of the Y Generation cohort born in the world – the United Nations has estimated as many as 1.8 billion (United Nations, 2005).

The United States Census Bureau (2006) predicts that part-way during their lifetime, members of the Y Generation will see in 2050 the world population rise to 9,536,111,257. This means that the first born of the Y Generation will, at age 68 and well before their life expectancy of 83 for females and 78 for males is reached, experience more than a doubling of the world population. However, the share of young people in the world's total population is gradually declining – the increase in world population is significantly attributable to increased health care and longer life expectancy, increasing the median age, rather than an increased birth rate. For example, in 2000, the median age of the Australian population was 35 years of age. It is projected to gradually increase to 44.6 years of age by the year 2050 (ABS, 2006). This pattern has intergenerational consequences, and the Y Generation is the first generation that will be impacted significantly by these events.

The unique character of the Y Generation

When the societal context and the demography of the generation are taken together, along with the patterns and behaviours that are predicted from the cyclical nature of generations, core traits have been formulated to represent the Y Generation. For this chapter, those developed by Howe (2006) will be utilized.

According to Howe (2006), there are seven core traits typifying the Y Generation. As a collective, they are:

1. Special.
2. Sheltered.
3. Confident.
4. Team-oriented.
5. Conventional.
6. Pressured.
7. Achieving.

Each trait will now be considered in turn.

Special

Y-Generation members regard themselves as special because of their digital capabilities and their membership of comparatively smaller family units. They are also considered by parents to be special because they typically belong to families with fewer children. Many Y-Generation children were planned, with the benefit of birth-control facilities. Individual Y-Generation members are often assigned high expectations and have been exposed to an environment where behaviour management has shifted from punitive to positive reinforcement in environments, such as schools.

Sheltered

Members of the Y Generation are protected by parents and wider community. This is evidenced through policy initiatives such as the mandatory wearing of bike helmets and seat belts, pool fencing and other initiatives that focus on the health and well-being of young people. While these laws apply across the generations, they have been introduced during the formative years of the Y Generation, naturalizing them for this cohort. As a generation they are particularly concerned with security issues such as crime and terrorism and school violence. Terms such as the 'cotton-wool generation' have been used to characterize this trait and to question whether they are overprotected. Generation Y often stay at home longer than members of previous generations have, mostly out of financial necessity. Regardless, this places them under the watchful eye of carers or parents and extends the dependency relationship.

Confident

They accept uncertainty and have experienced to this point a generally sound economic base, and hence a high level of confidence and optimism prevails. Recent economic changes have failed to impact on this confidence level and indeed confirm for Y-Generation members that the only certain thing is uncertainty.

Team-oriented

Experiences in their early years are more likely to predispose this generation to team activities when compared to other generations, examples include organized sports, opportunities for volunteerism, experiencing formal childcare, a focus on group work as a pedagogical strategy in schools and the like contribute to this character trait. Many schooling practices reinforce the value of teams and collaborative practices, impacting particularly during the formative years to consolidate this generational trait. That is not to say that members of Generation Y are effective team members – they still require skill development in this field.

Conventional

Members of the Y Generation cohort are regarded as having relatively conventional aspirations centred on career, work–life balance and citizenship. This is a response to the previous generations who have often committed excessively to achieve positive work outcomes at the expense of family balance (O'Reilly, 2000). They do not want these patterns repeated for themselves.

Pressured

Members of the Y Generation are regarded as being pressured, with formalized activities filling many hours of their days. Many have experienced busy social, school and after-school-care calendars, regardless of their socio-economic profile.

Achieving

This is the most education-minded generation that has lived. Much emphasis is placed on the relationship between education and success. Facilitating this education-mindedness are changes to the traditional school curriculum, with the inclusion of vocational and training possibilities in schooling culture. This trend started in the 1980s, which was a period of profound change in the nature and purpose of secondary schools in Australia. This was largely the result of declining youth-labour markets, combined with changes to student financial support. This is dramatically demonstrated by the national retention rate to year 12, which rose from 35% in 1980 to 77% by 1992 (Fullarton, 2001). Coupled with this trait is the vehicle for achieving higher education standards – typically an extended dependency on family support.

While these seven traits, based on the propositions of Howe (2006), have been utilized in this chapter, it is important to note that there is not a definitive list of character traits agreed to by generational theorists. The traits emerge over time, and are shaped by events and by time itself. Herein lies another of the challenges associated with the utilization of generational theory. Nevertheless, there is a growing interest in the use of generational theory with a focus on Generation Y as the succession generation entering the tourism workforce and as tourists now and in the future. So, what lessons might be learned by employing generational perspectives?

Y Generation and Tourism

The tourism industry has recently demonstrated a commitment to better understand generational differences to ensure both a strong workforce and a strong tourism market.

Y Generation as visitors

A recent study by the World Youth Student and Educational Travel Confederation (WYSETC) of more than 8500 Y-Generation travellers, for example, revealed the following key features about these travellers. They are: travelling more often; exploring more destinations; spending more on travel; booking more over the Internet; hungry for experience; hungry for information; intrepid travellers; and getting a lot out of their travel (Richards, 2007).

Table 1.6 provides an elaboration of each of these features, and makes connections with the seven character traits of the Y Generation.

In essence, Richards captures the spirit of the Y Generation in this statement: 'Travel is a way of life. A certain level of risk is part of travel, even though it can be minimised through careful planning' (Richards, 2007, p. 4). The World Tourism Organization (WTO) notes: 'The unique motivations of young travellers makes this niche market extremely important to the key objectives of the global tourism agenda' (WTO, 2008, p. i). Y-Generation travellers generate an estimated €109 billion annually (Richards, 2007), providing a strong impetus for Baby Boomer and Generation-X tourism owners and operators to understand the unique characteristics of these customers and potential members of the workforce, and to adapt practices and culture appropriately.

Y Generation in the workforce

With respect to the Y-Generation tourism workforce, Table 1.7 presents a collation of general population percentages for each generation

Table 1.6. Y-Generation travellers mapped against generational traits.

Features	Explanation of feature	Mapping against generational trait
Travelling more often	Average number of trips taken has increased in the last 5 years	Confident Pressured
Exploring more destinations	Take more trips outside the local region and explore new areas of the world	Achieving Confident
Spending more on travel	As a proportion of their income, spend more than any other group on international travel	Confident
Booking more over the Internet	Early adopters of new travel technology	Confident Special
Experience hungry	Want a range of different experiences often involving everyday life and culture of places visited, including contact with local people	Team-oriented Achieving Pressured
Information hungry	Consult a greater number of information sources to plan trips	Achieving
Intrepid travellers	Are not deterred by problems such as terrorism, natural disasters and epidemics – mitigate these risks through information	Confident Sheltered
Getting a lot out of their travel	Travel makes them want to travel more, serving as a stimulus to learn and develop, including developing greater cultural understanding	Achieving Conventional Team-oriented

Table 1.7. Generational patterns in the general work population. (From Brooks, 2006.)

	Current population (%)	Working-age adults (%)
GI	3	0
Silent	14	8
Baby Boomer	27	42
Generation X	15	24
Generation Y	41	26

and also the percentage in the workforce. These are American data, but provide a generally repeating pattern of the relative balance between the generations.

There is a growing corpus of theory on the work practices, values and motivators of the Y Generation (cf. Fields *et al.*, 2008). Boomer (2007) regards one of the priorities for attracting and retaining Y-Generational members to be embracing a 'training and learning culture' within the profession. The top three motivators for MilGens are:

1. Meaningful work that makes a difference to the world.
2. Working with committed co-workers who share their values.
3. Meeting their personal goals (Allen, 2004).

MilGens expect to be promoted quickly, to change jobs frequently, are motivated by training and education opportunities, respect leadership, expect flexibility and good working relationships. They promptly disengage if they are dissatisfied with their work situation (Salt, 2006). Long-term loyalty to one employer can carry a 'reverse stigma' for MilGens, the message being they are out of date and lacking in diverse experience (Robert, 2005).

In Table 1.8, key workplace generational traits and motivators are used to provide a basis for suggested strategies for attracting and retaining Y-Generation members in the tourism industry. This is not an exhaustive list, but a sample of the kind of possibilities that must be canvassed to make the profession viable for the MilGen to consider.

Table 1.8. Y-Generation values and motivators with workplace strategies. (From Pendergast, 2009.)

MilGen work values and motivators	Suggested strategies
Flexibility	Expectations of flexible working hours, job sharing, telecommuting
	Opportunity for part-time commitments to individual projects
	Conduct meetings, conferences and events during work days
	Provide virtual meeting opportunities, e.g. Skype and MSN
Networking and communicating	Utilize the latest available communications technologies such as web-based discussion forums, SMS and iPods
	Introduce an e-journal and other forms of e-communication as the professional 'face' of tourism peak bodies and associations
	Respond to communications quickly
Mentoring	Establish mentoring models that focus on individual development
	Use the timespan of 5 years for career planning
Ethics	Provide opportunities for individuals to make a difference – real capacity to action dreams
	Have high levels of morality and ethical standards
Education – lifelong learner and personal growth	Provide self-guided online workshops and the like
	Establish a training and learning culture
Authentic experiences	Connect theory with practice and ensure a global perspective
	Provide incentives that align with the real world
	Prioritize personal and family health and well-being
Collaborative teams	Use collaborative teaming as a basis for work tasks and structure these into projects
	Provide resources based on collaborative teams
	Facilitate leadership at team level
	Conduct collaborative teaming training programmes

Continued

Table 1.8. Continued.

MilGen work values and motivators	Suggested strategies
Instant results	Shift from function-based work to project-based work. This might mean restructuring committees and the like away from function to specific tasks
	Provide recognition and increased responsibility for results well received
Entrepreneurial	Provide opportunities for creativity and challenge – roles must be seen as important and as being valued
	Encourage members to make their own opportunities for advancement
	Provide a reward-for-performance system. This can mean that those teams that are performing should be resourced, while those that are underperforming should receive no support
	Additional responsibilities are welcomed as they are seen as a chance to aggregate new skills
Balance work and family	Unlike Baby Boomer and Generation X, family comes first, so workplaces need to be family friendly, e.g. provision of childcare facilities and a tolerant attitude to children
	Conferences and meetings should include family and provide childcare
	Programmes established that are geared towards health of Generation Y and their families
Multiple pathways: non-linear thinkers	Will be seeking opportunities to diversify
	Looking for opportunities to move in non-linear pathway
Technologically savvy	Access to information must be immediate and 24/7
	Internet is a main interface for communication

Conclusions

The WTO (2008, p. 73) concluded its recent report *Youth Travel Matters: Understanding the Global Phenomenon of Youth Travel* by emphasizing that youth and student travel is 'a major component of global tourism and a positive influence on the personal and social development of young people'. At the same time, the WTO recognized that student and youth travel is 'a unique market that must be understood for its specialist needs'.

This chapter approached an understanding of youth and travel through generational theory, positioning Y Generation in relation to other generational cohorts by age, shared social, economic and historical influences, and unique character traits of members. Generation Y members are identified as a hero generation, characterized as conventional and committed, with respect for authority and with civic pride. They are team-orientated, technically savvy and focus on how they feel and

experience events and workplaces. These characteristics are important to understand, both for the Y Generation as global tourists and as workers within the tourism industry. The following chapters expand these roles for the Y Generation.

Members of Y Generation are currently in the young adulthood phase of life, with the social role of vitality and testing of values. They are a cohort with a focus on brands, friends, fun and digital culture. They are also confident and relaxed, conservative and the most-educated generation ever. It is well accepted that the process of generational shaping has impacted the Y Generation in profound ways. They are the first generation of digital natives and the first cohort dealing with the age of terrorism in their formative years. Financially, Y-Generation members are credit-dependent and often financially dependent on parents and others much later in life than was typical for previous generations. The current global financial crisis will present a challenging time for them as travel consumers, though ironically there is anecdotal evidence that this generational group still prioritizes international travel above owning property, domestic travel and owning a car (TravelMole, 2008).

As the following chapters of this book reveal, tourism for the Y Generation is quite often a mixture of business and pleasure. For example, the WTO (2008) notes that 70% of all trips taken by young people are motivated by goals such as desire to explore, work or study abroad. Mapping Y-Generation travel and work characteristics against theoretical frameworks, such as that provided by Howe (2006), allows a greater understanding of this unique generation and ways to fully engage them within the tourism industry.

References

Allen, P. (2004) Welcoming Y. *Benefits Canada* 28(9), 51–53.
Australian Bureau of Statistics (2004). *Year Book Australia, 2004* (Cat 1301.0). Australian Government Publishing Service, Canberra.
Australian Bureau of Statistics (2006) *Population clock*. Available at: http://www.abs.gov.au/ausstats/abs%40.nsf/94713ad445ff1425ca25682000192af2/1647509ef7e25faaca2568a900154b63?OpenDocument. Retrieved 22 July 2006.
Beck, U. (1992) *Risk Society: Towards a New Modernity*. Sage, London.
Boomer, L.G. (2007) The 7 requirements of a training/learning culture. *Accounting Today* 21(6), 22.
Brooks, W. (2006) *Generations and the Future of Association Participation*. The William E. Smith Institute for Association Research, Chicago, Illinois.
Brooks, W. (2008) *Where the Winners Meet: Why Happier, More Successful People Gravitate Toward Associations*. The William E. Smith Institute for Association Research. Chicago, Illinois.
Donnison, S. (2007) Unpacking the millennial's: a cautionary tale for teacher education. *Australian Journal of Teacher Education* 32(3), 1–13.
Fields, B., Wilder, S., Bunch, J. and Newbold, R. (2008) *Millennial Leaders: Success Stories from Today's Most Brilliant Generation Y Leaders*. Ingram Publishing Services.
Fullarton, S. (2001) *VET in Schools: Participation and Pathways*. Australian Council for Educational Research, Camberwell, Victoria, Australia.
Howe, N. (2006) A generation to define a century. Paper presented to the Association for Supervision and Curriculum Development Annual Conference, Worldwide Issues, Chicago, Illinois, 1–3 April 2006. Available at: http://ascd.typepad.com/annualconference/2006/04/a_generation_to.html
Howe, N. and Strauss, W. (2000) *Millennial's Rising: The Next Great Generation*. Vintage Books, New York.
Huntley, R. (2006) *The World According to Y*. Allen & Unwin, Crows Nest, Australia.
Mannheim, K. (1952) *Essays on the Sociology of Knowledge*. Routledge & Kegan Paul, London.
McMahon, M. and Pospisil, R. (2005) Laptops for a digital lifestyle: millennial students and wireless mobile technologies. In: *Conference Proceedings. 22nd Annual Conference of the Australasian Society for Computers in Learning in Tertiary Education (ASCILITE) 2005: Balance, Fidelity, Mobility – Maintaining the Momentum*, 4–7 December 2005. Brisbane, Australia, pp. 421–431.
New Politics Institute. (2006) *The Politics of the Millennial Generation: A Survey Comparing Political Attitudes Between Generations*. New Politics Institute, Miami, Florida.
O'Reilly, B. (2000) Meet the future, it's your kids. The millennial generation has grown up with prosperity, the Internet, divorce and Columbine. They already know they don't want to live or work the way we do. *Fortune*, 24 July.
Pendergast, D. (2007) The MilGen and society. In: Bahr, N. and Pendergast, D. (eds) *The Millennial Adolescent*. Australian Council for Educational Research, Camberwell, Victoria, Australia, pp. 23–40. Available at: http://shop.acer.edu.au/acer-shop/product/0864316933
Pendergast, D. (2009) Generational theory and home economics: future proofing the profession. *Family and Consumer Sciences Research Journal* 37(4), 504–522.
Prensky, M. (2006) Listen to the natives. *Educational Leadership* 63(4), 8–13.

Reynol, J. and Mastrodicasa, J. (2007) *Connecting to the Net Generation: What Higher Education Professionals Need to Know About Today's College Students*. NASPA, Washington, DC.

Richards, G. (2007) *New Horizons II: The Young Independent Traveller, 2007*. World Youth Student & Educational Travel Confederation, Madrid.

Robert, S. (2005) *Millennial learning: On demand strategies for Generation X and beyond*. Available at: http://www.liimagazine.com/ltimagazine/article/articleDetails.jsp?id = 262368

Salt, B. (2006) *The Big Picture*. Hardie Grant, Sydney, Australia.

Strauss, W. and Howe, N. (2000) *Generations: The History of America's Future, 1584 to 2069*. William Morrow & Co, New York.

Thomson, S. and De Bortoli, L. (2007) *PISA 2003 Australia: ICT Use and Familiarity at School and Home*. Australian Council for Educational Research, Camberwell, Victoria, Australia.

TravelMole (2008) Travellers are young and green. Available at: http://www.travelmole.com/stories/1129435.php?news_cat = &pagename = searchresult

United Nations (2005) *World Youth Report 2005: Young people today, and in 2015*. Available at: http://www.un.org/esa/socdev/unyin/documents/wyr05book.pdf

United States Census Bureau (2006) *Total population for the world: 1950–2050*. Available at: http://www.census.gov/ipc/prod/wp02/wp-02001.pdf

World Tourism Organization (2008) *Youth Travel Matters: Understanding the Global Phenomenon of Youth Travel*. World Tourism Organization, Madrid.

2 Mythbusting: Generation Y and Travel

Gianna Moscardo and Pierre Benckendorff
School of Business, James Cook University

Introduction

Tourism is a complex, dynamic phenomenon with a relatively brief history of academic research attention, mostly in the social sciences. Like other areas of human activity, tourist behaviour exists in a constantly changing context and tourists have great capacity for social and personal adaptation and innovation within these contexts. In addition, given that the bulk of research into tourism has occurred since the late 1970s, there is little in the way of longitudinal research in this area, and as a result it is easy for tourism researchers to fall into the trap of premature cognitive commitment (Langer, 1997). Langer (1997) describes premature cognitive commitment as the inability to abandon existing assumptions about, or perspectives on, phenomena. Alternatively, it can be seen as a situation where individuals assume that an existing situation is set and this limits their ability to critically analyse underlying structures or situation-specific outcomes. These forces make the prediction of tourist behaviour difficult.

The key challenge for social scientists studying tourism is to look beyond the present manifestations of tourism and to use social science theories or conceptual approaches that can explain the underlying mechanisms of change rather than the specifics of the out-comes. One area that has received very little attention in tourism is that of change in tourist behaviour over time (Moscardo, 2004). Where it has been studied, the focus has been on changes in the supply of tourism rather than on the characteristics of tourists or the populations that tourists come from (Moscardo, 2004). One concept related to changes in consumption behaviour that has gained much attention in the broader social science literature is that of generational cohorts. The concept of generational differences in values and behaviours has potential power to explain and predict changes in tourist behaviour over time.

This chapter will introduce the idea of generational cohorts and discuss the challenges researchers face in using this concept before analysing in more detail the most recent generation to enter the world of travel – Generation Y (Gen Y). The chapter will critically examine the available evidence on Gen Y, its characteristics and what is actually known about its tourist behaviour.

Generational Cohorts

Generational labels such as Baby Boomers, Gen X and Gen Y have become commonplace in the popular media and used extensively in marketing and promotional materials. According to McCrindle and Beard (2007), this extensive coverage and discussion has been problematic because it has tended to be conducted by social commentators and journalists rather than social scientists, based on anecdotal evidence rather than sound empirical research, and speculative rather than critical and analytical. Not surprisingly, these kinds of popular discussions have attracted criticism and this criticism has often spilled over into the challenges to the concept of generational cohorts. McCrindle and Beard (2007) note, however, that while the discussions of specific aspects of particular generations may be suspect, it does not logically follow that the concept itself is flawed.

The concept is not a new one; it has a long history in sociology. Mannheim introduced the concept to sociology in German in the 1920s and then in English in 1952, and it has subsequently been used in sociology, psychology and related areas such as political science throughout the following years (Mannheim, 1952; Ryder, 1965; Elder, 1975; Braungart and Braungart, 1986; Whittier, 1997). Generations or generational cohorts can be defined as:

> proposed groups of individuals who are born during the same time period and who experienced similar external events during their formative or coming-of-age years (i.e. late adolescent and early adulthood years).
>
> (Noble and Schewe, 2003, p. 979)

The argument is that these similar experiences influence behaviours and values throughout the rest of the lifespan of these individuals (Lyons *et al.*, 2005). Each generation will have a different worldview compared to others because of these shared experiences (Mannheim, 1952). Table 2.1 provides an overview of the generations in current existence.

Two points are important to note about this generational theory. First, while external events are experienced by all people at the time, they are most critical for those individuals in their formative years, and these events continue to influence values and outlook throughout the lifespan. Second, this macro-level socialization influence does not determine all behaviour (Nobel and Schewe, 2003). Rather cohort or generation members are likely to share some common characteristics but they will also differ in many ways (Donnison, 2007).

The challenges of studying generational cohorts

Despite a lengthy history of use in sociology and psychology, generational cohorts can be difficult to study. Given the importance of particular external events in establishing cohort features, it is not surprising to find that they are not uniform across cultures and places. A study comparing European and American members of Gen Y noted that there are some core differences in the external events and social conditions that these two groups have been exposed to as they have grown up (Corvi *et al.*, 2007). More specifically, the groups differ in terms of family structures, parenting approaches, educational systems and exposure to terrorist attacks (Corvi *et al.*, 2007). This study raises a second challenge of studying generations – determining what the historical events or social conditions might be that define a generation. Schuman and Scott (1989) provide evidence that major events like World War II and the Vietnam War are clearly linked to the values and consciousness of older generations.

Table 2.1. Brief overview of proposed current generations. (From Strauss and Howe, 1992.)

Generation label	Approximate birth dates	Proposed critical features/ defining events
Silent Generation	1925–1945	Depression, World War II
Baby Boomers	1946–1964	Post-war economic growth, Vietnam War
Generation X	1965–1981	Economic instability
Generation Y	1977–2003	Internet, Baby Boomer-parenting

Evidence for significant events for younger generations is much less clear (Nobel and Schewe, 2003).

It can also be difficult to distinguish between the influence of generational cohorts and life-cycle stage (McCrindle, 2009). It is common to claim that a certain generation shares a set of characteristics by simply comparing the different generations at one point in time. However, the generations differ not only in age but also in terms of their life-cycle stages. Lyons, Duxbury and Higgins (2005), for example, claim to have tested generation differences in work-related values by surveying college students and workers, and comparing people in different age groups. The study found that the younger age groups were less interested in altruistic work values and more interested in social work values. However, it is not clear whether or not the difference in values detected reflect a generational difference or the difference between college students and workers. In order to claim a generational difference a study has to demonstrate not only that generations differ now but also across time. In other words, they have to show both that younger respondents are different to older groups now but also that they differ from previous generations when they were young. The large arrows in Fig. 2.1 demonstrate where the differences need to be to show a generational cohort difference.

A recent series of focus groups conducted by the one of the authors demonstrates this problem of confusing cohort with life stage.

The study was focused on understanding consumer perspectives on short-break holidays and involved several focus groups conducted in different Australian regions. One focus group was conducted with university students in a regional centre and another with members of the general public recruited through a local travel agency. The majority of the latter group was, however, within the same age range as the university student group. Qualitative analysis of the responses to questions about the importance of short-break holidays, the types of holiday taken in terms of destination, style of transport and accommodation and activities sought, and key features of positive holidays found three distinct patterns of responses – those of the university students (who gave a higher priority to spending spare money on holidays than the other groups, sought mainly social activities, used budget options and actively avoided structured events other than those related to contemporary music); those of younger workers (who were the same age as the university students, but who gave the lowest priority to spending money on holidays, sought luxury options and structured events, especially sporting ones); and other respondents (who were older, desired cultural events and were most flexible in their approach to the style of holiday sought). These results showed that cohort members differed in terms of factors such as access to money, education and restrictions of employment. McCrindle (2009) argues that it is important to remember that generational

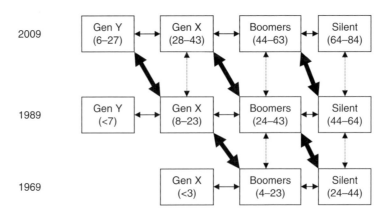

Fig. 2.1. Map of potential cohort differences.

cohort members will differ based on dimensions like culture, residence, gender, social class, levels of affluence and personality.

Generation Y

Gen Y is the latest generation to be labelled and examined in detail. This generational cohort is perhaps the most challenging to study of those listed in Table 2.1 because of considerable conflict over when its members were born, what they should be labelled and the fact that they are still very young. According to Donnison (2007), estimates of when the generation begins can vary between 1977 and 1983 and when it ends can vary between 1983 and 2009. A review of more than 15 papers on this generation found start dates as early as 1976 and the same range of end dates. The majority of definitions, however, fell between 1977 and 1995. Confusion over the defining birth dates creates two problems. First, it results in widely varying estimates of the size of the generation. Estimates within the US population, for example, can vary between 76 (Eisner, 2005) and 80 million (Mitchell, 2005) and these different estimates can make Gen Y larger than (Mitchell, 2005) or smaller than other cohorts (McCrindle, 2009). These differences are important when claims are made about potential future impacts of the generation especially in areas of consumption and travel.

Generations have typically been given labels that are meant to reflect key characteristics and generally there is little debate over the Baby Boomer and Gen X labels. Gen-Y members, however, are also known as Millennials, Echo Baby Boomers and the Net Generation (Eisner, 2005). Overall, Generation Y, usually shortened to Gen Y, is the most commonly used label, and according to McCrindle (2009), the label embraced by members of the cohort themselves. These varying labels reflect confusion over what the defining events or conditions are for this generation.

Table 2.2 summarizes both the events and social conditions that are said to be responsible for the generation's characteristics, and the characteristics themselves. An examination of this table reveals a number of issues. First, a wide range of events and/or conditions are claimed to be critical in defining this generation, but apart from the 11 September terrorist attacks no other extensive historical event is listed. There is also conflict between the claims made. For example, Baby-Boomer parents are often described as a critical influence (thus the justification for the Echo Boomer label) but not in a uniform way. Divorce and working mothers are variously seen as contributing to greater independence and autonomy as the children in these situations are left to look after themselves (ABS, 2006), or as trends contributing to anxious parents keen to make up for perceived neglect and creating sheltered and indulged offspring (Corvi *et al.*, 2007).

The table also indicates some confusion over what a characteristic resulting from a social condition is, versus what a defining social condition is. For example, evidence is presented that shows that Gen-Y members are typically living longer at home, delaying marriage and attaining higher levels of formal education than previous generations (Corvi *et al.*, 2007). But are these statements examples of characteristics of the generation or are they examples of the social conditions that influence the generation? These characteristics are also important because they reflect the fact that many members of this generation are still very young with the majority, according to most definitions, still in their teens or early 20s (NAS, 2006). Arguably many have not yet had their defining experiences. This argument could also be strengthened if we consider that this is a group which has been described as being in extended adolescence (Furstenberg *et al.*, 2003). If we see the progress of human development in social terms rather than simply biological maturation and or chronological age, then the majority of Gen-Y members can be classified as adolescents who have yet to achieve the key developmental milestones of independence from their family, making career choices and establishing intimacy in a long-term relationship (Sugarman, 2001). If it is the case that they are still forming their values and worldviews, then we might expect to find considerable confusion and contradiction in the research results to date.

The table also reveals that Gen Y is associated with a wide variety of defining characteristics, many of which appear to be

Table 2.2. Suggested defining events and distinguishing characteristics. (Sources: *Events* – AMP: NATSEM (2007); ABS (2007); Corvi *et al*. (2007); Donnison (2007); Eisner (2005); Lyons *et al*. (2005); McCrindle (2009); Mitchell (2005). *Features* – Clemmons (2008); Corvi *et al*. (2007); Donnison (2007); Eisner (2005); Howe and Strauss (2003); Jorgenson (2003); Krayewski (2009); Lyons *et al*. (2005); Martin (2005); McCrindle (2009); Mitchell (2005); NAS (2006); Saltzman (2007); Walker *et al*. (2006)).

Defining events	Distinguishing features
Internet and globalization • Global popular culture • Easy world travel • Rise of digital media	Technology savvy High levels of ICT usage Global cultural reference points Comfortable with and seek frequent change Flexible Multicultural, tolerant of diversity and inclusive in style Interested in creativity and innovation Team-oriented/socialize in groups Question rules and authority and would not defer automatically to authority Not brand loyal
Economic growth and prosperity • Affluence	Ambitious Seek status and prestige Highly brand conscious
Baby-Boomer parenting • Structured/scheduled lives • Active parenting • Fewer siblings • More divorced parents • More working mothers	Confident/strong-willed Optimistic Close to parents and family Respectful and trusting of authority Sheltered and indulged Seek constant feedback, rewards and recognition in the workplace See themselves as special and entitled Question rules and authority and would not defer automatically to authority
Baby-Boomer parenting • More divorced parents • More working mothers • Often latchkey kids	Seek autonomy Strong individualism Self-reliant and independent Questioning of authority Work–life balance is important – work to live
Higher levels of education • Staying in school longer • Staying at home longer • Marrying later	Want learning/education-oriented Pressured and competitive Team-oriented, group-focused Work hard at the expense of life, strong work ethic
Terrorism • 11 September attacks • Increased violence • Exposure to heroism	Civic-minded, volunteers, altruistic
Rise of environmentalism	Concerned about the world, volunteers Entrepreneurial Strong values Not interested in politics

contradictory. For example, Gen Y is claimed by some to be committed to finding a better work–life balance in which members primarily work to support a desired lifestyle (Howe and Strauss, 2003; Eisner, 2005; Lyons *et al*., 2005; Corvi *et al*., 2007) and by others to be ambitious overachievers prepared to sacrifice lifestyle for career goals (Jorgenson, 2003; NAS, 2006). They are described as strongly individualistic in their values (Mitchell, 2005), but also very social and group focused (Lyons *et al*., 2005; Clemmons, 2008). Furthermore,

Gen-Y members are described by some as deferential to, and respectful of, authority (Howe and Strauss, 2003; Eisner, 2005; Corvi *et al.*, 2007), but by others as questioning of authority and unlikely to easily accept existing social rules (Mitchell, 2005; NAS, 2006). In some cases there are explanations for these contradictions. Martin (2005) argues that Gen-Y members can be both respectful of authority and questioning of it at the same time. In this argument, Gen-Y members have confidence and awareness of multiple alternatives, which means that while they respect the right of authority figures to set tasks and make requests, they assume that it is useful and appropriate for them to question methods and traditions in order to achieve a better outcome (Martin, 2005).

At core there exists little reliable, valid evidence to support many of the claims that are made about Gen Y. Where such evidence does exist a more complex picture often emerges. For example, Macleod (2008) conducted an empirical study of Gen-Y managers with multiple data-collection methods over two time periods. This study found that while there was a trend towards shorter times spent in a job between the two study periods, 32% of the Gen-Y respondents had been in their current job for 3–5 years, 31% had been in their current position for more than 5 years and 39% expected to stay where they were in the future. This study also found that half of the sample was prepared to sacrifice their personal lives for their workplace. These results are inconsistent with the view that Gen-Y workers seek regular changes in jobs and careers and only work to live. The study did find, however, that the respondents were high Internet users, and 90% wanted to work for an organization that did something worthwhile or that they could believe in (Macleod, 2008), supporting other claims made about Gen-Y members being socially concerned and Internet savvy.

More detailed research into Internet use also reveals a more complex picture than is usually presented of Gen Y. Macleod's (2008) survey found that Gen-Y respondents could be further classified into three groups based on the patterns of their Internet usage with 26% labelled as 'uninvolved functionalists', who only used the Internet for work purposes; 34%

labelled 'viewers/readers', who were passive audiences for music, videos and photographs; and 26% were 'enthusiastic contributors' to Internet content. These findings suggest that Gen Y may not be uniform in its Internet usage or interest. It is also possible that being Internet savvy may not be as strong a defining feature of the generation as sometimes put forward. The Pew Research Center's 2008 survey of age and Internet use found that Gen Y did not dominate in all areas of Internet use, and the differences between the generations in terms of Internet use were not large, with little difference in the overall proportion of Internet users between Gen Y, Gen X and Baby Boomers, and the fastest-growing usage among people older than 70 (Pew Research Center, 2009). There were, however, major differences in the way in which the different groups used the Internet, with Gen Y distinctive in its use of the Internet for socializing and entertainment rather than research, shopping or banking (Pew Research Center, 2009). It is worth noting that the comparison of European to American Gen Y described earlier found a similar distinction, but in this instance between the cultural groups of the same age, with Europeans much less likely to use the Internet for socializing and entertainment. This latter finding raises the issue of the representativeness of the sample used in research into Gen Y. The bulk of the available literature comes from the USA and even within this geographic region is very much focused on college students, typically from more affluent backgrounds, and on studies investigating responses to education and marketing.

As noted previously, very few studies have been designed to distinguish between cohort and life-stage effects. An Australian study into financial and investment behaviour looked at Gen Y members in 2004 and compared their answers to those given by Gen X members in 1989 (AMP/NATSEM, 2007). The study found a slight increase in the likelihood that the respondents were living at home, with 46% of Gen X still at home in 1989 compared to 49% of Gen-Y respondents in 2004, and an increase in the number of respondents in full-time education (36% in 1989 and 47% in 2004). More interestingly, the study also found an increase in the number renting rather than buying their own home (47% in 1989 were homeowners while only 38% in 2004 were homeowners).

Many authors also go beyond the evidence that is available when drawing conclusions or setting out implications. For example an analysis of youth debt in Australia notes that one-third of new credit card applications in Australia came from 18–27 year olds and that one-third of credit card defaults also came from this age group (Veda, 2006). This evidence is then used to claim that Gen Y is a group with a problem in managing debt and credit (Veda, 2006). But arguably one would expect higher levels of applications for credit cards from younger people because older age groups already have them, and no evidence is presented to show that this level of credit card defaults is significantly higher for this age group than any others. The AMP/NATSEM (2007) analysed detailed data and found that Gen-Y respondents were no more or less in debt than Gen X had been when they were younger, and in 2004 as a group Gen Y had less debt than the other generations, and the majority of their debt (75%) was related to house mortgages. The researchers concluded that Gen-Y credit and debt was explained more by the relatively high cost of housing in Australia than by any other variable. There is clearly a tendency towards the presentation of negative stereotypes of Gen Y in the popular media and various studies reported on websites. Statements such as 'these kids are overindulged, overprotected and over-supervised' (NAS, 2006, p. 11) are not uncommon.

Given the existence of negative stereotypes, and the key argument in generational theory that the different generations have different patterns of values and unique worldviews, it could be argued that the study of Gen Y is a type of cross-cultural research. Howe and Strauss (2003) and Donnison (2007) caution Gen-Y researchers to recognize that they may be limited in their approach because of their own generational outlook, especially as most researchers in this area are Baby Boomers. Taking a cross-cultural perspective on this field may also explain some of the contradictions that are evident in Table 2.2. Gen Y is often described as oriented towards group, tribe or social networks, and this has been translated in educational practice into the argu-

ment that members prefer team approaches to learning and assessment. However, research into educational and learning preferences finds that Gen-Y respondents typically dislike teamwork (Walker *et al.*, 2006) and prefer mentoring or coaching (Macleod, 2008). The problem here lies in the different ways researchers and the researched interpret and use words like team, group, tribe and social network.

Overall, the evidence, both with regard to the events or conditions that have defined Gen Y and its characteristics, is limited in many ways and not surprisingly there is confusion and contradiction in what is claimed. However, despite this there is some consensus around four key themes. Donnison (2007) identifies three of these:

1. Its digital media use, especially for entertainment, social networking and creative endeavours.
2. It has positive attitudes towards diversity, flexibility, social issues and its own future.
3. It has an orientation towards family and social groups.

This chapter argues that a fourth key theme is the extension of adolescence, with longer time spent in formal education. It is not yet clear what, if any, consequences will arise from this extended adolescence, but it is clear that it influences current patterns of behaviour, particularly for consumption. While we may not yet understand Gen Y, it is worth remembering that the concept of generational cohorts has been used to explain a number of phenomena, and there is no evidence to suggest that generational theory should be abandoned for this group. Instead this review would suggest that we need to focus more research attention on this issue but with better methods, recognition of the possibility of cross-cultural issues and a more critical perspective on claims made.

Generation Y and Tourism

Like other areas of literature related to Gen Y, a number of claims and counterclaims have been made about Gen Y and tourism, but little evidence has been clearly presented to support the claims. Much of the discussion on Gen-Y members in tourism has been either about them as travellers or as workers. As the discussions about Gen Y as workers in tourism have generally paralleled those in other sectors, and as there is very little discussion of Gen Y as tourism managers, leaders, entrepreneurs, hosts or policy makers, this chapter will focus on what is presented about Gen Y as tourists or travellers.

There seem to be two main approaches to Gen Y as tourists – those who claim that they want to and do travel more than other generations, and those who argue that they want to and do travel less. As in previous sections the evidence to support either claim is not strong with mostly single surveys conducted at one point in time. Many of those who claim that Gen Y is travelling more tend to refer to one of a handful of empirical studies all conducted by organizations with a vested interest in youth or student travel, such as the World Youth Student and Educational Travel Confederation or the International Student Travel Confederation (Richards and Wilson, 2003; Richards, 2007; Contiki, 2008). In each of these surveys, the sampling is restricted to respondents who have either verified that they plan to travel in the future (Contiki, 2008) and/or those who travelled in the past and placed themselves on a mailing list of a travel organization (Richards, 2007; Richards and Wilson, 2003). So there is little evidence that Gen Y travels more than any previous generations. The evidence presented in these reports tells us that those Gen Y members already interested in, and experienced with, travel seem to be travelling more frequently and to a wider range of destinations.

Studies that look at a more broadly representative sample of Gen-Y respondents are limited but do suggest that they either travel no more than any other groups or are travelling less. A study by the Canadian Tourism Commission (2008) using a general resident sample of Quebec residents found the same rates of international travel participation for Gen-Y respondents (31%) as for the total sample (31%) and slightly lower rates of domestic travel participation by Gen Y (42%) than the total sample (46%). According to Japanese Tourism Marketing (2008), surveys of residents of major Japanese cities found an overall

decline in international travel among respondents in their 20s. An investigation of the Eurobarometer series of studies of young Europeans indicates a decline in international travel among 15–24 year olds. The 1987 survey, which would have been of Gen X, found that 71% of the sample had been on an international trip within Europe (Eurobarometer, 1989), while the 2001 survey, which was of Gen-Y respondents, found that this figure had decreased to 56% (European Union, 2001). There is also some indirect evidence in other sources that support a decreased interest in travel in general. Macleod (2008) found that only 16% of the American Gen-Y students or managers surveyed were interested in foreign travel as part of their job and the AMP/NATSEM (2007) Australian study found that Gen-Y respondents spent less of their income on recreation, including travel, than other generations.

In summary, there appears to be no evidence to support a claim that Gen Y is more interested in or likely to travel than any other current or previous generation. However, the studies that have focused on the Gen-Y members who do travel offer some insights into how the nature of Gen-Y travel may be changing over time. Clemmons (2008) proposes that there has been considerable growth in recent years in volunteer tourism and much of this growth is attributable to interest from Gen-Y travellers. According to Richards (2007) youth and student travellers are travelling more frequently to a wider range of destinations, looking for more cultural and social experiences and increasing their use of the Internet for travel information and booking. These findings are broadly consistent with those reported for Canadian and American youth travellers (Lang Research, 2002). Additional results from this study included an increase in holidays focused on personal indulgence and centred on shopping and fine dining, greater participation in outdoor and sports activities, higher levels of interest in music-related events, more independent travel and more interest in travel closer to home. The Contiki (2008) study also found an increased interest in local cultural experiences and more frequent but shorter trips, and a move towards spending longer in one country. Furthermore, this research found high levels of concern over the social and environmental impacts of travel (Contiki, 2008). Van Dyck (2008) focused on Gen-Y business travel, summarizing the results from consultant studies of Gen-Y perspectives on business hotel accommodation. In this summary, Van Dyck (2008) notes that although Gen-Y members currently make up only a small proportion of business travel (9%), they are likely to become more involved as they age and develop their careers. The research conducted shows that Gen-Y business travellers prefer more casual, home-like, self-service options for hotels and are seeking more opportunities for local cultural experiences while they travel.

While these findings are based on only a few studies and limited samples, there are patterns emerging in the results across different samples and these patterns are also consistent with the key themes identified in Gen-Y literature (see Table 2.3). First, the digital-media-use theme is consistently reported in all the studies of Gen-Y travellers. The second key theme of positive attitudes towards diversity, flexibility and social issues is reflected in the interest of Gen-Y travellers in volunteer tourism, their increasing levels of concern over the impacts of travel and their strong desire to experience local cultures. Their family and social orientation is also evident in the work on desired features of hotels and the consistent finding that

social interaction is a key element of a positive travel experience.

Conclusions

This chapter has examined the idea of generational cohorts and has discussed the challenges researchers face in using this concept. The chapter has also critically examined the most recent evidence on Gen Y, its characteristics and what is actually known about its travel behaviour. In doing so, this 'myth-busting' chapter has focused on separating the facts from some of the folklore surrounding Gen Y. Some consistent and enduring characteristics and themes have been identified, but the overwhelming conclusion is that more valid and reliable research employing established cohort analysis techniques is needed to better understand this generation.

There has been a tendency within the academic literature in general, and tourism more specifically, to dismiss Gen Y as a subject for research. Indeed the call for expressions of interest for the present volume generated some strong negative views on the value of the exercise. These views seem to be generated by either negative stereotypes of the generation or valid concerns over the quality of the evidence provided to back up many of the claims

Table 2.3. Key themes and supporting evidence from Gen Y and travel research.

Key themes	Supporting evidence
Digital media use	• Increased use of Internet to book travel (Richards, 2007) • Increased use of Internet to manage social interactions and networks while travelling • Increased use of Internet to share travel experiences (e.g. blogs, photos)
Positive attitudes towards diversity, flexibility and social issues	• Volunteer tourism (Clemmons, 2008) • Concern for impacts of travel (Contiki, 2008) • Seeking local culture and social experiences (Richards, 2007; Contiki, 2008; Van Dyck, 2008)
Family and social orientation	• Seeking local culture and social experiences (Richards, 2007; Contiki, 2008; Van Dyck, 2008) • Strong desire for social interaction • Seeking casual, home-like features in hotels (Van Dyck, 2008)

made about this generation. While it is true that the evidence to support many of the claims currently made about Gen Y is not strong, it is important to distinguish between the specific analysis of Gen Y and the use of the generational cohort theory. There is evidence to support generational theory and there are emerging patterns in the research into Gen Y that have been explored in this chapter as well as in Chapter 1.

It is often claimed in tourism that a particular market segment or type of tourism is growing faster than all others. This appears to be seen as necessary to justify the research into that form of tourism or market. Discussions of Gen Y as tourists also seem to feel this pressure with a common claim made that this is a generation that is travelling more than in the past. The available evidence does not, however, support these claims. However, it is not necessary to make these claims to justify research into the generation, as the available research does support the idea that they may have distinctive and new approaches to travel and this in itself is worthy of further consideration.

When Gen Y and tourism is considered, the overwhelming conclusion is that there exists very little research into any of the possible relationships between Gen Y and tourism. That is, research is needed into Gen-Y members as tourism staff, tourists, tourism managers, entrepreneurs, policy makers and hosts. This research also needs to use time series data and examine differences between the generations both in cross-sectional and longitudinal methods. Researchers also need to be careful to establish common understandings of terms and think about applying the criteria used to ensure sound cross-cultural research.

References

ABS (2007) *A Picture of the Nation – 2070.0 2006.* Australian Bureau of Statistics, Canberra.

AMP:NATSEM (2007) Generation whY? Available at: http://www.amp.com.au/ampnatsemreports

Braungart, R.G. and Braungart, M.M. (1986) Life-course and generational politics. *American Review of Sociology* 12, 205–231.

Canadian Tourism Commission (2008) Spotlight on Generation Y. Tourism online. Available at: http://www.corporate.canada.travel/corp/media/app/en/ca/magazine/

Clemmons, D. (2008) VolunTourism and the M3 travelers. Available at: http://www.voluntourism.oreg/news-feature224.htm

Contiki (2008) The shades of green report. Available at: http://contiki.com.au/pages/491-shades-of-green-report

Corvi, E., Bigi, A. and Ng, G. (2007) The European Millennials versus the US Millennials: similarities and differences. International Business Research Conference, Sydney, Australia.

Donnison, S. (2007) Unpacking the Millennials: a cautionary tale for teacher education. *Australian Journal of Teacher Education* 32, 1–13.

Eisner, S.P. (2005) Managing Generation Y. *S.A.M Advanced Management Journal* 70, 4–15.

Elder, G.H. (1975) Age differentiation and the life course. *Annual Review of Sociology* 1, 165–190.

Eurobarometer (1988) *Young Europeans in 1987.* Commission for European Communities, Brussels.

European Union (2001) *Young Europeans: Eurobarometer 47.2.* European Union, Brussels.

Furstenberg, F.F., Kennedy, S., McCloyd, V.C., Rumbault, R.G. and Settersten, R.A. (2003) *Between Adolescence and Adulthood: Expectations about the Timing of Adulthood.* Research Network on Transitions to Adulthood and Public Policy, University of Chicago Working Paper 1, Chicago, Illinois.

Howe, N. and Strauss, W. (2003) *Millennials Go to College.* American Association of Collegiate Registrars and Admissions Officers, Washington, DC.

Japanese Tourism Marketing (2008) JTM's survey results: consumption and travel trends for Japanese youth in their twenties (part 2). Available at: http://www.tourism.jp/english/report/2008/05/12/jtms-survey.php

Jorgenson, B. (2003) Baby Boomers, Generation X and Generation Y? Policy implications for defence forces in the modern era. *Foresight* 5, 41–49.

Krayewski, K. (2009) Generation Y and why they matter. Available at: http://internationalaffairs.suite101.com/article.cfm/generation_y

Langer, E.J. (1997) *The Power of Mindful Learning.* Addison-Wesley, Reading, Massachusetts.

Lang Research (2002) *TAMS: Lifecycle Markets.* Canadian Government, Ottawa, Canada.

Lyons, S., Duxbury, L. and Higgins, C. (2005) An empirical assessment of generational difference in work-related values. *Human Resources Management* 26, 62–71.

Macleod, A. (2008) *Generation Y: Unlocking the Talent of Young Managers.* Chartered Management Institute, London.

Mannheim, K. (1952) The problem of generations. In: Mannheim, K. (ed.) *Essays on the Sociology of Knowledge.* Routledge and Kegan Paul, London, pp. 276–322.

Martin, C.A. (2005) From high maintenance to high productivity. *Industrial and Commercial Training* 37, 39–44.

McCrindle, M. (2009) Seriously cool: marketing, communicating and engaging with the diverse generations. Available at: http://www.mccrindle.com.au

McCrindle, M. and Beard, M. (2007) In defence of Gen Y. Available at: http://internationalaffairs.suite101.com/article.cfm/generation_y.pdf

Mitchell, S. (2005) The Millennial generation: its demographics, market preferences, productivity and global impact. In *Managerial Excellence and Networked Collaboration for Global Competitiveness.* International Training Center, Chula Vista, California.

Moscardo, G. (2004) Exploring change in Asia Pacific tourism markets. In: Chon, K., Hsu, C. and Okamoto, N. (eds) *Globalization and Tourism Research: East Meets West.* Asia Pacific Tourist Association, Hong Kong, pp. 369–378.

NAS (2006) Generation Y: the Millennials. NAS recruitment. Available at: http://www.nasrecruitment.com/talenttips/NASinsights/GenerationY.pdf

Noble, S.M. and Schewe, C.D. (2003) Cohort segmentation: an exploration of its validity. *Journal of Business Research* 56, 979–987.

Pew Research Center (2009) Generations online in 2009. Available at: http://www.pewinternetr.org/Reports/2009/Generations-online-in-2009/

Richards, G. (2007) *New Horizons II: The Young Independent Travellers 2007.* WYSE Travel Confederation, Amsterdam.

Richards, G. and Wilson, J. (2003) *New Horizons in Independent Youth and Student Travel.* International Student Travel Confederation, Amsterdam.

Ryder, N.B. (1965) The cohort as a concept in the study of social change. *American Sociological Review* 30, 843–861.

Saltzman, D. (2007) 'Younthanize' your travel agency. *Travel Trade,* 9 November. Available at: http://www.traveltrade.com/news_article.htm?id=238

Schuman, H. and Scott, J. (1989) Generations and collective memories. *American Sociological Review* 54, 359–381.

Strauss, W. and Howe, N. (1992) *Generations: The History of America's Future 1594–2069.* William Morrow, New York.

Sugarman, L. (2001) *Life-span Development,* 2nd edn. Routledge, London.

Van Dyck, D. (2008) The Generation Y hotel. *Time Magazine.* Available at: http://www.time.com/time/magazine/article/0,9171,1813977,00.html?imw=Y

Veda (2006) Call for 'Gen Y' to get credit wise. Available at: http://www.vedaadvantage.com

Walker, J.T., Martin, T., White, J., Elliott, R., Norwood, A., Mangum, C. and Haynie, L. (2006) Generational (age) differences in nursing students' preferences for teaching methods. *Journal of Nursing Education* 45, 371–374.

Whittier, N. (1997) Political generations, micro-cohorts, and the transformation of social movements. *American Sociological Review* 62, 760–778.

3 Generation Y's Travel Behaviours: a Comparison with Baby Boomers and Generation X

Yu-Chin Huang and James F. Petrick
Department of Recreation, Park and Tourism Sciences, Texas A&M University

Importance of Market Segmentation

Over the next decade, tourism growth will depend on how well tourism products and service providers understand the social and demographic trends influencing traveller behaviours (Horneman *et al.* 2002). In recent years, tourism marketers have recognized the need to target homogenous components of a heterogeneous market, rather than the market as a whole. This strategy called 'segmentation' (Pennington-Gray *et al.* 2003) is a technique used to identify different visitor types and groups with the goal of predicting who will respond favourably to a particular promotion programme (Harmon *et al.*, 1999).

Demographics are frequently the first criterion used in marketing decisions that involve product characteristics and features, personal selling strategies and advertising. For consumer marketers and researchers, it has been argued that no demographic characteristic is more important than age (Roberts and Manolis, 2000). Although such variables as education, income, gender, occupation, family life cycle, social class, place of residence and marital status have all been suggested to influence perceptions and images, age appears to be a major determinant of image and has an effect on travel behaviours. For example, Nickel and Wertheimer (1979) studied the effects of age, education, occupation, income, marital status

and size of the family on consumer images of drugstores and found that age was the only variable affecting the process.

When conceptualizing age as a demographic variable, it is important to consider not only chronological age, but also age cohorts and time periods (Stevens *et al.*, 2005). While marketing research has typically focused on changes in consumption rates based on age classes, it has been argued that this approach fails to account for cohort succession effects (Rentz and Reynolds, 1991). This suggests that in order to develop an accurate understanding of a consumer segment and subsequent effective marketing and promotion strategies, it is imperative to take into consideration both age segments and cohort characteristics to fully understand consumer preferences. In the travel literature, few studies exist that look at cohorts (Pennington-Gray *et al.*, 2003). Therefore, the sample in this study is described not only in cohort terms as Generation Y, Generation X and Baby Boomers, but also in terms of three age-segments. This enables both cohort-based and age-based explanations to be addressed in the discussion.

Researchers who study population effects on society use the term 'generation' to refer to people born in the same general timespan and experience the same key historical or social life events (Gursoy *et al.*, 2008). Generation has also been defined as a group of people with certain attitudes and behaviours in common that are different from the generation before it (Beirne, 2008). Strauss and Howe (1991, p. 60) defined a generation as 'a cohort-group whose length approximates the span of a phase of life and whose boundaries are fixed by peer personalities'. Strauss and Howe's definition includes two important points: the length of a generational cohort and its peer personality. Different from other social philosophers, they based the length of a generation cohort on the length of a phase of life (Pennington-Gray et al., 2003). They determined that each cohort-group will last for 22 years maximum and possess a unique unified personality that will later differentiate it from other age-brackets (Pennington-Gray et al., 2003). Each generation develops a unique personality that determines its feelings towards authority and other generations based on these distinct critical life events. An era in which a person was born shapes their early life and creates in them a worldview that can affect their value system and the way they view and interact with the environment around them (Wolf et al., 2005). Behavioural sociologists suggest that each generation lasts around 20 years and fades into the background as the next generation emerges (Gursoy et al., 2008).

Three Age-Cohort Markets: Baby Boomers, Generation X-ers and Generation Y-ers

Three potential important age cohorts, representing three separate generations, are Baby Boomers, Generation X-ers and Generation Y-ers. The Baby Boomer generation is defined as the members of the US population born between 1946 and 1964, and comprises the largest single generation in America (Mitchell, 1995). Due to its massive size, this generation has had, and will continue to have, an enormous influence on the US economy (Roberts and Manolis, 2000). Generation X is defined as the members of the US population born between 1965 and 1976, and consists of approximately 49.3 million consumers comprising 17% of the US population approximately (Reynolds, 2004). Generation Y is

defined as the members of the US population born between 1977 and 1994 (Harmon et al., 1999), includes approximately 60 million US citizens (Newborne and Kerwin, 1999), and will comprise 41% of the population by the year 2009 (Noble et al., 2009).

Characteristics of Baby Boomers and Generation X-ers

These three groups represent large segments of opportunity for marketers. The Baby-Boomer generation is important because of its size (76 million) and discretionary income. The oldest Baby Boomers have now reached retirement age and many are finding that they have a greater amount of discretionary time. Some of the research that has been conducted on senior travels encompasses older members of the Baby-Boomer generation. The research suggests that senior travellers tend to travel greater distances and stay away longer than any other age cohort (Horneman et al., 2002). The senior market impact becomes even more substantial with the increased opportunities to travel based on health improvement and potential financial surplus of future seniors over the current senior market (Horneman et al., 2002).

Generation X-ers are just now entering their peak-earning years and are future business travellers. According to D.K. Shifflet Associates (De Lollis, 2005), Generation X is already the most free-spending of leisure travellers and outspends Baby Boomers on trips involving hotel stays. In 2004, Generation X spent roughly US$1297 per trip per person, compared with Baby Boomers who spent US$1155 (McMahon, 2005). Generation Y-ers are predicted to have the biggest spending potential since teenagers currently spend an estimated of US$153 billion a year on everything from computers to cars to clothes (Brand, 2000), and they have tremendous potential for becoming lifetime consumers (Wolburg and Pokrywczynski, 2001).

Literature from marketing shows that Baby Boomers want more input and control of the buying process, and that marketing strategies should include messages tailored directly to the ageing Baby-Boomer generation

(Kahle, 1995; Kass, 1996). Ageing Boomers prefer information-intensive advertising that identifies a product's benefits as opposed to image-oriented marketing that usually targets younger consumers (Roberts and Manolis, 2000). Good value is the most important factor for this generation when they make a purchase (Wolf *et al.*, 2005), and they also value brand name.

Generation X is more media savvy; although television is the main source of advertising to this group, only the suitable advertising that is right for their tastes and preferences can best reach this target market (Freeman, 1995). Members of Generation X view marketing as a highly manipulative practice, but they are not hostile towards advertising. They understand that the purpose of advertising is to sell products, so their attitude towards advertising is: 'tell me more about your product, give me information, and reasons for buying it' (Roberts and Manolis, 2000). They prefer promotional messages to be blunt and kinetic (Francese, 1993). Advertising messages and promotion themes that will attract the attention of Generation X should stress safety, security and self-sufficiency (Francese, 1993). Generation X needs convincing proof that a product is reliable and will simplify rather than complicate life. Additionally, Generation-X consumers rate premium quality as the most desirable characteristic when they buy a product, and prefer the prestige of the brands (Francese, 1993; Wolf *et al.*, 2005). Typically, Generation X is looking for activities that suggest comfort and relaxation (Beverland, 2001).

Characteristics of Generation Y

Generation Y has been acculturated into an environment that provides more opportunities and reasons to shop than ever before. Additionally, the television and the Internet, as well as the more traditional catalogue-based shopping forms, offer additional consumption opportunities. Generation Y has been socialized into shopping as a form of leisure, and spends more time in the mall than other generation groups (Belleau *et al.*, 2007). Generation-Y customers also demonstrate a

general liking for purchasing, have ample discretionary time for shopping, and are likely to spend freely and quickly (Ma and Niehm, 2006). This has led researchers to believe that shopping is an important activity for this group when choosing a destination (Martin and Turley, 2004). Described as media savvy and very comfortable with electronic commerce, Generation Y has been raised on the premise of choice and is equipped with the expertise regarding information access, and hence, members of Generation Y are considered to be the most independent decision makers (Alch, 2000; Stevens *et al.*, 2005). Therefore, Generation Y is thought to exhibit a growing sophistication of products, brands, advertising, shopping, pricing and decision-making strategies, and influence approaches compared with the previous generations (Stevens *et al.*, 2005).

As the newest wave of the youth consumer market, Generation Y has caught the attention of researchers due to the sheer size of this consumer segment and also its significant spending power (Kueh and Voon, 2007). Generation Y-ers are therefore legitimate targets of research in service marketing. Generation Y is usually defined as those born between the years 1977 and 1994; the youngest in this generation is 15 years old in the year 2009, the oldest 32. More than 70% of this generation has reached adulthood (Paul, 2001). Generation Y represents a highly valued youth market since it is three times the size of its Generation-X predecessor (Stevens *et al.*, 2005) and is expected to be as large and influential as the Baby Boomers (Sullivan and Heitmeyer, 2008).

Consumerism is the central feature of this generation's life (Belleau *et al.*, 2007). It has been projected that by 2020, the influence of Baby Boomers will decrease, the impact of Generation Y-ers will increase and the spending power of this demographic will grow to approximately US$300 billion (Stevens *et al.*, 2005).

The youth market has been characterized as one of the most coveted segments because of its spending powers, ability to be trendsetters, receptivity to new products and tremendous potential for becoming lifetime customers (Belleau *et al.*, 2007). The challenge to marketers is that today's teens and 20-somethings are very demanding (Brooks, 2005), and they are considered the hardest to reach through advertising (Sullivan and Heitmeyer, 2008). Researchers have found that Generation Y is individualistic, anti-corporate and resistant to advertising efforts (Wolburg and Pokrywczynski, 2001; Belleau et al., 2007).

As research shows, children of the Baby Boomers (mostly Generation Y) who are employed and have access to money from both parents and grandparents have an estimated US$150 billion in direct purchasing power and around US$500 billion in indirect purchasing power in the USA (Stevens et al., 2005). Generation Y-ers typically spend about US$187 billion annually or US$260 per person, per month (Kumar and Lim, 2008). Additionally, Generation Y is important for marketers due to its impact on its families' purchase decisions. Among all the purchases Generation Y-ers make, clothing, entertainment and food are the top three purchases (Alch, 2000).

More than one third of the Generation-Y members are minorities compared to 27% of the total population, and they have a growing tolerance for diversity in both public and private areas of life and also create a global mix and match culture (Morton, 2002). Many of them have grown up in a 'nontraditional family', which gives them a broader definition of what constitutes a family. Wolburg and Pokrywczynski (2001) describe Generation Y as the best educated and most culturally diverse generation in history, which makes it more tolerant and open-minded towards different lifestyles and family structures.

Members of Generation Y think they are special and smart, are more community-minded and are more focused on teamwork, achievement, modesty and good conduct than previous generations (Beirne, 2008). As a group, Generation Y is different from any other youth in history; it is more numerous, more affluent, better educated, more ethnically diverse and more interested in positive social habits than the previous generations (Beirne, 2008). Generation-Y members celebrate individuality and diversity, but still seek group association (Sullivan and Heitmeyer, 2008). Since members are community-minded, they are

rule-followers, and accept authority. Research shows that rates of: violent crime among teens has fallen by 70%; teen pregnancy and abortion by 35%; high school sexual activity by 15%; and alcohol and tobacco consumption have been reaching all-time lows over the past 10 years (Beirne, 2008).

Kueh and Voon (2007) examined the influence of individual-level cultural dimensions on Generation-Y consumers' expectations of service quality. Their results revealed that the Generation-Y consumers in Asia are likely to have higher expectations of service quality than Generation Y-ers in other parts of the world. Additionally, Generation-Y consumers expect prompt and reliable service with visually appealing facilities and well-groomed staff (Kueh and Voon, 2007). Stevens et al. (2005) revealed similar results that technical and aesthetic features, in addition to price and brand, are important product features that should be included in contemporary youth consumer investigations.

Generation Y-ers rarely participate in active leisure pursuits such as tennis and motorcycling. Most of them are pragmatic, like convenience, and are value-oriented (Morton, 2002). They are brand- and fashion-conscious, and prefer brands with a core identity based on core values (Morton, 2002). Word of mouth is the best marketing method to target this group of people since they value friends' opinions enormously (Morton, 2002), and like to have friends around wherever they go (Rowe, 2008). Research suggests that Generation Y-ers use radio as their major medium for music and information, but are loyal to only a few stations (Morton, 2002). They also like apparel that reflects their lifestyles more than their outward appearance, and respond to humorous and emotional advertising the best when it uses real people in real-life situations (Kumar and Lim, 2008). It has further been suggested that advertising aimed at Generation Y should focus on lifestyle and fun rather than product features and specifications (Morton, 2002).

Overall, Generation-Y members are risk-adverse, mistrustful of mass media and can best be reached via word-of-mouth promotion, celebrity testimonials, loud and quick visuals and advertisements that reflect their lifestyles and core values in humorous and emotional ways (Morton, 2002). Additionally, Generation Y values diversity and equality; loves music, movies, television shows, friends and dining out (Paul, 2001; Brooks, 2005; Noble *et al.*, 2008). Members have money to spend but they change their tastes consistently (Morton, 2002; Belleau *et al.*, 2007), which suggests that generating repeat patronage will be a big challenge for marketers. Since it has been argued that service companies can boost profits by almost 100% by retaining only 5% of their customers (Ma and Niehm, 2006), it is believed to also be important for destination marketing organizations to identify potential Generation-Y travellers' preferences and tastes in relation to their future travel intentions.

Because each generation has its own characteristics, it is important to consider how each generation behaves in terms of information search behaviour, preferred activities and perception of destination characteristics. The literature reveals numerous studies on the travel behaviours of seniors and Baby Boomers. Yet, there is a lack of studies investigating Generation Y, and few studies have made comparisons between Baby Boomers, Generation X-ers and Generation Y-ers (Harmon *et al.*, 1999; Bakewell and Mitchell, 2003; Pennington-Gray *et al.*, 2003). Opperman (1995) suggested that cohort analysis is needed to examine changes in travel behaviours. Additionally, the majority of authors studying Generation Y as a whole have focused more on demographic and attitudinal characteristics, and shopping behaviours of this generation rather than its travel behaviours. Thus, the object of this study is to investigate and compare the differences in travel behaviours of Generation Y, Generation X and Baby Boomers.

Methodology

The data for this chapter are drawn from a broader study, analysing the travel behaviours of both current and future markets for the state of Texas. Monthly household telephone surveys were conducted on Texas travel advertising awareness and literature conversion. The study was designed to measure Texas tourism advertising awareness and literature conver-

sion and provide a general market profile of the leisure travellers within the USA. The most recent and relatively stable 2 years' (2005–2006) data were merged and only variables (including travel information resources, preferred activities while on a leisure trip and factors that may influence travel decisions) relevant to the current study were used. The sample for analysis (n = 3458) was respondents, aged 25 or older, who had taken a leisure out-of-state trip in the last 24 months or were planning a trip in the next 24 months. Since respondents had to be aged 25 or older to be included in the data utilized, only a portion of Generation Y was sampled in this study.

The analysis of variance procedure (ANOVA) and Tukey's post-hoc tests were performed to determine if there were significant statistical differences in the level of importance of information sources, as perceived by the three groups. The same methods were used to determine the differences on preferred activities to participate in while on a leisure trip and factors that influence trip decision.

Findings

The sample for this study consisted of 37.4% males and 62.6% females, and more than half of the respondents (52.3%) had an annual household income of US$35,000–US$99,999. More than three-quarters (78.3%) of the respondents were Caucasians, two-thirds (67.4%) were employed full-time and a majority of the respondents (70.0%) were married. Baby Boomers accounted for 62.4% (n = 2158) of the respondents, Generation X-ers accounted for 28.4% (n = 982) and Generation Y-ers accounted for 9.2% (n = 318) of the sample. A summary of the demographic information is presented in Table 3.1.

Respondents were asked to rate the importance of 11 information sources when planning an out-of-state leisure trip among destinations, where 1 = not at all important and 5 = very important. ANOVA was used to test for differences between the means of the responses and the importance of information sources across generational subgroups. Analysis revealed that nine of the 11 information

Table 3.1. Demographic characteristics of the sample.

Variable	Categories	Frequency	(%)
Gender	Male	1295	37.4
	Female	2163	62.6
Ethnicity	African-American	294	8.5
	White	2709	78.3
	Hispanic	125	3.6
	Asian/Pacific Islander	21	0.6
	Native American/Alaskan Native	77	2.2
	Prefer not to answer	125	3.6
	Other	20	0.6
	Multiple responses	87	2.5
Income	Less than US$10,000	73	2.1
	US$10,000–19,999	120	3.5
	US$20,000–34,999	343	9.9
	US$35,000–49,999	551	15.9
	US$50,000–74,999	749	21.7
	US$75,000–99,999	509	14.7
	US$100,000 or more	567	16.4
	Prefer not to answer	546	15.8
Marital status	Married	2420	70.0
	Single, never married	971	28.1
	Prefer not to answer	67	1.9
Employment	Employed full-time	2330	67.4
	Employed part-time	374	10.8
	Not employed	631	18.2
	Prefer not to answer	123	3.6
Generation	Baby Boomers (mean age = 52)	2158	62.4
	Generation X (mean age = 37)	982	28.4
	Generation Y (mean age = 29)	318	9.2

sources were rated as significantly different between the three groups (Table 3.2). To examine individual differences between groups, Tukey's post-hoc test was utilized (Table 3.2). Results found that Generation X and Generation Y evaluated phone access to travel consultants, travel packages including transportation and lodging and price discounts and coupons as more important than Baby Boomers. Generation Y evaluated a central reservation number for flights, hotels and car rentals and a calendar of events and information from friends and relatives as more important than Baby Boomers. Baby Boomers evaluated newspapers as more important than Generation X, while Generation Y evaluated television/radio broadcasts as more important than Baby Boomers (Table 3.3).

Respondents were additionally asked what activities they like to do while on a leisure trip, and ANOVA revealed significant statistical differences between activities. To examine indi-

Table 3.2. Results of ANOVA for importance on information sources.

Information sources	Significances
Travel literature	0.707
Phone access to travel counsellors	0.000
Travel packages including transportation and lodging	0.000
Price discounts and coupons	0.000
A calendar of events	0.030
A central reservation number for flights, hotels and car rentals	0.017
Information from friends and relatives	0.002
The Internet	0.034
Newspapers	0.020
Magazines	0.072
Television or radio broadcasts	0.046

vidual differences between groups, Tukey's post-hoc test was utilized and a summary of findings can be seen in Table 3.4. Results found

Table 3.3. Summary of Tukey's results of information sources.

Information sources			Mean differences	Significance
Phone access to travel counsellors	Baby Boomers	X-ers	−0.171	0.023
		Y-ers	−0.342	0.002
Travel packages (including transport and lodging)	Baby Boomers	X-ers	−0.297	0.000
		Y-ers	−0.473	0.000
Price discounts and coupons	Baby Boomers	X-ers	−0.213	0.000
		Y-ers	−0.336	0.000
A calendar of events	Baby Boomers	Y-ers	−0.229	0.022
A central reservation number for flights, hotels and car rentals	Baby Boomers	Y-ers	−0.280	0.012
Information from friends and relatives	Baby Boomers	Y-ers	−0.238	0.007
Newspaper	Baby Boomers	X-ers	0.125	0.034
Television or radio broadcasts	Baby Boomers	Y-ers	−0.189	0.046

Table 3.4. Summary of Tukey's results of preferred activities.

Activities			Mean differences	Significance
Amusement/theme parks	Baby Boomers	X-ers	−0.07582	0.000
		Y-ers	−0.06697	0.001
Art gallery/museum	Baby Boomers	X-ers	0.03297	0.004
		Y-ers	0.05948	0.001
Golfing/tennis	Baby Boomers	X-ers	0.03118	0.002
Hunting/fishing	Baby Boomers	X-ers	−0.02715	0.042
		Y-ers	−0.04369	0.035
Nightclubs/dancing	Baby Boomers	Y-ers	−0.01331	0.044
Sightseeing in cities	Baby Boomers	X-ers	0.07193	0.000
		Y-ers	0.12682	0.000
Visiting historical places	Baby Boomers	X-ers	0.03352	0.002
		Y-ers	0.05392	0.002

that fewer Baby Boomers participated in amusement/theme park activities than both Generation X-ers and Y-ers and that significantly more Baby Boomers participated in visiting museums than both Generations X and Y. Additionally, Baby Boomers participated in golfing and tennis more than Generation X and Boomers also participated in hunting and fishing more than both Generations X and Y. Generation Y-ers were also more likely to have participated in night clubs and dancing activities than Baby Boomers, while Baby Boomers were more likely to go sightseeing in cities and visit historical places than both Generations X and Y.

Respondents were also asked to rate the importance of various destination attributes on a 5-point scale. Results indicated that each group of respondents evaluated the importance of each factor differently. To examine individual differences between groups, Tukey's post-hoc test was utilized, and a summary of the results can be found in Table 3.5. Results found that Baby Boomers evaluated beaches, amusement park/theme parks and spectator sports such as baseball, basketball and football as less important destination attributes when choosing a destination than Generations X and Y, while Generation Y thought having big cities in a destination was more important than Generation X and Baby Boomers. Furthermore, Generation Y evaluated activities like tennis and golf and weather as more important than Baby Boomers while Baby Boomers evaluated good highway as more important than Generation X. Additionally, Baby Boomers

Table 3.5. Summary of Tukey's result of preferred destination attributes.

Activities			Mean differences	Significance
Beautiful beaches	Baby Boomers	X-ers	−0.261	0.007
		Y-ers	−0.333	0.046
Large cities	Baby Boomers	Y-ers	−0.678	0.000
Activities such as tennis and golf	Baby Boomers	Y-ers	−0.386	0.017
Amusement/theme parks	Baby Boomers	X-ers	−0.524	0.000
		Y-ers	−0.664	0.000
Good highways	Baby Boomers	X-ers	0.237	0.001
Historical sites	Baby Boomers	X-ers	0.332	0.000
		Y-ers	0.279	0.046
Museums	Baby Boomers	X-ers	0.259	0.003
Pretty scenery	Baby Boomers	X-ers	0.189	0.002
Shopping opportunities	Baby Boomers	Y-ers	−0.420	0.008
Spectator sports such as basketball,	Baby Boomers	X-ers	−0.251	0.022
baseball and football		Y-ers	−0.543	0.001
Weather	Baby Boomers	Y-ers	−0.246	0.039
Western image	Baby Boomers	X-ers	0.334	0.001

evaluated historical sites and western image as more important than Generations X and Y, furthermore, Baby Boomers evaluated museum and pretty scenery as more important than Generation X. Meanwhile, Generation Y evaluated shopping opportunities as more important than Baby Boomers.

Conclusions

This current study explored the differences in each group's use of different sources of information, participation in activities and the importance of characteristics for a destination to possess. The findings of this study may provide insightful information for destination-marketing organizations interested in targeting preferred visitors based on age differences. To target Baby Boomers more effectively, destination marketing managers should place more adverts in newspapers and emphasize attractions including museums, hunting/fishing and historical places, since research results revealed that more Baby Boomers participated in these activities. They also placed importance on these attributes when choosing a leisure vacation destination. The research findings are similar to Pennington-Gray *et al.* (2003).

If Generation X is the preferred market, destination-marketing managers should place more emphasis on travel counsellors, travel packages, price discount/coupons and highlight attractions such as beaches, amusement/theme parks and spectator sports. To target Generation Y more efficiently, promotion messages should be focused more on calendar of events, a central reservation number for booking hotels, flights and car rental, word of mouth, and television/radio broadcast and show images related to night clubs, big cities and shopping opportunities.

Clearly, this study is just one step towards a thorough understanding of the generational differences and similarities among travellers. Identification of generational issues is likely to result in development of marketing strategies that increase travel intention and preferences by offering destination attractiveness. Therefore, this study holds the potential for helping destination marketing organizations to better understand generational issues. Additionally, the results of the study will, hopefully, serve as a base for more comprehensive research in the future.

Marketing implications

Understanding the various attitudes associated with travel preferences across three distinct generations of consumers clearly has important implications for researchers and practitioners alike. For example, an understanding of exactly how each generation searches for travel information, in addition to what activities it likes to do while on a leisure trip, and what the factors are that a destination needs to have to attract its customers represent important insights on the part of destination-marketing organizations as they prepare an effective marketing plan.

As the research findings of the current study reveals, word of mouth is a reliable source of information for Generation Y. Marketers trying to reach out specifically to members of Generation Y are more likely to be successful if they act as their friends or assume they are their friends, to find out what they think (Beirne, 2008; Rowe, 2008). Additionally, Generation Y-ers want to answer as a group, and not as individuals (Beirne, 2008); they prefer directness over subtlety, action over observation and cool over all else, which means marketers could translate this mindset into an effective marketing strategy (Stevens *et al.*, 2005). In this way, marketing can be used to target quality services for customers to build positive relationships, and satisfied customers are likely to spread positive experiences to their peer groups.

Current research shows that Generation Y prefers to use a central reservation number for flights, hotels and car rentals and a calendar of events for information sources. Therefore, Generation-Y members expect a much greater array of product and service selectivity from one information source, and desire consumer control. With this number, they can find all the information they need to make a travel decision. Generation-Y members prefer to keep their time and commitments flexible, they also expect travel services to have as many personalization and customization features as possible to meet their consistently changing needs, interests and tastes (Sweeney, 2006). Destination marketing organizations should also be able to provide a much wider array of cost-effective travel packages, itineraries and services. As the current research revealed, Generation Y reported that phone access to travel counsellors is an important and preferable information source. Generation Y expects instant service; hence,

marketers should have 24/7 service personnel available to serve this target group to give them constant feedback on any questions they may have for their destinations. For advertising, Generation Y prefers constant interactivity, full motion multimedia, colourful graphics and audio (Sweeney, 2006). Thus, marketers should incorporate a multimedia advertisement campaign to attract Generation Y's attention. Generation Y is technologically savvy, therefore, to sell a destination or travel service to this target group, creating and increasing a positive attitude through the Internet and other technological innovations may offer an increase in sales (Belleau *et al.*, 2007).

In conclusion, there are several practical implications arising from these findings. First, the study provides an understanding of travel behaviours among three distinct generational groups. The study demonstrates that there are a number of differences in travel behaviours among these three groups of people. Second, destination-marketing organizations can apply current study findings to target markets. For example, marketing materials can be focused on newspapers as the medium when Baby Boomer is the desired market. Another practical implication of this research lies in the activities that people like to do while on a leisure trip. Destination-marketing organizations can emphasize their advertising on amusement/theme parks if Generations X and Y are the preferred travellers. Amusement/theme parks can arrange different themes and special events during each different holiday to create more diverse activities for its visitors. Last, destination-marketing organizations can tailor their attractions to meet the needs of different target audiences. Big city, nightclubs, dancing activities and shopping opportunities will be very appealing to Generation Y, if they are the preferred target market.

Limitations

Like any other study, this study is not free from limitations. Data for this study were gathered through a secondary data set. Since respondents had to be aged 25 or older to be included in the data utilized, only a portion of Generation Y was sampled in this study. Therefore, this excludes other age groups also falling under the Generation Y category, such as younger school-going teenagers. The generalizability of our findings should therefore be treated cautiously as further studies examining a broader range of Generation-Y travellers with larger and more representative sample sizes are still pending. However, the majority of research on this generation assumes Generation-Y consumers are all alike, though the generation includes 15-year olds to 32-year olds. A 15-year old will most surely have different travel behaviours from a 32-year old. Thus, a need exists to understand narrower segments of Generation Y's travel behaviours. For marketers to effectively target and position their destinations for travellers, more information is needed about specific age groups, especially when people who are aged 25 or older are more financially stable and have the ability to make travel decisions on their own.

An additional limitation is that this study did not actually compare generational cohorts, it only compared three different age groups. While these age groups correspond with different generational cohorts, many of the observed differences may simply be due to different life-cycle stages. If this study had surveyed the Baby Boomers in the late 1970s, when they were the same age as Generation Y, would this study have found that they also liked theme parks and more active leisure activities? To be certain of generational differences, it is better to have a data set stretching back 30–40 years, where the author could compare the different generations when they were at the same age.

References

Alch, M.L. (2000) The echo-boom generation. *Futurist* 34, 42.

Bakewell, C. and Mitchell, V.W. (2003) Generation Y female consumer decision-making styles. *International Journal of Retail & Distribution Management* 31(2), 95–106.

Beirne, M. (2008) Generation Gap. *Brandweek* 49, 16–20.

Belleau, B.D., Summers, T.A., Xu, Y. and Pinel, R. (2007) Theory of reasoned action: purchase intention of young consumers. *Clothing & Textiles Research Journal* 25(3), 244–257.

Beverland, M. (2001) Generation X and wine consumption. *Australian and New Zealand Wine Industry Journal* 16(1), 91–96.

Brand, R. (2000) Advertisers examine teens and their spending clout. Available at: http://www.tcpalm.com/business/01jteenu.shtml

Brooks, S. (2005) What's so special about Echo Boomers? *Restaurant Business* 104(15), 34–36.

De Lollis, B. (2005) Hotels loosen their ties for a younger crowd. *USA Today*.

Francese, P.A. (1993) Rising stars in the consumer constellation: a peer personality profile of the post-baby boom generation. *Hospitality Research Journal* 17(1), 17–27.

Freeman, L. (1995) No tricking the media savvy. *Advertising Age* 6, 30.

Gursoy, D., Maier, T.A. and Chi, C.G. (2008) Generational differences: an examination of work values and generational gaps in the hospitality workforce. *International Journal of Hospitality Management* 27, 448–458.

Harmon, H.H., Webster, R.L. and Weyenberg, S. (1999) Marketing medium impact: differences between baby boomers, and generation Xers in their information search in a variety of purchase decision situations. *Journal of Marketing Communications* 5, 29–38.

Horneman, L., Carter, R.W., Wei, S. and Ruys, H. (2002) Profiling the senior traveler: an Australian perspective. *Journal of Travel Research* 41, 23–37.

Kahle, L.R. (1995) Role-relaxed consumers: a trend of the nineties. *Journal of Advertising Research* 35(2), 66–71.

Kass, G. (1996) Call me mature. *American Demographics* 18, 11.

Kueh, K. and Voon, B.H. (2007) Culture and service quality expectations: evidence from generation Y consumers in Malaysia. *Managing Service Quality* 17(6), 656–680.

Kumar, A. and Lim, H. (2008) Age differences in mobile service perceptions: comparison of Generation Y and baby boomers. *Journal of Services Marketing* 22(7), 568–577.

Ma, Y.J. and Niehm, L.S. (2006) Service expectations of older Generation Y consumers: an examination of apparel retail settings. *Managing Service Quality* 16(6), 620–640.

Martin, C.A. and Turley, L.W. (2004) Malls and consumption motivation: an exploratory examination of older Generation Y consumers. *International Journal of Retail & Distribution Management* 32(10), 464–475.

McMahon, S. (2005) Going the X-tra mile. Available at: http://www.signonsandiego.com/uniontrib/20050424/news_mz1b24going.html

Mitchell, S. (1995) *The Official Guide to Generations: Who They Are, How They Live, What They Think*. New Strategist Publications, Ithaca, New York.

Morton, L.P. (2002) Targeting Generation Y. *Public Relations Quarterly* 47(2), 46–48.

Newborne, N. and Kerwin, K. (1999) Generation Y. *Business Week* 15, 80–88.

Nickel, P. and Wertheimer, A.I. (1979) Factors affecting consumers' images and choices of drugstores. *Journal of Retailing* 55(2), 71–78.

Noble, S.M., Haytko, D.L. and Philips, J. (2009) What drives college-age Generation Y consumers? *Journal of Business Research* 62(6), 617–628.

Opperman, M. (1995) Family life cycle and cohort effects: a study of travel patterns of german residents. *Journal of Travel and Tourism Marketing* 4(1), 23–45.

Paul, P. (2001) Getting inside Generation Y. *American Demographics* 23(9), 42–49.

Pennington-Gray, L., Fridgen, J.D. and Stynes, D. (2003) Cohort segmentation: an application to tourism. *Leisure Sciences* 25, 341–361.

Rentz, J. and Reynolds, F. (1991) Forecasting the effects of an aging population on product consumption: an age-period-cohort framework. *Journal of Marketing Research* 28, 355–360.

Reynolds, C. (2004) Overlooked and Under X-Ploited. Available at: http://findarticles.com/p/articles/mi_m4021/is_4_26/ai_n6047692

Roberts, J.A. and Manolis, C. (2000) Baby boomers and busters: an exploratory investigation of attitudes toward marketing, advertising and consumerism. *Journal of Consumer Marketing* 17(6), 481–499.

Rowe, M. (2008) Generation Revelation. *Restaurant Hospitality* January, 26–30.

Stevens, J., Lathrop, A. and Bradish, C. (2005) Tracking Generation Y: a contemporary sport consumer profile. *Journal of Sport Management* 19, 254–277.

Strauss, W. and Howe, N. (1991) *Generations: The History of America's Future, 1584–2096*. Quill, New York.

Sullivan, P. and Heitmeyer, J. (2008) Looking at Gen Y shopping preferences and intentions: exploring the role of experience and apparel involvement. *International Journal of Consumer Studies* 32, 285–295.

Sweeney, R. (2006) Millennial behaviors and demographics. Available at: http://library1.njit.edu/staff-folders/sweeney/

Wolburg, J.M. and Pokrywczynski, A. (2001) A psychographic analysis of Generation Y. *Journal of Advertising Research* 41(5), 33–53.

Wolf, M.M., Carpenter, S. and Qenani-Petrela, E. (2005) A comparison of X,Y, and Boomer generation wine consumers in California. *Journal of Food Distribution Research* 36(1), 186–191.

4 Understanding Generation-Y Tourists: Managing the Risk and Change Associated with a New Emerging Market

Pierre Benckendorff and Gianna Moscardo
School of Business, James Cook University

Introduction

A number of marketing companies and social commentators have begun to discuss in the broader public arena the notion that there exists a generational cohort that is profoundly different from those that have preceded it. This cohort is variously referred to as Generation Y, the Net or Web generation, the Echo Boomers or the Millennials. Donnison (2007) found that estimates of when Generation Y started can vary between 1977 and 1983, with end dates varying between 1983 and 2009. The majority of definitions, however, fell between 1977 and 1995. This generational cohort is therefore now reaching adulthood, creating new opportunities for exploring their characteristics, values, attitudes and consumption patterns in tourism.

At the core of the descriptions of Generation Y is a belief that this cohort exhibits a distinctive and unique pattern of values, attitudes and behaviours that have important implications for how it will respond to, and create change in, a number of public and social arenas. Generation Y has become more than simply a label used to describe people born between 1980 and 1994, it has become a symbol of a new 'culture' with a unique set of values, skills and behaviours that transcend geography and ethnicity. The consequences of this emerging culture are only just beginning to be discussed in higher education, as these individuals become the core group of college students, and in human relations, as they enter the workforce. But Generation Y also represents a significant market for tourist operations. So are the claims made about this group true? And what are the implications of these claims for tourism managers? Will Generation Y travel more or less, or take longer or shorter trips? What types of products will Generation Y demand? Both longitudinal and cross-sectional research is needed to reduce the risks that tourism managers face in dealing with this new generational cohort.

The idea of using age and/or generation as a market segmentation tool is not new to tourism research. The increasing attention being paid to senior tourists, for example, both reflects and recognizes that the ageing of Baby Boomers creates new tourism markets and that these Baby Boomer seniors are different from older travellers in the past (Gilleard and Higgs, 2002). Baby Boomers have captured the attention of tourism researchers and managers because of the large size of this generational cohort and their affluence (Shoemaker, 2000) and because many tourism researchers and managers are themselves Baby Boomers. More recent generational cohorts, such as Generation Y, have yet to be given the same sort of research attention in tourism.

Much of the material currently available that describes Generation Y has been provided by the commercial consultants and social-survey research companies focused on specific populations and client issues. Much of the information that is publicly available on Generation Y is about brand perception and attitudes towards work. This information is, however, limited in that few, if any, methodological details are provided and often quite contradictory claims are made leading to very disparate conclusions and recommendations. Generation Y is also emerging as a topic of interest in the academic literature, but the focus has been primarily on information and technology use (Gardner and Eng, 2005) and attitudes to learning and education (Oblinger and Oblinger, 2005). Very little is known about Generation Y in terms of travel and tourism behaviour and, as in other areas, many contradictory claims have been made. For example, a recent Australian news article reporting on a tourist survey claimed that Australian Generation-Y members were travelling less than previous younger age-groups (a decline of 15% over a 5-year period) and instead spending discretionary income on entertainment media and electronic equipment (Burke, 2007). This claim contrasts with another article published 2 months earlier claiming that 70% of Australian Generation-Y members had already travelled internationally (Sydney Morning Herald, 2007).

For tourism managers, Generation Y represents a substantial market, and having contradictory and limited information about its values, characteristics and attitudes towards travel limits the manager's abilities to effectively market to, and manage, this travel segment. If youth travel markets are changing, then doing business without information detailing these changes is risky. Change and risk are two closely linked concepts in all aspects of human life, including tourism. Typically we assume risk is a necessary companion to management or business change and often the risk associated with a change is used as a reason for not changing. What is problematic for many people to evaluate is the risk of not changing, as we have difficulty analysing trends and predicting future conditions. This is particularly true in tourism where consistent time series or longitudinal data are difficult to find, because tourism has only recently been recognized as a major social and economic phenomenon worthy of study by the government and other researchers. One way to reduce this risk is to examine the nature of these changes and explore the processes underlying them.

This chapter seeks to demonstrate the value of longitudinal generational research by describing a specific study that utilized time series data to examine the emergence of a particular generational cohort, Generation Y, in a major tourist destination in Australia, the Great Barrier Reef. The chapter compares and contrasts tourists in different age groups over time, in order to determine if and how Generation-Y travellers differ from other age groups and generational cohorts. The overall goal of the analysis is to determine what, if any, changes may be required from tourism managers to meet the requirements of this emerging tourism market.

Understanding Generation-Y Tourists

The data that form the basis of this chapter were collected in a series of surveys conducted over an 8-year time period from 1996 to 2002 with tourists visiting the Great Barrier Reef (GBR) region on the north-eastern coast of Australia. A total of 6431 survey questionnaires were completed by visitors on commercial tour operations to the GBR with an overall response rate of 73%. The surveys were conducted in English, German, Mandarin and Japanese with passengers on a wide variety of reef tours in a range of locations throughout the region and were distributed in two ways. The first method of distribution involved direct contact with visitors on day trips. As these boats returned to the coast, research interviewers approached all passengers judged to be older than 18 years. The second method of distribution relied on the support of tourism staff and was used with overnight and extended tours, and in these cases the staff approached visitors at the end of the trips and asked them to participate. These visitors completed the survey and posted it back to the research team. The survey questionnaire included questions gathering demographic information, travel behaviour (including travel party, previous experience in the region and type of reef travel undertaken), reef-travel motivation, activity participation and satisfaction with the reef tourism experience.

The GBR is a world heritage site covering an area of nearly 350,000 km[2] and is one of Australia's leading tourist attractions. Loker (1993) and Buchanan and Rossetto (1997) report that the GBR is a particularly important destination for younger, international, long-stay, independent travellers. These 'backpackers', as they are commonly labelled in Australia, are aged 31 years or less and are the main markets for specialist reef tours and dive trips (Moscardo, 2006).

A framework for understanding generational cohort differences

The challenge in studying age cohorts over time in tourist settings is to distinguish between three processes: maturation of individual travellers as they move through different lifecycle stages; changes across generations or cohorts; and development of the destination. Figure 4.1 sets out the six groups used in the present study with their sample sizes and the key comparisons that could be made between them. Each of the three processes proposed as potentially underlying change should exhibit a different pattern of results. If there are generational or cohort differences then the analyses should find key significant differences for those comparisons highlighted by the thickest arrows. That is, the youngest age groups should be significantly different from each other over time and there should be significant differences between the first two groups and the rest of the sample in 1996, but between the first and second groups in 2002. If maturation or development across the life cycle is the key process then the major significant differences would lie between each of the three age groups regardless of the year of the survey. If destination development is the key then the main differences should lie across the 2 survey years with minimal differences within each year.

It is most likely that more than one process is involved and so the analyses were conducted in two main stages using a series of analyses of variance and chi-square statistics, to compare and contrast the different age groups across the two time periods examined. The first stage looked at the three age groups within each of the survey years to check for maturation versus cohort differences. The second stage of the analyses compared all groups to each other and over time.

Table 4.1 provides a summary of the results of analyses conducted on travel behaviour variables. A detailed examination of the pattern of results in this table shows evidence for all three possible patterns of change. For example, the usual place of residence has changed substantially for all age groups across the 2 years, reflecting the development of the destination in different origin markets. But there were also substantial differences between the age groups within each year, suggesting

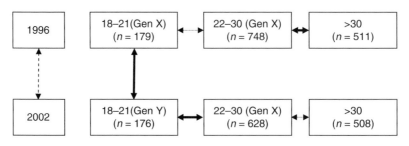

Fig. 4.1. Main groups and possible comparisons.

Table 4.1. Age-cohort differences over time for travel behaviour variables.

	1996			2001		
	18–21 (Generation X)	22–30 (Generation X)	>30	18–21 (Generation Y)	22–30 (Generation X)	>30
Usual place of residence						
Australia (%)	20	26	26	15	26	55
North America (%)	16	24	29	45	13	15
Europe (%)	30	19	22	30	52	18
Asia (%)	34	31	23	10	9	12

Overall chi-square = 705.1, $p < 0.05$; chi-square between age groups in 1996 only = 58.2, $p < 0.05$; chi-square between age groups in 2001 only = 338.3, $p < 0.05$

Previous visits to GBR						
0 (%)	70	64	65	81	62	60
1 (%)	17	20	23	8	16	17
2 (%)	3	3	3	3	5	7
>2 (%)	1	7	5	1	5	10
Regional resident (%)	9	6	4	7	12	6

Overall chi-square = 147.2, $p < 0.05$; chi-square between age groups in 1996 only = 25.9, $p < 0.05$; chi-square between age groups in 2001 only = 63.7, $p < 0.05$.

Visited other coral reefs (%)	37	44	47	26	38	42

Overall chi-square = 34.4, $p < 0.05$; chi-square between age groups in 1996 only was not significant; chi-square between age groups in 2001 only = 15.9, $p < 0.05$

Travel party						
Alone (%)	7	9	6	5	11	5
As a couple (%)	14	51	61	4	35	37
With a family group (%)	28	10	21	33	13	29
Family and friends (%)	4	2	2	7	5	9
Friends (%)	37	26	16	25	31	13
Organized group (%)	15	7	8	22	3	3

Overall chi-squares were significant for all the travel party categories; chi-squares between age groups in 1996 were significant for categories except alone and family and friends; chi-squares between age groups in 2001 were significant for all categories

Time spent away from home						
<1 week (%)	35	40	38	23	30	37
1–2 weeks (%)	15	30	35	13	11	24
2–3 weeks (%)	10	6	13	34	12	15
>3 weeks (%)	40	24	14	30	47	24

Overall chi-square = 585.8, $p < 0.05$; chi-square between age groups in 1996 only = 180.7, $p < 0.05$; chi-square between age groups in 2001 only = 185.3, $p < 0.05$

maturation effects. Finally, there were also differences between the age groups across the years, supporting an argument that there are cohort changes as well. In general, across all the variables in Table 4.1 the largest differences were between the youngest group in 1996 (Generation X) and the youngest group in 2001 (Generation Y) and then between the Generation Y and Generation X groups in 2001. In summary, the core differences between Generation-Y reef visitors and other groups appeared to be that they were more likely to come from North America, have less experience with reef destinations and take shorter trips.

Table 4.2 provides a summary of the differences in the target groups on information source usage. The cohort differences are not so clear in this table, with the largest differences being between the two time periods with all the 2001 groups more likely to use the Internet and guidebooks for information, and less likely to use travel agents. Generation-Y respondents were, however, distinctive in their low usage of travel agents. While Generation Y reported the highest usage of the Internet, the actual rate of 21% seems low given that widespread Internet use is often cited as a factor underlying the distinctive attitudes and behaviours of this cohort (Gardner and Eng, 2005).

The next set of analyses is summarized in Table 4.3 and focuses on what the respondent actually did while visiting the GBR region. Again, while all three change processes are evident, the largest changes were between the two youngest groups across the 2 years and between the Generation-Y and Generation-X respondents. In this case, Generation-Y respondents were less likely to participate in self-contained underwater breathing apparatus (SCUBA) diving and sailing, choosing instead larger boats with a focus on more general marine activities. Generation Y also appeared to be less interested in adventure activities and specialist tour operations than earlier groups of younger travellers.

The survey respondents were also asked to rate the importance of a number of reef trip motivations on a scale from 1 = not at all important, to 5 = very important. The use of rating scales allowed the researchers to employ a two-way analysis of variance procedure (ANOVA) to simultaneously explore the effects of age, time of survey and the interaction between these two independent variables. All the results of these ANOVAs are presented in Table 4.4. These results suggested that overall the largest differences in motivation ratings lay between the 2 years with much more varied scores across all the age groups in the 2001. Despite these year differences, two motivations were still significantly different between the youngest age groups across the 2 years. These were experiencing excitement and rest and relaxation, which were both more important for Generation-Y respondents.

The final analyses, presented in Table 4.5, were of differences in reef trip evaluations. The results for the first two trip evaluation variables showed no cohort or maturation effects. Across all the age groups it seems that reef visitors in 2001 were more satisfied with their experience, suggesting improvements in the tour operations in general. The patterns for the second two variables were less clear. These variables could not be subjected to significance

Table 4.2. Age cohort differences over time in information source use.

	1996			2001		
	18–21 (Generation X)	22–30 (Generation X)	>30	18–21 (Generation Y)	22–30 (Generation X)	>30
Auto association (%)	0	4	4	2	1	3
Brochures from outside region (%)	18	21	22	14	15	17
Brochures from inside region (%)	25	29	19	26	28	29
Internet (%)	4	4	2	21	15	16
Television (%)	1	0	1	4	4	6
Friends/family (%)	56	50	45	50	43	37
Travel agents (%)	34	50	50	15	20	20
Newspapers (%)	18	16	22	18	22	32
Guidebooks (%)	15	16	19	29	28	27

Overall chi-squares were significant for all the information source categories except guidebooks; chi-squares between age groups in 1996 were significant for all categories except brochures outside the region, Internet, television and guidebooks; chi-squares between age groups in 2001 were significant only for family/friends, travel agents and newspapers

Table 4.3. Age cohort differences over time in reef trip behaviours.

	1996			2001		
	18–21 (Generation X)	22–30 (Generation X)	>30	18–21 (Generation Y)	22–30 (Generation X)	>30
Reef trip type						
Large boat to reef (%)	44	31	46	70	46	55
Small boat to reef (%)	25	26	26	5	13	9
Island trip (%)	17	37	26	22	25	24
Dive trip (%)	14	6	2	3	16	11

Overall chi-square = 496.4, $p < 0.05$; chi-square between age groups in 1996 only = 104.9, $p < 0.05$; chi-square between age groups in 2001 only = 61.2, $p < 0.05$

	1996			2001		
Reef activity participation						
Swimming (%)	67	72	63	65	56	47
Fishing (%)	6	10	3	3	6	7
Sailing (%)	28	13	9	1	1	1
Snorkelling (%)	68	79	63	75	71	62
SCUBA diving (%)	38	31	15	23	35	16
Glass-bottom boat (%)	45	47	59	28	19	375

Overall chi-squares were significant for all the participation categories; chi-squares between age groups in 1996 were significant for all categories; chi-squares between age groups in 2001 were significant for all categories except fishing and sailing

Table 4.4. Age cohort differences over time in reef trip motivations.

	1996			2001		
	18–21 (Generation X)	22–30 (Generation X)	>30	18–21 (Generation Y)	22–30 (Generation X)	>30
Motivation						
Be with family/friends	2.7	2.8	2.3	2.4	2.1	2.3
Escape from everyday stresses	2.7	2.9	2.8	3.9	3.9	3.9
Do something new and different	3.5	3.4	3.3	4.5	4.4	4.4
Be physically active	3.6	2.9	2.8	3.2	3.2	3.2
Experience nature	3.5	3.4	3.4	4.6	4.6	4.6
Experience some excitement	3.3	3.1	2.9	4.2	3.6	3.6
Rest and relax	3.0	3.2	3.1	3.7	3.8	3.8

Numbers are mean ratings on scale from 1, not at all important, to 5, very important

Results of ANOVA	Overall F	F for age groups	F for year	F for interaction of age × year
Statement				
Be with family/friends	38.9	2.6	85.0	2.6
Escape from everyday stresses	178.0	1.8	494.3	1.8
Do something new and different	355.4	9.6	842.1	0.3
Be physically active	22.5	3.8	45.1	0.9
Experience nature	557.4	0.7	1467.4	0.9
Experience some excitement	176.1	86.0	440.5	10.2
Rest and relax	96.6	1.2	255.0	3.1

Results significant at the $p < 0.05$ level are in bold

Table 4.5. Age cohort differences over time in reef trip evaluations.

	1996			2001		
	18–21 (Generation X)	22–30 (Generation X)	>30	18–21 (Generation Y)	22–30 (Generation X)	>30
Mean overall enjoyment (0 not at all – 10 very much)	8.2	8.2	8.2	8.7	8.5	8.7

Overall $F = 13.3$, $p < 0.05$, F for age not significant, F for year = 42.5, $p < 0.05$, F for interaction not significant

Recommend reef trip						
No (%)	2	1	1	0	1	1
Do not know (%)	10	7	7	6	3	3
Probably (%)	22	32	27	28	24	20
Definitely (%)	66	60	65	66	72	76

Overall chi-square = 88.9, $p < 0.05$; chi-square between age groups in 1996 not significant, $p < 0.05$; chi-square between age groups in 2001 only = 16.2, $p < 0.05$

Best features						
Activities available (%)	56	58	54	72	69	69
Reef-educational (%) experiences	2	2	2	1	0	0
Reef itself (%)	13	11	14	6	7	7
Wildlife (%)	23	23	21	17	19	15
Service quality (%)	2	2	45	2	1	1
Suggested improvements						
More planning information (%)	22	40	32	34	24	19
More reef education (%)	16	17	14	10	14	16
More facilities (%)	6	6	7	10	17	18
Improved safety (%)	7	4	5	10	11	10
Better service quality (%)	4	2	2	5	6	6

testing as they were answers given to open-ended questions. Multiple answers were possible and all the answers were recorded according to the major themes that were identified, and these are listed in Table 4.5. The two most obvious features of Generation-Y visitors in these two variables were a greater emphasis placed on activities and a lesser emphasis on experiencing the reef itself in terms of the best feature of the reef trip, and a greater emphasis on trip-planning information and a lesser emphasis on reef education in suggested improvements.

Conclusions

The results provided evidence of all three processes – changes resulting from development of the destination, changes resulting from the maturation or development of tourists as they age and move through different lifecycle stages, and cohort or generational differences. However, when both destination and individual maturation are taken into account, Generation-Y tourists still displayed significant differences to the other age cohorts on a number of variables. The results also provided some consistency with previous claims about Generation Y. For example, this group was more likely to travel in a family group, which is consistent with a tendency for Generation-Y individuals to stay at home longer (Huntley, 2006). They were also more interested in escape, novelty and excitement, a pattern consistent with their early exposure to a wide range of entertainment and leisure experiences (Aleh, 2000). There were also some findings that were not consistent with previous claims. The relatively low rate of Internet usage, for example, seems not to support claims made about Internet usage as a defining feature of this cohort. It has been suggested elsewhere that Internet usage may have been overstated and may appear so because of a heavy reliance on online survey methods to study this group (Broos and Roe, 2006).

In the specific destination that was studied, the GBR, a number of characteristics that were found to be associated with Generation-Y reef visitors can be linked to particular challenges for tourism managers. In particular, this group was more likely to use the Internet and guidebooks for travel information, take shorter trips and have less travel experience. The Generation-Y respondents in this study also differed significantly from all other groups in that they were less interested in nature education activities and much more concerned about gathering specific tour information in order to plan their reef experiences to maximize value for money. The first of these challenges presented by these Generation-Y characteristics relates to the importance of nature education as a tool to support sustainable tourism to this destination. Nature education or interpretation has been used as a key strategy to influence tourist behaviour and minimize negative impacts. The Generation-Y tourists in this study were significantly less interested in this aspect of their reef experiences, suggesting that reef tourism managers may need to reconsider strategies for communicating with tourists and influencing their behaviour. Second,

the Generation-Y tourists were also more demanding in terms of organizing their reef experiences to maximize value for money. Reef tour operators who can provide for this need are likely to gain a competitive advantage with this group.

Finally, the changing pattern of behaviours has implications for a number of smaller and more specialized reef tour operations. As noted earlier, since the late 1990s, tourism in this destination region has relied heavily on longer-stay visitors and in particular on the young independent travellers referred to as backpackers. The data in the present study suggest that emerging youth markets to this destination are not like the backpackers that have dominated in the past, and this has implications for the provision, marketing and sustainability of current tourism activities in this destination.

The overall pattern of results suggested that the use of generational cohorts as a market segmentation tool is valid and that Generation Y is emerging as a group of travellers with a unique pattern of characteristics, motivations and expectations. The study showed that not all claims made in the media about Generation Y are supported by evidence and that not all claims may apply to specific tourism destinations. This study also demonstrated the value of longitudinal data sets in providing the information necessary to evaluate and describe changing patterns of tourist behaviours. There is a risk associated with misunderstanding Generation Y, and tourism research is a key element in managing this risk.

References

Aleh, M.L. (2000) The Echo-boom generation. *The Futurist*, 42–46.

Broos, A. and Roe, K. (2006) The digital divide in the playstation generation: self-efficacy, locus of control and ICT adoption among adolescents. *Poetics* 34, 306–317.

Buchanan, I. and Rossetto, A. (1997) *With My Swag Upon My Shoulder: A Comprehensive Study of International Backpackers to Australia*. Bureau of Tourism Research, Canberra, Australia.

Burke, N. (2007) Singles favour gadgets over travel. *The Advertiser* 26 March. Available at: http://www.news.com.au/travel/story/0,23483,21454287-27977,00.html

Donnison, S. (2007) Unpacking the millennials: a cautionary tale for teacher education. *Australian Journal of Teacher Education* 32, 1–13.

Gardner, S. and Eng, S. (2005) What students want: generation Y and the changing function of the academic library. *Portal: Libraries and the Academy* 5(3), 405–420.

Gilleard, C. and Higgs, P. (2002) Concept forum: the third age: class, cohort or generation? *Ageing and Society* 22, 369–382.

Gorman, P., Nelson, T. and Glassman, A. (2004) The millennial generation: a strategic opportunity. *Organizational Analysis* 12(3), 255–270.

Howe, N. and Strauss, W. (2000) *Millennials Rising: The Next Great Generation*. Vintage, New York.

Huntley, T. (2006) A job for life? Attitudes to work amongst Generation Y. *Reform* 88, 24–27.

Loker, L. (1993) *The Backpacker Phenomenon II*. James Cook University, Townsville, Queensland, Australia.

Moscardo, G. (2006) Backpackers and other younger travellers to the Great Barrier Reef: an exploration of changes in characteristics and behaviours 1996–2002. *Tourism Recreation Research* 31(3), 29–38.

Oblinger, D.G. and Oblinger, J.L. (eds) (2005) *Educating the Net Generation*. Educause. Available at: http://www.educause.edu/educatingthenetgen/

Shoemaker, S. (2000) Segmenting the mature market: 10 years later. *Journal of Travel Research* 39, 11–26.

Sydney Morning Herald. (2007) Generation Y stay Home? Sydney Morning Herald, 16 January. Available at: http://www.smh.com.au/news/travel/generation-y-stay-home/2007/01/16/1168709730245.html

5 Generation Y as Wine Tourists: Their Expectations and Experiences at the Winery-cellar Door

Joanna Fountain[1] and Steve Charters[2]

[1]Environment, Society and Design Faculty, Lincoln University; [2]Reims Management School and Edith Cowan University

Introduction

Wine tourism and research surrounding it has developed substantially since the mid-1990s. The importance for wineries of visitation to cellar doors is recognized by both the tourism and wine industries (Carlsen and Charters, 2006; Mitchell and Hall, 2006), and the need to understand the expectations and experiences of wine tourists has driven much of the research that has been conducted. Ensuring a match between expectations and experience of the cellar door will affect not only the tourists' satisfaction with the experience but their emotional attachments to the brand and, by implication, their future purchase intentions (Dodd and Bigotte, 1997). It is important to note, however, that wine tourists are not a homogeneous grouping (Mitchell *et al.* 2000; Charters and Ali-Knight, 2002), and the importance of understanding the differences between them is increasingly recognized.

Anecdotal evidence suggests that Baby Boomers, particularly males, have been viewed as the typical, and perhaps most desirable, wine tourists in the past (Charters and O'Neill, 2000). This is due to a range of factors, including their role in driving the growth in wine consumption in the anglophone world, their perceived level of wine knowledge and wine involvement, and greater disposable income. However, it is now becoming clear that a younger generation of wine consumers and wine tourists need to be considered if the industry is to have a long-term future (Koerber, 2000). This will require an understanding of the relationship of Generation Y to the winery experience. To this end, this chapter explores the attitudes, expectations and behaviour of Generation Y at the winery-cellar door. In particular, the focus is on their preferences regarding the interaction they seek with cellar-door staff, their needs with regards to the type of education and/or information sought during a winery visit and their overall attitude to a winery experience. The chapter is based on fieldwork conducted in Swan Valley, Western Australia, Yarra Valley, Victoria and Waipara Valley, New Zealand. It is worth noting that Generation Y has been defined in this chapter as those born between 1978 and 1994 (Sheahan, 2005).

Generation Y, Wine and Wine Tourism

A growing body of research has explored the significance of age or generational groupings as a factor in the wine tourism experience over the past decade (Mitchell, 2002; Treloar, 2004; Treloar *et al.*, 2004; Charters and Fountain, 2006; Dodd *et al.*, 2006; Nowak *et al.*, 2006). In relation to younger wine tourists' experience at the winery-cellar door, Mitchell's (2002) study found no significant generational differences in satisfaction. However, glimpses of age-related factors affecting cellar-door experiences have at times emerged from other more general investigations of the characteristics and experiences of wine tourists. For example, Dodd and Bigotte (1997) found evidence of a variation in perception of winery experiences based on the age of winery visitors, suggesting that older visitors were generally less critical than younger ones. The same study also suggested that younger wine tourists rated service quality as a more important factor in determining satisfaction with the winery visit than their older counterparts. What was not investigated, however, was whether the lower satisfaction of younger wine tourists was due to differing priorities at the cellar door, or to differential experiences of service quality at the winery visited.

Additionally, there has been research conducted into the importance of generational cohorts in relation to wine consumption, with growing recognition of the need to foster an interest in wine among younger consumers in order to ensure the long-term survival of the wine industry (Beverland, 2001; Howard and Stonier, 2001; Treloar, 2004; Nowak et al., 2006; Thach and Olsen, 2006; Olsen et al., 2007).

Generation Y has been portrayed by some as a confident cohort – comfortable with evolving technologies, self-reliant, ambitious, tolerant of others and eager for a challenge (Martin and Tulgan, 2001). However, it has also been described as lazy, self-absorbed, inpatient and ill-mannered (Martin and Tulgan, 2001). Sheahan (2005) counters this by suggesting that Generation Y is perceived this way because it is not prepared to compromise or sacrifice lifestyles for career ambitions. Members expect (and demand) enjoyment from their employment, and seek meaningful and interesting work in which they experience some control over their working environment. Generation Y seeks similar stimulation in its leisure environments through multi-sensory experiences, entertainment, fun and variety. This generation has been raised to be demanding; members want 'instant gratification' and enjoy getting 'something for nothing'. In this regard, they may see little connection between effort and results. Researchers report that this cohort has high self-confidence, expecting respect and carrying a sense of entitlement into most encounters. However, it also needs validation from others, suggesting the self-confidence noted above may not yet be very robust (Sheahan, 2005).

As stated above, limited research has been conducted into the wine involvement of Generation Y (Treloar, 2002, 2004; Thach and Olsen, 2006), and no in-depth study has been completed into the expectations and experience of this generational cohort as wine tourists. This is partly due to the fact that members of Generation Y, outside Europe at least, are currently irregular wine drinkers (Scalera, 2002). Their early experience of alcohol begins with experimenting with alcoholic beverages in pubs, clubs and bars where the expectation to drink wine is lower than it is to consume beer and spirits (Scalera, 2002; Treloar, 2004). This does not mean that members of Generation Y are not drinking wine at all; Treloar (2004) reports that over 60% of his Australasian Generation-Y respondents drank wine at least once a month, and almost a third drank wine weekly. According to his research, the most common environment in which this group consumes wine is while having an 'intimate dinner', where the wine adds to the atmosphere of the occasion. These findings are echoed in research in the USA, which found that a similar proportion of their sample drank wine (66%); however, this is much higher than the national average of 26% (Thach and Olsen, 2006). Thach and Olsen (2006) report that among their young respondents there was a preference for red wine over white, and they drank wine because they liked the taste, its relationship with food and its ability to help them relax. While they associate wine with 'nice dinners', there was a perception that wine is not 'cool or hip', and it was seen by some to be 'expensive, snobby and snooty' (p. 319). However, it is also seen to be a natural product.

Treloar (2004) observes that a significant proportion of Generation-Y respondents show an interest in wine tourism. In fact, 59% of his respondents had visited a winery at least once in the past, and 67% of his sample thought visiting wineries was an appealing activity. As a result of this finding, Treloar et al. (2004) suggest that an emphasis on the leisure and social aspects of wine tourism rather than more wine-related aspects, such as production techniques, wine styles or cellaring practices may be more effective in marketing to this segment. Similarly, other authors have suggested that social activities, such as wine events and festivals, may prove an important avenue through which to introduce younger wine tourists, including the Generation-Y cohort, to the wine tourism experience (Houghton, 2001; Dodd *et al.*, 2006). There is evidence also that a positive experience at the cellar door will stimulate a long-term sense of attachment and brand loyalty in Generation-Y tourists (Nowak *et al.*, 2006).

While these findings provide a useful starting point, it is clear that further research into this cohort at the winery-cellar door would be beneficial. Furthermore, given that this generation has grown up with ever-changing technologies (Hofman, 1999; King, 2000; Thach and Olsen, 2006), their openness to change may provide an important opportunity for wine marketers and cellar-door managers if they are able to identify products and experiences which appeal to these young adults.

Exploring Generation-Y Wine Tourists: a Modified Mystery Shopping Approach

A modified mystery shopping approach was developed and applied to the exploration of the experience of Generation Y at the winery-cellar door. Mystery shopping is a form of covert participant observation in which researchers take on the role of customers or potential customers in order to monitor the processes and procedures involved in service delivery (Wilson, 1998). Most significantly, this approach enables the researcher to get first-hand knowledge of the service environment as it unfolds in a natural and uncontrived setting (Grove and Fisk, 1992; Wilson, 1998). The potential of observational methods, including mystery shopping, for investigating service provision is increasingly acknowledged and has been used extensively in the services industry to investigate service quality (Jorgensen, 1989; Grove and Fisk, 1992; Wilson, 1998), yet it has rarely been used in tourism research to date (Hudson *et al.*, 2001; Thach *et al.*, 2007).

Typically, the goal of commercial mystery shopping is to *reduce* the impact of the shopper's personal characteristics and subjectivity on the assessment of a service encounter (Morrison, Colman, and Preston, 1997; Wilson, 1998; Hudson *et al.*, 2001), but in the current context the differences in perceptions and expectations of the mystery shoppers based on individual characteristics, particularly as they related to generational groupings, were of central importance. Consequently, the research sought to explore both the supply and the demand sides of the service encounter, using a modified mystery shopping approach that returns the methodology to its qualitative origins, brings a phenomenological emphasis on the consumer's experience, and prioritizes the subjective and affective components of the visitor experience of the winery-cellar door (Charters *et al.*, 2009).

This research consisted of two main processes. First, a short, open-ended questionnaire was developed to assess the participants' experience of the winery-cellar door during the mystery shopping exercise. Second, focus groups were used to revisit the questions covered in the questionnaire in more detail.

The participants involved in the encounter were recruited using convenience sampling among residents in the cities adjacent to the winery regions (Perth, Melbourne and Christchurch), and specifically with a form of snowball sampling. The Generation-Y participants included students and recent graduates of the researchers' universities, plus friends of those students, and friends and children of work colleagues. Participants were selected by virtue of having visited a winery, having some interest in wine, and to represent a range of generational cohorts. While a range of interest levels was felt desirable to offer some form of triangulation (Denzin, 1989; Thach and Olsen, 2006), participants with a high degree of involvement that could skew the findings were avoided.

Fitting with the phenomenological approach of this research, before visiting the winery, the participants were briefed to treat the experience as a normal and pleasurable experience. They were then sent out to visit wineries in teams of six. In general the teams comprised a pair of each of three 'generational groups': one pair of Baby Boomers, one from Generation X and one from Generation Y. All participants were sent out in pairs to ensure alternative perspectives on a single encounter, again increasing trustworthiness of data (Wallendorf and Belk, 1989). The teams, although at the winery at the same time, were sent in a staggered way to avoid any appearance of acting as one homogeneous group. On leaving the cellar door the participants individually completed a questionnaire about their experience before returning to the project headquarters where the focus group debriefing, facilitated by one of the researchers, took place. The focus groups tended to last for between 20 and 40 min and they were recorded on audiotape, and then transcribed for later analysis. The analysis involved the close examination of both the transcriptions and the questionnaires for patterns of behaviour and for emergent themes – as well as for any apparent contradictions.

In total, 82 participants were involved in this research, and teams made 28 winery visits (16 in Australia and 12 in New Zealand). Forty-eight of these encounters were undertaken by 24 Generation-Y participants, with a fairly even split between males (11) and females (13). This cohort of participants generally had relatively low subjective wine knowledge; 9% reporting no knowledge at all, 68% reporting basic knowledge and the remaining 23% reporting intermediate knowledge. They did drink wine, however; almost three-quarters (74%) drank wine at least monthly, and 47%

drank wine weekly or more often. To this extent, as one would expect within a wine tourism setting, the participants generally showed a higher level of involvement with wine than would be normal for their age group.

Generation-Y Wine Tourists: Some Characteristics

Table 5.1 provides a summary of some key findings relating to the experience of Generation Y at the cellar door in comparison to the other generational groupings. These will be explored in more detail with a consideration of the cohort's need for a total experience and for interaction, the desire to learn and to gain a connection, and the fact that differing experiences are sought at differing wineries. While a percentage is given to the number expressing a preference in each category, this is merely indicative of relative importance, as this was not a quantitative study, so no statistical significance is implied.

Generation Y wants a total experience

Initial findings from the research reveal some interesting characteristics of Generation-Y wine tourists, which tend to support some of the more general assessments of the cohort. First, Generation Y-participants clearly placed an emphasis on enjoying the entire experience

Table 5.1. A comparison by generational grouping of the importance of aspects of the cellar-door experience.

Rating activity as important when visiting a winery (%)	Gen Y	Gen X	Baby Boomer
Wine tasting	75	76	85
Wine buying	25	40	40
Learning about wine tasting	63	43	24
Learning about winemaking	56	29	14
Learning how to cellar	25	38	14
Touring the winery	38	19	24
Atmosphere location	63	76	62
Enjoying day out with friends	94	95	85
Attending wine event festival	25	14	5
Eating a meal	44	67	60

of the winery, rather than explicitly focusing on wine tasting (and even less on buying wine), although wine tasting was still important. A number of participants commented that a significant aspect of their visit was that it was relaxed, inviting and 'fun'. As an example of this, one male wrote in his questionnaire: 'When wine tasting with friends, having a good time...is more important than tasting the wine.' This informant stated subsequently in the focus group that he 'didn't like the wines' this winery offered, but liked the atmosphere as it was not 'too posh'; therefore he would return with friends. This seems to support the findings of previous research that enjoying a day out is a more important motivator for cellar-door visitation than wine tasting alone (Treloar *et al.*, 2004; Dodd *et al.*, 2006).

As indicated above, the atmosphere of a winery was very important for these young participants, and they appreciated an environment that was not intimidating. An important point in this context was that wineries with imposing buildings, or which seemed too 'refined' or 'upmarket' to Generation Y, were seen as potentially more intimidating than small family-run establishments. A number of participants acknowledged that they felt apprehensive approaching larger, more imposing winery structures. By comparison, the smaller establishments, with their less sophisticated surroundings, were less threatening, and in some ways were more appealing:

> At [the smaller winery]...I didn't feel as intimidated by the whole situation...the building was not as nice looking but it does the job (male).

While all of the young participants in this research had visited a winery before, many considered themselves inexperienced wine tasters and appreciated efforts to reduce the 'intimidation factor'. Thus, the welcome received from cellar-door staff was crucial in relaxing these visitors. Participants unanimously agreed that an appropriate and proactive greeting from cellar-door staff made them feel much more relaxed in the setting on arrival. Other things could also set them at ease, for example, having a dog at the door or music playing were two ways some participants felt wineries had reduced their initial tension on arrival.

Generation Y seeks interaction

In keeping with their focus on the overall experience, Generation-Y participants expressed a strong desire for interaction with cellar-door staff during their winery experience; as one respondent said 'the more interaction there is the better'. Thus, it was important that their cellar-door experience involved a personalized service – rather than merely exchanging information or goods. This point is summarized as follows:

> It's more about having a conversation with them....It's like getting to know you and your wine habits....Not trying to sell you anything, but trying to see what you like, and what might suit you (female).

This prior expectation of interaction with cellar-door staff was most apparent in accounts from participants who had not had this need met:

> She didn't ask anything about us...about what we were doing, or try to make it more personal, it was very much just 'taste the wines' (female).

Generation-Y participants sought a wine-tasting experience that was more flexible than that desired by Baby Boomers, however they did desire some structure in their cellar-door experience (more than Generation X), due to their lack of confidence about the wine-tasting experience. In focus group discussions, they questioned their ability to 'do the tasting right', as the following quotation indicates:

> I felt really intimidated because she just goes 'Do you want to try the wines? There's the list' and I was looking at the list, going 'this is just complete gibberish to me, I have no real idea of what's going on', so I sort of blindly pointed at one (male).

For this reason, Generation-Y participants seemed happiest with a partially structured process, involving more reassurance or guidance from the cellar-door staff to account for their lack of experience. This reassurance and more interaction, in general, were additional ways in which staff could reduce the intimidation factor. Thus, a number of young participants thought an opening question from the staff member – similar to that experienced in other retail settings – would have been useful to ascertain visitors' interests and existing knowledge of wine. In light of this requirement, Generation-Y participants rated their experience very highly in situations where they did not feel uncertain about the process. They also sought advice from the cellar-door staff in order to find a wine that would suit them:

> The whole reason that you go to the cellar door is to try and find wines that you enjoy drinking. So, as far as I'm concerned, they're the experts, they're the ones who know what their talking about, so…they can help you find out what you want in a wine (female).

There were other ways in which they sought this guidance too, including using displays of awards won to indicate which wines they should taste.

Generation Y wants to learn

A key finding in this study is the interest these participants expressed for learning more about wine, reflecting their openness to a challenge and to new experiences. This tends to contradict previous research that suggests that the social, enjoyable element is more important to young people's winery experience than wine tasting and related activities (Treloar et al., 2004). In fact, this study seemed to suggest that Generation Y is *more* interested in learning from its winery experience than either the Generation X or Baby Boomer participants, perhaps due to these other cohorts having more existing knowledge. Despite evidence of a lack of self-confidence about the wine-tasting process, these participants were willing to confront their ignorance by asking questions, sometimes of a fairly basic nature:

> I'm not a big wine connoisseur or anything, so I…asked her the difference between Pinot Noir and Riesling and stuff like that and she was really helpful. I learnt a few things. She answered my questions really well (female).

In order to feel comfortable asking these questions, Generation-Y participants had to feel as if the staff members treated them seriously and with respect; this was an issue to which they seemed particularly sensitive. At the outset of this study, the researchers were interested to explore whether younger people were treated differently from older visitors at the cellar door. While at some cellar doors, Generation-Y participants perceived that they received different and inferior service to their older counterparts (Fountain and Charters, 2004), there were also occasions when the youngest pairing in a team received superior treatment to the others, so there was little consistency in this regard. However, where Generation-Y participants did feel less well treated, or treated in a different way, their interpretation of this situation differed markedly to that of the older cohorts. On receiving what they felt was inferior service, older participants would explain this difference of treatment in structural terms – for example, their positioning at the tasting bar was disadvantageous or their arrival at a busy time precluded better treatment. By comparison, Generation-Y participants took it personally, often blaming their different treatment on their age, their probable financial status or their lack of wine knowledge; the following quotation is typical:

> She may not have been quite so at ease with us, or maybe not so interested in talking to us, because it was probably unlikely that we would be buying, or able to hold a conversation to the same extent that perhaps [the others] could (male).

Where they did feel respected, however, Generation-Y participants were keen to seek more information from the cellar-door staff:

> We were asking some pretty silly questions and he wasn't laughing about it or anything – he was giving a serious response back (male).

Another important prerequisite for members of Generation Y to feel comfortable asking questions was the feeling that the staff had the time to talk to them. Again, the atmosphere had to be non-intimidating, and not feeling rushed was an important part of this.

Generation Y seeks a connection

Despite an assumption in some quarters that Generation Y may be a 'self-absorbed' cohort, this did not seem to be the case; these participants did not want 'one-way conversations' where the emphasis was only on them and their needs. Through interacting with the cellar-door staff they were seeking more meaningful encounters and experiences and a sense of 'connection' to the winery itself – a quality linked to Generation Y in previous research (Sheahan, 2005). Consequently, many participants expressed a strong desire to find out more about the history of the winery and winemaker in order to give their experience that more meaningful, personal touch (Charters *et al.*, 2009). In this desire, the youngest participants were joined by their Generation-X counterparts, but it did not seem to be as important to the Baby Boomers.

This connection seemed much more likely to occur at smaller wineries, where many young participants felt that they were having a genuine conversation with the staff members, rather than a commercial transaction. Comments about the personal and 'real' nature of the interaction between the visitor and staff of smaller cellar doors were frequently made, and there was a sense that participants were made to feel special at these smaller wineries. As one female said of a smaller winery visited: 'it was just that family feel: it was her wine, and her photo and her bottles…so there was just a personal touch to it'. Other participants linked these smaller, family run wineries to a less commercial experience:

> I enjoyed the boutique experience there. Because going to a commercial winery and then a boutique one, it is interesting to note the differences. Just chatting to the guy, his knowledge was fantastic. I really enjoyed that, compared to the commercial ones with just staff who don't know a huge amount whereas this chap just seemed to know everything (male).

Money, or lack of it, was explicitly an issue for these participants, and their lack of funds was mentioned frequently, particularly in relation to buying wine. Having said this, many of the Generation-Y participants *did* buy wine. In deciding to buy wine not only was the taste and price important, but also the feeling of connection that had developed with the cellar-door staff or the winery itself. As one male succinctly put it 'if the service is excelling then it is easier to get your wallet out'. Further, the role of a bottle of wine as a souvenir of an enjoyable experience was explained by a young participant:

> [You'd buy a bottle of wine] and then you'd drink that wine, and you'd remember the experience, and if you were drinking it with friends you'd say 'oh, I bought this at [the winery]. I remember we had a great experience; this is what we did' (female).

Different wineries for different experiences

It was clear that different types of wineries served very different functions for these young participants. Smaller wineries were environments in which younger wine tasters felt less rushed, and where a personal connection with the staff enabled them to feel comfortable and offered them the opportunity to ask more questions. Thus, it is not surprising that many participants explicitly stated a preference for visiting smaller wineries in the future:

> With the bigger winery you feel like you are pushed in the door, and pushed out again. It's like there's only a set time they really want you in there, then you kind of do the loop and then you're out again. But here you wander around, and it's small, but you feel like you can ask questions, it does make you want to come back and learn a little more from the guy. So yeah, I would go back and I would purchase their wine (male).

This preference for small wineries is not as clear-cut as it might seem. While many participants stated that they much preferred their experience at the smaller wineries – they felt like lingering, they learnt a lot, they would buy the wines again – many of these same people stated that they wouldn't necessarily visit the *same* small winery again, as 'you've seen what there is to see and there's not much else' – perhaps highlighting Generation Y's need for variety in leisure activities (Sheahan, 2005). The issue seemed to be that once they had tasted the wine and learnt what they could from the cellar-door staff, there was little more the winery could offer in the way of a 'total experience'. This was a viewpoint heard repeatedly from Generation-Y participants; while they preferred their experiences at small wineries, their encounters at larger wineries did not necessarily leave them disappointed, and the wider range of attractions at larger wineries meant that they were more likely to consider revisiting them. However, few of those who said they would return to a larger winery stated that they would come again to taste wine, reporting instead that a future visit would be for a social occasion, particularly for a meal. The exception to this was where a smaller winery was hosting a social event, such as a music festival, which Generation-Y participants stated *would* draw them back for the social occasion it offered.

Lessons for Wine Tourism

The findings summarize the experience of only 24 Generation-Y participants visiting a small number of wineries in Australasia. Nevertheless, there are important implications of the expectations of the winery-cellar door experience among this group with much broader significance.

First, despite their reputation as a 'confident' and 'self-reliant' group (Martin and Tulgan, 2001), there is evidence that when faced with experiences and situations with which they are not overly familiar, such as the winery-cellar door, Generation Y participants appreciate efforts made to put them at ease and to guide them through the tasting process in a setting that is relaxed and informal. In general, they find the environment of a winery-cellar door potentially intimidating, whether that is due to the grand, imposing appearance of the winery or the 'mysteries' of the tasting process. For this cohort a relaxing, fun atmosphere at the cellar door is very important; probably more important than the wines themselves. The efforts of the cellar-door staff contribute significantly to this atmosphere, but so too does the setting, the decor and the music being played. Anything that a winery or the cellar-door staff can do to put them at ease is greatly appreciated. This may be as simple as a friendly smile and welcome on entry, or good signage indicating where to go and the process

to be followed. These efforts will be appreciated and are crucial considerations for wineries providing cellar-door facilities.

Second, members of Generation Y want to be treated as individuals when they visit a winery-cellar door. They expect cellar-door staff to ascertain their needs and tailor an experience to suit their level of wine and tasting knowledge. There is no doubt that the Generation-Y participants in general had much less confidence in the cellar-door setting than their older counterparts. In general, they recognize that they currently have quite limited wine knowledge and are somewhat uneasy about the visit due to their perception that their youth, inexperience and lack of funds make them less appealing clients. In this way, they appreciate personalized guidance through the process in a way that is respectful and which shows they are valued as customers.

Third, Generation Y wants to interact and 'connect' with cellar-door staff. This is not just a matter of staff listening to participants' needs but a meaningful two-way conversation. For this reason they find the experience more rewarding at small, family-run wineries where there is time for this dialogue and a less scripted, more interactive approach is available. Smaller wineries introduce a 'human element', which is less intimidating and may be more difficult to uncover at larger commercial operations. These smaller wineries tend to offer a more relaxed environment, which is more conducive to taking one's time and asking questions.

This is connected with a crucial element in the Generation-Y approach to the winery-cellar door; they wish to learn and again this may be more important than tasting the wine for them. They are willing students, and want to extend their knowledge of wines and winemaking. They do not want cellar-door staff to use 'technical jargon', but they do appreciate being given information about the wine and the process at a level that they can understand. Learning may include gaining knowledge about wine generally; this is a generation for whom 'life-long learning' is important. They are seeking a simple but not condescending introduction into the mysteries of producing and tasting wine. Additionally, they want to learn the story of the winery, its history, why it is there and what makes it different.

Fourth, it is clear that members of Generation Y seek different types of experiences at different types of wineries. While younger wine tourists clearly appreciate the 'whole wine tourist' experience available at the larger, commercial wineries, this has to be balanced against a desire for a personalized, intimate experience, where these other features may not be available. Nevertheless, there is some evidence that while Generation-Y members prefer the experience available at the smaller wineries, this may not be enough to get them to return to the same winery again; instead, they talk about visiting other small cellar doors for a similar but different experience, highlighting their need for variety.

This preference is nuanced, however; there were many occasions when a positive experience was rewarded with the intention to return. This suggests a significant impact on their purchase decisions and future brand loyalty, confirming the conclusions of Nowak *et al.* (2006). A good experience where they 'connect' with the wines and the wineries can have a lasting impact on these young people at the outset of their wine-drinking career.

What More Do We Need to Know About Generation Y as Wine Tourists?

There is scope for further research in this area. For example, this project has only focused on Australasian respondents, who live in a culture where wine is not the drink of choice for young people, and for many of whom wine drinking and tasting is still a relatively new experience. For this reason it would be interesting to replicate such a study in a different cultural context such as Europe where perspectives on wine may be different. For example, Smiley (2004) reports that young consumers in France and Italy are drinking less wine, as wine is the beverage of their parents so it is considered 'old-fashioned'. It is likely, as Thach and Olsen (2006) suggest, that a wider comparative study would be useful.

Furthermore, it is unclear which of the trends apparent in the expectations and requirements of Generation-Y participants is a factor of them being young and inexperienced when it comes to wine specifically, as opposed to a general feature of their generational cohort. In relation to this, a characteristic of the wine tourist gaining attention in tourism literature is that of wine involvement (Charters and Ali-Knight, 2002; Brown *et al.*, 2006). There is little doubt that most of the Generation-Y participants in this study had less experience of wine and wineries than their older counterparts, although all participants had visited a winery at least once before. Thus, some of the differences identified between cohorts might be attributed to differences in wine knowledge and wine involvement and interest. In association with this it would be interesting to explore the influence of other personal characteristics on their expectations and experiences, such as gender, educational level and personality type.

More exploration of the different experiences sought at different types of wineries and how to leverage off the varying factors that improve brand loyalty would be useful. Currently, it seems that larger wineries might be more likely to draw Generation Y back for a repeat visit, but this visit would be for a social occasion, and may not do much for brand loyalty. By comparison, it is clear that brand loyalty seems stronger at the smaller wineries, but these young people may not revisit the winery unless there is something new to experience.

Overall, however, there is cause to be optimistic about the potential of Generation Y to become an important market for wine tourism in the future, and the wine industry must do what it can to foster brand loyalty among this cohort. The participants in this research revealed themselves to be eager to try new experiences and to learn, and despite their lack of experience and a tendency to feel a little intimidated they are not afraid to express what they want from a winery experience. It is important that wineries do not offer a 'one size fits all' approach to the cellar door; it is clear that Generation Y want a personalized and flexible service responsive to their needs. An environment in which younger visitors feel at ease, and from which they leave satisfied, is crucial to developing long-term brand loyalty for the wine and wine-tourism industries; it is up to winery operators and managers to make the changes to ensure this happens.

References

Beverland, M. (2001) Generation X and wine consumption. *Australian and New Zealand Wine Industry Journal* 16(1), 91–96.

Brown, G., Havitz, M.E. and Getz, D. (2006) Relationship between wine involvement and wine-related travel. *Journal of Travel and Tourism Marketing* 21(1), 31–46.

Carlsen, J. and Charters, S. (eds) (2006) *Global Wine Tourism: Research, Management and Marketing.* CAB International, Wallingford, UK.

Charters, S. and O'Neill, M. (2000) Delighting the customer – how good is the cellar door experience? *Australian and New Zealand Wine Industry Journal* 15(4), 11–16.

Charters, S. and Ali-Knight, J. (2002) Who is the wine tourist? *Tourism Management* 23(3), 311–319.

Charters, S. and Fountain, J. (2006) Younger wine tourists: a study of generational differences in the cellar door experience. In: Carlsen, J. and Charters S. (eds) *Global Wine Tourism: Research, Management and Marketing.* CAB International, Wallingford, UK, pp. 153–160.

Charters, S., Fountain, J. and Fish, N. (2009) 'You felt like lingering…': experiencing 'real' service at the winery tasting room. *Journal of Travel Research*, 48(1), 122–134.

Denzin, N.K. (1989) *The Research Act.* Prentice-Hall, Englewood Cliffs, New Jersey.

Dodd, T. and Bigotte, V. (1997) Perceptual differences among visitor groups to wineries. *Journal of Travel Research* 35(3), 46–51.

Dodd, T., Yuan, J. and Kolyesnikova, N. (2006) Motivations of young people for visiting wine festivals. *Event Management* 10(1), 23–33.

Fountain, J. and Charters, S. (2004) Younger wine tourists: a study of generational differences in the cellar door experience. In: Carlsen, J. and Charters, S. (eds) *Proceedings of the International Wine Tourism Conference, 2–5 May, 2004.* Vineyard Publishers, Margaret River, Western Australia.

Grove, S.J. and Fisk, R. (1992) Observational data collection methods for services marketing: an overview. *Journal of the Academy of Marketing Services* 20(3), 217–224.

Hofman, M. (1999) Upstarts: tapping Generation Y. *Inc. Magazine, December.* Retrieved from http://www.inc.com/magazine/19991201/15689.html

Houghton, M. (2001) The propensity of wine festivals to encourage subsequent winery visitation. *International Journal of Wine Marketing* 13(3), 32–41.

Howard, R. and Stonier, S. (2001) Marketing wine to Generation X: the way ahead. *The Australian Grapegrower and Winemaker, December.* Retrieved from http://www.grapeandwine.com.au/dec02/011211.htm

Hudson, S., Snaith, T., Miller, G.A. and Hudson, P. (2001) Distribution channels in the travel industry: using mystery shoppers to understand the influence of travel agency recommendations. *Journal of Travel Research* 40, 148–154.

Jorgensen, D.L. (1989) *Participant Observation: A Methodology for Human Studies.* Sage, Newbury Park, California.

King, D. (2000) Defining a generation: tips for uniting our multi-generational workforce. Retrieved from http://www.careerfirm.com/generations.htm

Koerber, K. (2000) Fueling increased. *Wine Business Monthly* 2. Retrieved from http://winebusiness.com/html/MonthlyArticle.cfm?Aid = 121andissueId = 25886

Martin, C.A. and Tulgan, B. (2001) *Managing Generation Y: Global Citizens Born in the Late Seventies and Early Eighties.* HRD Press, Amherst, Massachusetts.

Mitchell, R. (2002) The generation game: generation X and baby boomer wine tourism. *Proceedings of the New Zealand Tourism and Hospitality Research Conference.* Waiariki Institute of Technology, Rotorua, New Zealand.

Mitchell, R. and Hall, C.M. (2006) Wine tourism research: the state of play. *Tourism Review International* 9, 307–332.

Mitchell, R., Hall, C.M. and McIntosh, A. (2000) Wine tourism and consumer behaviour. In: Hall, C.M., Sharples, L., Cambourne, B., Macionis, N., Mitchell, R. and Johnson, G. (eds) *Wine Tourism Around the World: Development, Management and Markets.* Elsevier Science, Oxford, pp. 115–135.

Morrison, L.J., Colman, A.M. and Preston, C.C. (1997) Mystery customer research: cognitive processes affecting accuracy. *Journal of the Market Research Society* 39(2), 349–361.

Nowak, L.I., Thach, L. and Olsen, J.E. (2006) Wowing the millennials: creating brand equity in the wine industry. *Journal of Product and Brand Management* 15(5), 316–323.

Olsen, J.E., Thach, L. and Nowak, L.I. (2007) Wine for my generation: exploring how US wine consumers are socialized to wine. *Journal of Wine Research* 18(1), 1–18.

Scalera, B. (2002) New ideas for a new generation. *Harpers* [Online]. Retrieved from http://www.winexwired. com/archives/harpers2.htm

Sheahan, P. (2005) *Generation Y: Thriving and Surviving with Generation Y at Work*. Hardie Grant Books, Prahran, Victoria, Australia.

Smiley, R. (2004) Industry trends mail survey. *Presentation made at Wine Industrial Financial Symposium 22* September, Napa, California.

Thach, L., Mason, B. and Amspacher, W. (2007) Perceptions of cellar door hospitality: lessons for improving customer service and sales. Paper presented at the Bacchus at Brock Conference.

Thach, L. and Olsen, J.E. (2006) Market segment analysis to target young adult wine drinkers. *Agribusiness* 22(3), 307–322.

Treloar, P. (2002) An investigation into the significance of relationship marketing on the young winery tourist. *Proceedings of the New Zealand Tourism and Hospitality Research Conference*. Waiariki Institute of Technology, Rotorua, New Zealand.

Treloar, P. (2004) The youth market, wine and wine tourism: a behavioural context for wine tourism potential. M.Tour thesis, University of Otago, Dunedin, New Zealand.

Treloar, P., Hall, C.M. and Mitchell, R. (2004) Wine tourism and the Generation Y market: any possibilities? Paper presented at the CAUTHE Conference, Brisbane, Queensland, Australia.

Wallendorf, M. and Belk, R.W. (1989) Assessing trustworthiness in naturalistic consumer research. In: Hirschman, E. (ed.) *Interpretive Consumer Research*. Association for Consumer Research, Provo, Utah, pp. 69–83.

Wilson, A.M. (1998) The use of mystery shopping in the measurement of service delivery. *The Services Industries Journal* 18(3), 148–162.

6 Generation Y: Perspectives of Quality in Youth Adventure Travel Experiences in an Australian Backpacker Context

Gayle Jennings[1], Carl Cater[1], Young-Sook Lee[1], Claudia Ollenburg[2],
Amanda Ayling[1], and Brooke Lunny[3]
[1]*Griffith Business School, Griffith University;* [2]*School of Hotel, Resort &
Tourism Management, Bond University;* [3]*Gold Coast City Council*

Introduction

Generation Y (Gen Y), Echo Boomers, Nexters, dot-coms, Net Gen, N.Gen, Millennium, Thumb or Paradoxical Generation, as noted elsewhere in this book, are variously classified by developed nations around the world. Given that this chapter is contextualized within an Australian setting, and specifically focuses on the youth adventure travel market within a popular Australian east coast tourism destination, Queensland's Gold Coast; we shall adopt the Australian Bureau of Statistics' (ABS, 2002) and Cooke's (2006) definition based on the following years of birth: 1980–1994 in order to distinguish Generation Y-ers. In this chapter, the terms Generation Y and Gen Y refer to the generation as a collective, while Generation Y-ers and Gen Y-ers refer to individuals in Generation Y. At the time of writing, Gen Y-ers' ages were distributed between 14 and 28 years. Given this chronological age categorization, there is some complementarity with young tourists, youth tourism segments and Gen-Y tourists. Young tourists have been described as people under 26 years of age (Bywater, 1993), 18–35 years (Kale *et al.*, 1987), and 15–25 years of age (Aramberri, 1991). More recently, the United Nations World Tourism Organization (UNWTO, 2006) found that youth tourists tended to be categorized in two ways: 15 to 24–26 and 15–30, although in

1991, the World Tourism Organization, as a consequence of the New Delhi Declaration of Youth Tourism, framed the age as between 15 and 29 years (WTO, 1991b). Obviously, there is some ambiguity between what age categories constitute 'young' and 'youth' tourists as well as the extant interchangeable use of the terms. In addition to age ambiguity, a number of earlier writers have criticized the use of age as the only classifier for young and youth (Roberts, 1983; Aramberri, 1991; Clarke, 1992). Other considerations include sociological and psychological factors. Subsequently:

> although age may be the main distinguishing factor, psychological and sociological characteristics of youth, their status in society, and their economic capacity are also important considerations.
>
> (WTO, 1991a, p. 5)

Given this statement, we return to consideration of generational population cohorts of youths and young people, and Gen Y in particular. As noted in generational studies, each successive generation will demonstrate differing and similar sociological and psychological characteristics. These characteristics have been influenced by society, cultures, political and economic circumstances of their time (Schewe and Noble, 2000). Earlier chapters have distinguished some of these specific features of Gen Y. The purpose of this chapter is to further extend qualitatively our understandings of Gen Y as adventure travellers with regard to the nature and meaning of quality tourism experiences. Some of these travellers also used backpacker accommodation and facilities. In order to advance our purpose, first we will revisit some of those attributes and findings from the extant literature about Gen Y. We recognize that Gen Y is 'fundamentally different in outlook and ambition from any group of kids in the past 50 or 60 years' (O'Reilly and Vella-Zarb, 2000, p. 146). They have been described as the 'healthiest and most cared for generation' and one which perceives itself as 'global' (Howe and Strauss, 2000, p. 76 and 46). Core values of Gen Y-ers are 'freedom, flexibility and choice' (Huntley, 2006, p. 18). From a sociopsychological perspective, they have been described as a generation possessing the following attributes: optimism, materialism and consumerism. They value relationships, experiences, travel and being active. While we acknowledge that these attributes or characteristics tend to homogenize the generation, we also acknowledge that the generation does exhibit heterogeneity. The homogeneity of the generation, which we describe, is connected to the social and resulting psychological 'moments' inherent in framing generationally their place in time.

What Else Do We Know About Generation Y?

They are the progeny primarily of Baby Boomers. Gen Y follows Gen X, the latter having been the first to grow up with computers. Apart from this similarity, Gen Y-ers' social life experiences are somewhat different to their Gen X counterparts. Gen Y-ers more than Gen X-ers have been born into either one-child or novel, blended and complex family compositions, situations and relationships (Hill, 2002; Huntley, 2006) with working parent(s) (Bakewell and Mitchell, 2003). As a consequence, this generation strives for community primarily with their peers aided by the connectivity afforded by social networking and computer technology. These are critical for maintaining Gen Y-ers' sense of community and belonging (Saatchi and Saatchi, 1999; O'Reilly and Vella-Zarb, 2000) and sense of self.

Gen Y's life experiences have also been informed and shaped by consumer culture, which has engendered a strong desire to 'fit in' (Huntley, 2006). This generation has been saturated by multimedia influences on their life experiences, which have served to tailor and commodify their life experiences (Bakewell and Mitchell, 2003). Additionally, Gen Y-ers' life experiences, socialization and acculturation processes have emphasized living life as a series of multiple experiences as evidenced, for example, in suburban malls where 'leisure activities, shopping and social encounters' are combined (Bakewell and Mitchell, 2003, p. 95). Consequently, Gen Y-ers are multitaskers (Teenage Research Unit, TRU, 2000). Celebrity and brand awareness are firmly planted in their psyches (Bakewell and Mitchell, 2003). They have also been exposed to more brand choices (Fielding, 1994; Quelch and Kenny, 1994; TRU, 1999) than any other youth generation. Moreover, their consumer behaviour has been patterned by (multiple) experiences (Hill, 2002) and a search for what may be termed fulfilling 'peak' experiences (Csikszentmihalyi, 1975), with these often being associated with personal fulfilment (O'Reilly and Vella-Zarb, 2000). Subsequently, while Gen Y-ers look for community and a sense of belonging, they also seek experiences where they can individually experience 'activity, excitement, and movement' (Bennett and Lachowetz, 2004, p. 241). Their experiences with regard to leisure accord more with individual rather than team-based sports. Relatedly, Gen Y-ers 'consume action sports more than any preceding generation, leading some to label action sports as "Gen-Y sport"' (Gordon, 2000; Petrecca, 1999, quoted in Bennett and Lachowetz, 2004, p. 239). Gen Y-ers use the Internet, are technologically knowledgeable and engage in and with various forms of media (Bennett and Lachowetz, 2004). As a generation, Gen Y-ers accept that living in today's world means dealing with uncertainty. That being said, to reiterate, Gen Y-ers are optimistic and 'place a big premium in having fun' (Huntley, 2006, p. 9) and are passionate about 'personal freedom' (Huntley, 2006, p.3).

Financially, they have grown up in affluent and stable times, at least until October 2008. They have also observed that credit – rather than savings – finances consumption (Bakewell and Mitchell, 2003). They tend not to have substantive housing loans, many of them are still living at home with parents and they are not committing to long-term relationships until later in life (see Huntley, 2006). They have also been independently spending since a very young age (Bakewell and Mitchell, 2003). They are reported as working to live rather than living to work in order to support the style of life that they desire (McCrindle, n.d.). Consequently, as travellers they may combine travel and work with the latter supporting their ability to sustain continuous travel.

Generation Y: Debates and Contexts

While there has been a debate as to whether Gen Y is a significant generation or not, we know that it is a significant proportion of populations in developed worlds. It constitutes approximately 25% of the population in Australia, which puts it on parity with Baby Boomers and Gen X. In the USA, Gen Y constitutes 25% of the population (Gardyn and Fetto, 2000) and is larger in size than Gen X (Huntley, 2006), specifically, 76 million and 50 million respectively (Trunk, 2007). In the UK, Gen Y currently makes up 22.9% of the population (ONS, 2008), and over 20% of the workforce, a figure that will increase further as Baby Boomers retire (*The Times*, 2008). Another current debate about Gen Y-ers is about what they have contributed as a generation. They have as yet to move into this space, and some suggest that they are already making their mark with regard to volunteerism (Huntley, 2006) and climate changes issues. Regardless of their mark as a generation, globally from a tourism perspective, Gen Y, as part of young and youth travel, has been recognized as big business (Bennett and Lachowetz, 2004; UNWTO, 2008). Currently, youth tourism accounts for 20% of international arrivals and constitutes one of the fastest-growing tourism sectors (UNWTO, 2008). A substantive number of government

tourism authorities perceive youth/student markets as being very important to tourism industries' futures (UNWTO, 2008).

Generation Y: Young and Youth Travel, Backpacker Tourism

Within Australia (and New Zealand), youth tourists constitute a large component of adventure travel and the backpacker markets. Indeed, Australia had already recognized the value of youth tourism as an important sector as early as 1995, as demonstrated in its development of the *Australian National Backpacker Tourism Strategy* (1995). Though at that time, age was not a component of defining backpackers; youth tourists, however, did constitute part of backpacker market segmentation. It is within the context of Australia's focus on youth tourism and, in particular, adventure travel experiences and backpacker tourism that this chapter is contextualized. Many Gen Y-ers visiting Australia may not yet have entered permanent employment work (with a high proportion on 'gap-year' or working holiday-maker programmes), and if they have, their position on the career ladder may dictate more budget-oriented forms of travel, of which the backpacker is the most readily recognized segment. However, there has been somewhat of a sea change in attitudes to this segment from industry, policy and academic perspectives in recognizing their economic value, as previously noted with regard to tourist authorities. As Richards and Wilson found in their extensive survey of backpackers carried out in 2002, via the International Student Travel Confederation, they were 'highly oriented towards experiencing as much as possible during the trip' (2004, p. 25). Furthermore, although they may be interested in value for money, they are not adverse to spending significant amounts on signature experiences that provide value (Loker-Murphy and Pearce, 1995). Indeed, in 2007, in Australia, the backpacker industry was worth 20% of total tourism industry earnings, despite only making up around 10% of arrivals (Tourism Research Australia, 2007). Our research (described later) suggests that Gen Y constitutes part of the overall backpacker market in Australia (and New Zealand). Additionally, like the backpackers market, which we acknowledge is constituted of several generations (Gen Y, Gen X and Baby Boomers), specific characteristics of Gen Y as youth travellers have complementarity with backpacker characteristics: specifically longer stay patterns and a high experiential imperative.

As a result, youth travellers do have considerable power in shaping the characteristics and development of tourism destinations. Desforges (1998, p. 183) points out:

> young travellers have the power to determine which places are brought into the tourist economy (and which places are excluded), which put simply means incorporating those places which conform to notions of authenticity.

In addition, 'young travellers determine the *terms* by which peoples and places are included in the tourist economy' (Desforges, 1998, p. 183; see also Horak and Weber, 2000). While the backpacker market constitutes only part of the youth tourism market, and vice versa, it should be noted that one-third of youth tourists classify themselves as backpackers (Richards and Wilson, 2004). In addition, as these authors discuss, the label 'backpacker' has some negative social connotations, with many youth travellers not willing to immediately identify with this moniker, despite fitting most of the classifications outlined by Pearce (1990). Irrespective, for Australia, youth tourism is particularly important as 'a growth segment . . . with huge "life time value"' due to potential return visitation associated with youth tourists as they move through their life cycles (UNWTO, 2006, p. 199). It is suggested, however, that given the core priorities of Gen Y outlined earlier, these return visits will only flow if the initial one is perceived to have delivered a high-quality tourism experience.

Quality Tourism Experiences: Extant Literature

Recent academic work has sought to investigate the taken-for-granted nature of the term 'quality', for example in the edited work, *Quality Tourism Experiences* by Jennings and Nickerson (2006). Additionally, component parts of the term 'quality tourism experiences' have also been studied. 'Quality' has also been commented on by Rathmell (1966), Crosby (1979), Parasuram *et al.* (1985) and Zeithaml *et al.* (2002). 'Experiences' have been discussed by Holbrook and Hirschman (1982), Pine and Gilmore (1999) and Kotler *et al.* (2001). 'Visitor experiences' have been considered by Borrie and Birzell (2001) as well as Andereck *et al.* (2006). 'Tourism experiences' have been portrayed by Killion (1992) and Craig-Smith and French (1994). 'Travel experiences' literature includes writings by Clawson (1963), Cohen (1972, 1979) and MacCannell (1973), while Ryan (1997, 2002) has focused on 'tourist experiences'. An extended review of the related literature appears in Jennings *et al.* (2009) and Ritchie and Hudson (2009).

Quality Tourism Experiences: Industry Schemes

There has also been a number of quantitative industry schemes developed to assess tourism quality in Australasia, which by default includes youth adventure as well as youth backpacker tourism. As a national accreditation scheme, the related Quality Tourism (QT) might best represent such assessment and accreditation processes for tourism business in Australia. QT assesses a tourism business by its core business standards, such as risk management, customer handling and/or facilities, amenities, level of maintenance and cleanliness of the property, upon which appropriate stars or ratings are given to the business (Quality Tourism, 2008). Similarly, Qualmark® is New Zealand tourism's official mark of quality. Individual properties are evaluated and accredited by cleanliness, safety, security and comfort (Qualmark, 2008). When accredited and given a certain level of star grade, provision of 'quality services' adequate to the star grade given to the property is then promised (assured) by Qualmark®. This, however, may lead to contested perceptions of 'quality experiences' of particular star grades, for example, 'promising a four-star level of quality' from the industry perspective, may be different from a four-star-level experience from tourists' and travellers' perspectives. In the UK, the National

Quality Assessment Scheme (NQAS) evaluates a set of mainly physical attributes and amenities of accommodation places, including numbers of bedrooms, brand identity and/or own kitchen facilities, etc. (NQAS, 2008). The European Hospitality Quality (EHQ) scheme focuses on the management processes of businesses, including one quality-coordinator per establishment, written reports of mystery checks and internal/self-assessments of the establishment (EHQ, 2008). Across various nations, current quality tourism accreditation schemes are invariably focused on the properties' physical facilities and amenities and/or management processes of the business. Such quantitative schemes and measures have been critiqued and countered by a need to use emic (insider) and qualitative approaches (Arnould and Wallendorf, 1994; Andereck, et al., 2006; Bricker and Kerstetter, 2006; Nickerson, 2006).

Generation Y: Quality in Youth Adventure Travel Experiences, Towards an Alternate View

To reiterate, the purpose of this chapter is to further extend understandings of the nature and meaning of quality tourism experiences for Gen-Y (youth) adventure travellers using an insider and qualitative research approach. The chapter focuses on the youth adventure travel market within a popular Australian east coast tourism destination, Queensland's Gold Coast. The study was undertaken over a period from January to May 2007, thus incorporating busier and slower times of the year. For the purposes of the sample, the youth adventure travel market was defined as:

> people aged between 18–29 years, who are travelling in Australia outside of family units, not for business, and not primarily to visit friends or relatives, whose travel includes at least one overnight stay and purchase of adventure travel products, services, or experiences.

This construction is a blend of definitions drawn from Youth Tourism Consortium of Canada (2004), Tourism Research Australia (2005), and Tourism Queensland (2003, 2005). Quite clearly, this definition fits a large section of contemporary Gen-Y travellers, including our Australian-framed definition noted at the beginning of this chapter. Subsequently, the preceding discussion has served to situate our focus on Gen Y within youth tourism. The chapter will now turn its attention to consideration of youth adventure travellers' experiences within Australia as specifically associated with the generational cohort: Gen Y.

The key focus of this chapter is to critically examine the nature of quality, as assessed by Gen-Y travellers while undertaking adventure tourism experiences in Australia. Some of the Gen-Y travellers used backpacker accommodation. Subsequently, from time to time, we will refer to youth adventure travellers and youth backpackers. The latter are, in theory, parenthetically framed since our focus was youth adventure travellers; albeit some of these travellers may be categorized as youth backpackers and Gen-Y backpackers. Regardless of their categorization, all fit generationally a Gen-Y classification. Our aim is to show that these particular Gen-Y travellers are critically reflexive about notions of quality, a characteristic not previously ascribed to this particular market segment. Thus, a conceptual model, derived from consumer narratives, is presented that suggests a range of higher-order concepts that form the basis for assessments of quality tourism experiences. Understanding what these concepts are, and how they shape the values, attitudes and behaviours of the Gen-Y tourist is vitally important, as the authors of this chapter believe that the formation of these during such youth travel practices, such as adventure travel and backpacking, provides the foundation for understanding their future tourism behaviour. Therefore, we include a range of sector-specific suggestions for catering to the needs of this youth travel market, while noting that these have broader ramifications for future tourism industry development.

Generation Y: Quality in Youth Adventure Travel Experiences – Study Design

A social constructivist paradigm (see Lincoln and Guba, 2005) was used to inform our research as it enabled both insider perspectives as well as a multiplicity of interpretations to be gathered. The methodology was qualitative in nature. A variety of methods was used for empirical material collection including focus groups, semi-structured interviews, and quality-related travel experience diaries. Additionally, researchers used individual and team reflexive practices throughout the course of the research and development of the grounded theory. Purposive sampling was used to recruit participants via backpacker accommodation providers and an adventure travel provider. An industry group of small- to medium-level adventure travel enterprises that had formed a network charged with 'developing quality backpacker product' (Gold Coast City Council, 2005) provided the 'sampling frame' and facilitated access to their guests – the youth adventure travellers (and youth backpackers). Fourteen youth adventure travellers in total participated in three focus groups, another 16 travellers participated in semi-structured interviews and 8 youth adventure travellers completed travel diaries. The youth adventure travellers were mostly international tourists with a smaller number of domestic tourists also participating in the study. The international youth travellers were primarily from England, as this market makes up approximately a quarter of backpacker visitors to the Gold Coast (GCATG, 2007). A number of tourists came from Germany, Korea, Japan, Canada, the Netherlands, Denmark and New Zealand. Domestic tourists were from western Australia and Victoria. All travellers were English speaking.

Generation Y: Quality in Youth Adventure Travel Experiences – Study Interpretations

Empirical materials were interpreted using a grounded theory tradition (see Charmaz, 2003a,b), particularly the work of Rynehart (2004). The grounded theory of what constitutes quality for Gen-Y adventure travellers is summarized in Fig. 6.1. Root concepts and higher-order concepts emerged from lower-order common themes. The higher-order concepts highlight that the nature of quality for these Gen-Y travellers was determined by 'personal connectivity', 'social connectivity', 'combining experiences', 'experience delivery' and 'interconnectivity of the entire adventure travel experience'. Several root concepts also include 'having fun'.

However, before we turn to the higher-order concepts, it is interesting to note the prominence of several root concepts concerning 'value for money', 'cleanliness' and 'safety', which are connected to the higher-order concept 'experience delivery'. Perhaps contrary to some myths about the youth and backpacker segments, contemporary Gen-Y travellers are very conscious about basic needs such as value for money, cleanliness and especially personal safety, perhaps, as a result of the (generally) high degree of safety and caring provided by their parents, as discussed previously. Numerous respondents pointed to the importance of a clean kitchen where they could prepare their own food and would even 'pay an extra few dollars to have a clean and tidy place'. Thus, a few travellers expressed displeasure at some hostels that 'felt like a prison', 'had one poxy fan' or 'you could tell that thousands of people had been there before you'. Indeed, having some comfort facilities such as air conditioning, television and Internet access was deemed important, the latter especially so in an era where these travellers spend a significant amount of time updating friends and relatives through blogs or social-networking sites. Safety was deemed important, not only for adventure activities, where respondents were conscious of appropriate and well-maintained equipment, but also in the hostels where they could feel that they and their belongings were safe. Indeed, it is important to note that the hostels often function as a 'home away from home', so are much more than just a bed for the night for these individuals. The emergence of the so-called flashpacker, a Gen-Y individual who is more willing to pay a premium for comfortable experiences is evidence of this trend (*Courier Mail*, 2007). These host locations are thus central to the travel experience itself, and this links to higher-order concepts of personal and social connectivity.

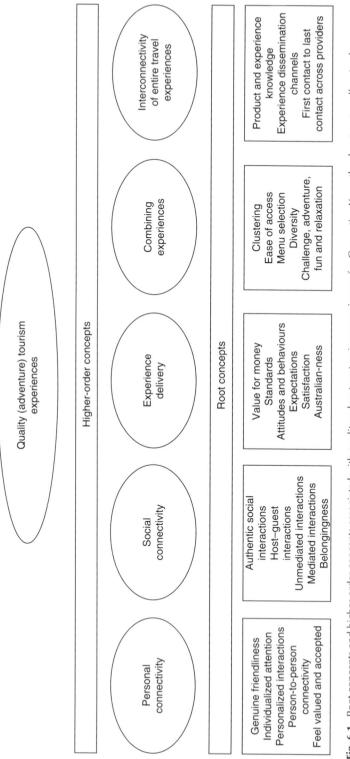

Fig. 6.1. Root concepts and higher-order concepts associated with quality adventure tourism experiences for Generation Y: youth adventure travellers (and backpackers).

Personal connectivity

Personal connectivity represents a strong inter-personal connection between industry provid-ers and their staff with the Gen-Y traveller, and is core to generational characteristics of valuing relationships and experiences. This connection is more than good customer service and more than just being friendly. It is an authentic inter-action which is person-to-person related rather than business-provider- to customer-related. It incorporates a strong host–guest relationship, which merges social, cultural and business prac-tices within an authentic, in this case, Australian context. Here we do see evidence of Gen Y putting 'personal' value above commodified experiences. So although this generation is highly consumerist, it strives for authentic tailor-made experiences that symbolize the 'freedom, flexibility and choice' that Huntley described (2006, p. 18). Thus, individuals might value the experience of being taken surfing by an accom-modation provider over visiting one of the com-mercial water parks.

However, a large part of this connectivity is built around relationships of trust and hon-esty, particularly through what might be prom-ised in advertising and delivered through the actual product, as shown by the following examples:

> I don't like...when you go to the tour operator, whether it be Whitsundays or whatever, and they say, or you see it on the leaflet $95 to do the Whitsundays. When you get down there then its an additional charge of $20 which they never mentioned, or like this hostel hasn't got air-conditioning, and like a lot of hostels adver-tise they got this, they got that.

> Even in there it says this one comes with air-conditioning and other accommodation has a gym and I saw the gym and it's a dumb-bell...it's not a gym, they kind of hype it up a bit. Every hostel is portrayed as the best hostel in Australia like...

Therefore, it would appear that having respon-sible and ethical business practices is very important to Gen Y, and operators should con-sider the breadth of their responsibilities in this area. These might fit within a broader remit of sustainable business operations in this sector.

For example, given the ethical concerns of this population relating specifically to volunteerism and climate change identified earlier in the chapter, there is scope for attention to these areas from experience providers.

Social connectivity

The second related aspect to quality for this Gen-Y cohort of youth adventure travellers (and backpackers) was social connectivity, which is associated with the provision of spaces and opportunities for social interac-tions between travellers, host-community members, and travel providers as well as vari-ous mixes of these. Pearce's early definition of backpackers noted their social orientation, with one of their five identifying characteristics being 'an emphasis on meeting other travel-lers' (1990). This 'emphasis' might be argued as a resonating backpacker and/or youth travel theme, or a life-cycle characteristic. However, given the qualitative nature of this study and its focus on both Gen-Y youth adventure travellers (and backpackers), the concept 'social connectivity' emerged and was grounded in the discourses of those Gen-Y participants in this study. Extrapolation to backpackers and youth travellers more broadly and/or over time as well as linkages to life-cycle characteristics requires further research. As identified, a need to 'fit in' and access a sense of community and belonging (O'Reilly and Vella-Zarb, 2000; Saatchi and Saatchi, 1999) is central to this generation's needs. One consequence of this is that it is apparent that as an information channel for Gen-Y trav-ellers, 'word of mouth', and increasingly 'word of web' is an important and trusted source. These global interactions provide the connec-tivity that these travellers actively seek. Thus, providers need to be acutely aware of their reputation in these areas, and need to monitor and evaluate carefully the personal and social connectivity that is provided and delivered in their adventure travel experiences. This could include employee/staff self-reports, peer reviews and line manager assessments of social and emotional capabilities of staff. Such monitoring and evaluation should be connected to staff development activities, particularly developing capacity with regard to understanding staff's own and customers' emotional intelligence (see Goleman, 2005) and social intelligence (see Goleman, 2006). There is clearly a question of capacity to perform these functions in small business enterprises, where staff turnover is extremely high (and is often made up of youth travellers and backpackers). However, evidence suggests that maintaining quality connections in these areas is of paramount importance.

The difference between personal and social connectivities is that the former is person to person related and the latter is constituted of an individual's interaction within social groups. What is interesting in this study is a desire for relaxed social connection opportunities, and a somewhat lower interest in adventure and ecotourism experiences, where respondents would rather 'kickback and have a laugh with their mates, not sit in a tent'. This would seem to reflect the strong desires for personal freedom identified in this generation. However, one should also bear in mind the sample being located on the Gold Coast, a destination where, despite the efforts of the industry group mentioned earlier, travellers are seduced primarily by the beach and party lifestyle. It may be that in an alternative destination, themes of 'eco' and adventure involvement may be higher.

Nevertheless, in line with this ease of opportunity for social connections is ease of access to experiences. As intimated earlier, the popularity of Australia with western youth travellers and backpackers is partly due to a familiar cultural environment, especially for native English speakers. The developed nature of the destination, good transport links and ease of finding work were all part of this connectedness:

> Compare Australia to other countries, Australia's a good country, a good country to travel, because obviously there's no language barrier from our point as well. Work is a lot easier and you have got so much to do and see at the Gold Coast and Cairns, and so many activities and stuff going on in Australia. It's easy enough done, work's easy done and it wouldn't be in other countries. That's why a lot of people I think choose Australia.

Combining experiences

As identified previously, Gen Y seek multiple experiences and quite often attempt to 'multitask' in their pursuit, so having an experiential smorgasbord is undoubtedly one of the major attractions of destinations. Nevertheless, some study participants were still frustrated by the relative difficulty of accessing certain tourist locations; for example, one individual felt that visiting the theme park enclave in the study setting would take too long by public transport:

> Maybe if the theme parks were a bit closer, they'd get a bit more use or something you know. If you have to travel an hour or hour and a half to a park to actually get there, I mean, a lot of people when they come to Surfers Paradise stay around this area because it's the main area, to get to theme parks you still gotta do a fair bit of travelling, out there to actually get to them, so if they were closer they would get more use.

Thus, the identified theme here is that of combining experiences, which refers to clustering of experiences, and echoes concerns with efficiency possessed by Gen Y. Clustering facilitates ease of access and provision of multiple connected experiences, which also provides choice and balance between challenge, adventure, fun and relaxation, as well as opportunities to socialize. Furthermore, combining accommodation and adventure experiences, for example, was associated with contributing to quality tourism experiences. To develop clustered products, services and experiences, action research approaches (see Kemmis and McTaggart, 2005) could be used. This would enable the industry to continuously monitor and evaluate the contributions of combinations to quality (adventure) tourism experiences, through the reflexive processes associated with action research. The incorporation of benchmarking processes with related and divergent industry sectors and groups would also provide comparative platforms and models.

Experience delivery

Subsequent to identifying how quality tourist experiences for Gen Y are associated with convenience is attention to how that experience is delivered. Experience delivery is the delivery of an experience rather than goods, a product or a service. It may, however, package within the experience various goods, products and services. Experience delivery was also associated with component experiences within overall travel experiences. Despite the growth of networks in youth travel and backpacker segments, some travellers expressed a frustration with 'going round in circles' in their quest for personal fulfilment. This was also felt to extend, on occasion, to the product itself, particularly manifested through the lack of interpretative or cultural material:

> Maybe have like descriptions of different plants and stuff. Like when you go on walks they don't really explain it very well. Like if you didn't know, you would walk straight past.

It would seem that hostels and activity operators occasionally took for granted this Gen-Y cohort of youth adventure travellers' (and backpackers') familiarity with the destination and products, when these contemporary travellers were expecting the experience to be highly tailored to their needs. Again, this is an expression of the desire for personal fulfilment and connected experiences shown by this generation. There are a number of ways that operators could monitor and evaluate their experience delivery. It is suggested that these be undertaken conterminously with traditional service delivery mechanisms, as well as the accreditation standards and their measurements described earlier. Monitoring and evaluation could include, for example, the use of reflexive journals by travellers for extended periods of time. Additionally, providers could issue invitations to travellers and staff to participate in quasi-focus groups, that is, 'conversation-based working breakfast/lunch/evening meals' in order to reflect on the quality of tourism experiences delivered.

Interconnectivity of the entire adventure tourism experience

Relatedly, 'experience delivery' links to the 'interconnectivity of the entire adventure tourism experience' and thereby encompasses an overall framing from the first to last contact point of experience delivery. Interconnectivity of the entire adventure tourism experience recognizes that quality tourism experiences begin prior to the initial point of contact through to, and inclusive of, the point of departure and beyond. This interconnectivity is directly related to generating lasting memories of a quality adventure tourism experience. It was here that study participants emphasized the importance of taking away signature narratives of Australia, and the drive for memorable adventure experiences as suggested above. Here, Gen-Y travellers were not afraid to spend money if they perceived that this would be the main 'souvenir' that they would take home with them:

> When you are backpacking and that, it [experiences] is all the stuff like that eats up a big part of your money like. We come over here and we do want to do Fraser Island, Whitsundays, bungy, sky-diving and do all these things and they'd be the most expensive part of your trip, apart from the accommodation. What eats your money, what you save for I suppose, and work for.

> I went SKYDIVING today. Fuckin-A! It was the most amazing thing ever! It was pretty pricey ($500 for everything), but it was worth it. They even picked us up at our hostel.

This latter quote shows a concern not only with the desire for 'peak' quality experiences, but remains reflexive about the connectivity of the service delivery described previously. Such consumer sophistication, perhaps as a result of the early independence, financial security and credit awareness highlighted in the introduction makes Gen Y highly reflexive about quality attributes.

What Australia might lack in terms of historical connections to the experience, it does make up for in scenic and natural beauty, which is an important framing point. In common with previous work on the youth adventure experience (e.g. Cater, 2007), respondents clearly pointed to the importance of this backdrop to the quality of their experiences, and how important it was to facilitate this connection.

Say like Fraser Island, Whitsundays, Great Barrier Reef...they are the things you can't do back home, it's only in Australia that can offer them sort of things.

You can sky-dive anywhere else I mean around the world, but might not be as nice as Mission Beach or somewhere like that.

Furthermore, as for many travellers this may be their first independent travel experience, these experiences have the potential to be the quality benchmark for all subsequent travel. Thus, the degree to which the interconnectivity of the entire adventure tourism experience 'works', is what Gen Y will judge by in the future:

So Australia sort of becomes to you, is a barometer to actually measure. Ok this is what you can get if you go somewhere else like Thailand and China and then you see it's not like that at home, and it becomes a barometer. It's the measuring point.

Subsequently, to ensure the interconnectivity of entire travel experiences, accommodation and experience providers need to ensure that they are adopting a whole of destination approach, which includes working closely with neighbouring destinations, as shown by this participant:

The Gold Coast is nice, but the only two things that stick out on the Gold Coast for me are Surfers Paradise and Byron Bay. They are the two sort of like spots that travellers will go and get on the way down. They haven't really got no natural attractions like on the Whitsunday, Fraser Island and like that.

Of note with regard to this comment is first, Byron Bay is not part of the Gold Coast, and is across a state boundary, yet in the youth adventure traveller's perception the region comes across as one. Second, one of the industry group's aims has been to promote the presence of world heritage rainforest and other attractions in the Gold Coast hinterland, which does not seem to have worked on this occasion. Consequently, while interconnectivity might be difficult to achieve, youth travellers on extended trips will perceive these connections via their own travel

patterns. As this generation becomes more and more 'globalized', recognizing the scale at which these interactions are played out is highly important. In addition, the strategies already suggested for industry with regard to personal and social connectivity, experience delivery, as well as combining experiences, have relevance with regard to understanding how the interconnectivity of entire travel experiences contributes to and influences the overall quality of tourism experiences. Strategies used should be team-based within organizations and between sector enterprises in order to emphasize the interconnectivity of individual actions and providers impacting on the entire travel experience. Auditing team capabilities would also identify team-building skills and repertoires that are under-utilized and overutilized by team members. This may lead to the matching of a range of team-building skills and activities to build positive interconnectivity outcomes for travel experiences as well as to influence the overall quality of tourism experiences for travellers.

Having fun

Last, we wish to focus on one of the root concepts that is linked to the higher-order concept of 'combining experiences'. Specifically, we wish to comment on 'having fun', a facet that was especially strong in the reflective journals. Again, it is important to note that the selected destination has a strong 'fun' reputation, but the fact that Gen-Y travellers were reflexive about the possibilities for this as part of their experience is notable.

I took my first surf lesson today...those guys are great! I had so much fun...I am totally addicted.

Today I went to one of the theme parks for the first time. It was lots of fun and I enjoyed the **** ride the most. When I returned to the hostel I was tired so slept all afternoon and night.

Today we just bummed at the beach then went on a club crawl till early morning, was lots of fun.

Thus, the experiences that these travellers undertake can express widely varying degrees of 'activity, excitement and movement' (Bennett and Lachowetz, 2004, p. 241) at alternative times during travel experiences. What is clear, however, is that they are willing to suspend normative codes of conduct in the search for individually fulfilling experiences. This may have similarity to the 'other' prominent youth tourists on the Gold Coast, the Gen-Y school leavers or 'Schoolies' who traditionally visit in November in search of a suspension of norms (Winchester *et al.*, 1999, p. 68). Indeed, those Gen Y-ers, who were intending on undertaking employment under the working holiday-maker programme enjoyed the ability for casual work, but were under no illusions about the primary purpose of their trip. For them, quality employment in Australia was 'like easy come, easy go', as opposed to their home where 'it's like I have a job at home, and it's like, if you have a job you keep it, yeah cause everyone wants it'. Again, this demonstrates the themes of 'working to live' as a generational trait, with many of them utilizing the former as a means to travel experiences. As has been shown elsewhere, such travel practices 'are fundamentally about pleasure and fun...to ignore the importance of hedonism is to miss the principal aim of such pursuits' (Cater and Cloke, 2007, p. 16). Therefore, operators should actively reflect on the role of fun in the experience that they are providing.

Generation Y: Quality in Youth Adventure Travel Experiences – Conclusion

This chapter has given an insight into the importance of quality to Gen-Y youth adventure travellers (and backpackers) in Australia. These modes of travel are important for understanding Gen-Y tourism because they are the foundation for the formation of travel attitudes and practices in the future. Perhaps contrary to popular belief, we have shown how concerns with quality tourism experiences are at the forefront of these travellers' minds. The nature of 'quality tourism experiences' for the youth adventure travellers (and backpackers)

who participated in this study was associated with 'personal connectivity', 'social connectivity', 'combining experiences', 'experience delivery', 'interconnectivity of the entire adventure travel experience' and 'having fun'. Gen-Y travellers are highly informed, making the most of the great variety of information sources they can access, but are critical and reflexive about the delivery of those experiences. As shown by the preceding discussion, Gen-Y adventure youth adventure travellers (and backpackers) are connected and they want their tourism to be, although not in a traditional packaged sense, as they have highly individualized needs. They value integrity and honesty in their assessments of quality, are voracious in their appetite for experiences but are also happy to relax when it suits them. In particular, themes of fun and play, on terms which suit them, are strong, as shown by the previous section.

Indeed, the nature of 'experiences are inherently personal, existing only in the mind of an individual' (Pine and Gilmore, 1998, p. 99), and for Gen Y this is especially so. Thus, in order to understand experiences, industry and 'researchers need to interact [and connect!] with the [travellers, who are] using the term' (Jennings and Weiler, 2006, p. 59). Additionally, an emic (insider-perspective based) design will serve to achieve personal and multiple meanings associated with quality tourism experiences as provided in the recently termed 'emotional economy' (Gobe *et al.*, 2001, p. x, 47) or emotion-based economies of a globalized world and 'markets of one' (Gilmore and Pine, 2000). Finally, in order to keep up to date with the changing nature and manifold meanings of quality tourism experiences, research agendas need to be longitudinal in design in order to embed monitoring and evaluation. Agendas also need to be responsive to change and flexible in methods for empirical material collection and interpretations to accommodate the changing world milieux in which tourism operates. As this chapter and volume demonstrates, as Gen-Y travellers move beyond adventure travel and backpacker experiences, they will continue to have significant power to shape notions of quality in tourism destinations and experiences in the coming years.

References

Aramberri, J.R. (1991) The nature of youth tourism: concepts, definitions and evolution. Unpublished paper presented at the World Tourism Organization International Conference on Youth Tourism, New Delhi, India.

Andereck, K. Bricker, K.S. Kerstetter, D. and Nickerson, N.P. (2006) Connecting experiences to quality: understanding meanings behind visitors' experiences. In: Jennings, G.R. and Nickerson, N. (eds) *Quality Tourism Experiences*, Elsevier, Burlington, Massachusetts, pp. 81–98.

Arnould, E.J. and Wallendorf, M. (1994) Market-oriented ethnography: interpretation building and marketing strategy formulation. *Journal of Marketing Research* 31, 484–504.

Australian Bureau of Statistics (ABS) (2002) *Australian Year Book*. 1301.0 – Year Book Australia, 2002. Available at: http://www.abs.gov.au/ausstatsABS.nsf/94713ad445ff1425ca25682000192af2/d3b9f d318e7d8f46ca256b3600032287!OpenDocument

Bakewell, C. and Mitchell, V-W. (2003) Generation Y female consumer decision-making styles. *International Journal of Retail & Distribution Management* 31(2), 95–106.

Bennett, G. and Lachowetz, T. (2004) Marketing to lifestyles: action sports and Generation Y. *Sports Marketing Quarterly* 13, 239–243.

Borrie W.T. and Birzell, R. (2001) Approaches to measuring quality of the wilderness experience. In: Freimund, W.A. and Cole, D.N. (eds) *Visitor Use Density and Wilderness Experience: Proceedings*, 2001 June 1–3; Missoula, Massachusetts. Proceedings of RMRS-P-20, pp. 29–38, Ogden, Utah: US Department of Agriculture, Forest Service, Rocky Mountain Research Station.

Bricker, K.S. and Kerstetter, D. (2006) Saravanua ni naua: exploring sense of place in the rural highlands of Fiji. In: Jennings, G.R. and Nickerson, N. (eds) *Quality Tourism Experiences*, Elsevier, Burlington, Massachusetts, pp. 99–111.

Bywater, M. (1993) Market segments: the youth and student travel market, *Travel and Tourism Analyst* 3, 35–50.

Cater, C. (2007) Adventure tourism: will to power? In Church, A. and Coles, T. (eds) *Tourism, Power and Space*. Routledge, London, pp. 63–82.

Cater, C. and Cloke, P. (2007) Bodies in action: the performativity of adventure tourism. *Anthropology Today* 23, 6.

Charmaz, K. (2003a) Grounded theory: objectivist and constructivist methods. In: Denzin, N.K. and Lincoln, Y.S. (eds) *Strategies of Qualitative Inquiry*. Sage, Thousand Oaks, California, pp. 249–291.

Charmaz, K. (2003b) Qualitative interviewing and grounded theory analysis. In: Holstein, J.A. and Gubrium, J.F. (eds) *Inside Interviewing: New Lenses, New Concerns*. Sage, Thousand Oaks, California, pp. 311–330.

Clarke, J.A. (1992) Marketing spotlight on the youth 'four s's' consumer. *Tourism Management* 13(3), 321–327.

Clawson, M. (1963) *Land and Water for Recreation: Opportunities, Problems and Policies*. Rand McNally, Chicago, Illinois.

Cohen, E. (1972) Toward a sociology of international tourism. *Social Research* 39, 164–182.

Cohen, E. (1979) A phenomenology of tourist experiences. *Sociology* 13, 179–201.

Cooke, G. (2006) *DR Dossetor Address*. Housing Industry Commission. Available at: http://housing.hia.com.au/July06Edition/media/Dossetors Report.pdf

Craig-Smith, S. and French, C. (1994) *Learning to Live with Tourism*, Pitman, Melbourne, Australia.

Cravatta, M. (1997) Online adolescents. *American Demographics*, August, p. 29.

Crosby, P.B. (1979) *Quality is Free: The Art of Making Quality Certain*. McGraw-Hill, New York.

Csikszentmihalyi, M. (1975) *Beyond Boredom and Anxiety*, Jossey-Bass, San Francisco, California.

Courier Mail. (2007) Age of the flashpacker. *Courier Mail*, 27 January 2007, pp. M32. Brisbane, Australia.

Desforges, L. (1998) Checking out the planet: global representations/local identities and youth travel. In: Valentine, G. and Skelton, T. (eds) *Cool Places: Geographies of Youth Cultures*. Routledge, London, pp. 175–194.

European Hospitality Quality (2008) *European Hospitality Quality*. Available at: http://www.iha-hotelfuehrer.de/home/page_sta_3900.html

Fielding, H. (1994) Spoilt for choice in all the clutter. *Independent*, 3 June, p. 23.

Gardyn, R. and Fetto, J. (2000) Demographics: it's all in the rage. *American Demographics* 22(6), 72.

Gold Coast City Council (2005) *Gold Coast Backpacker Industry Development Project*. Regional Partnerships Project 2005 Progress Reports No. 3 (18 May 2005). Gold Coast City Council, Queensland, Australia.

GCTAG (2007) *Gold Coast Adventure Travel Group's Achievements 2007 – A Year In Review*. Gold Coast City Council, Queensland, Australia.

Gilmore, J.H. and Pine, B.J. (2000) *Markets of One: Creating Customer-Unique Value Through Mass Customization*. Harvard Business School Press, Boston, Massachusetts.

Gobe, M. Gob, M. and Zyman, S. (2001) *Emotional Branding: The New Paradigm for Connecting Brands to People*. Allworth Press, New York.

Goleman, D. (2005) *Emotional Intelligence*. Bantam Books, New York.

Goleman, D. (2006) *Social Intelligence: The New Science of Human Relationships*. Bantam Books, New York.

Hill, R.P. (2002) Managing across generations in the 21st century: important lessons from the ivory trenches. *Journal of Management Inquiry* 11(1), 60–66.

Holbrook, M.B. and Hirschman, E.C. (1982) The experiential aspects of consumption: consumer fantasies, feelings and fun. *Journal of Consumer Research* 9(2), 132–140.

Horak, S. and Weber, S. (2000) Youth tourism in Europe: problems and prospects. *Journal of Recreation Research* 25(2), 37–44.

Howe, N. and Strauss, W. (2000) *Millenials Rising: The Next Great Generation*. Random House, New York.

Huntley, R. (2006) *The World According to Y*. Allen & Unwin, Crows Nest, Australia.

Jennings, G.R. and Nickerson, N. (eds) (2006) *Quality Tourism Experiences*, Elsevier, Burlington, Massachusetts.

Jennings, G.R. and Weiler, B. (2006) Mediating meaning: perspectives on brokering quality tourism experiences. In: Jennings, G.R. and Nickerson, N. (eds) *Quality Tourism Experiences*. Elsevier, Burlington, Massachusetts, pp. 57–78.

Jennings, G.R., Lee, Y-S., Cater, C., Ayling, A., Ollenburg, C. and Lunny, B. (2009) Quality tourism experiences: reviews, reflections, research agendas. *Journal of Hospitality and Leisure Marketing*, Special Issue – *The Marketing of Hospitality and Leisure Experiences*, pp. 294–310.

Kale, S.H., McIntyre, R.P. and Weir, K.M. (1987) Marketing overseas tour packages to the youth segment: an empirical analysis. *Journal of Travel Research*, 26(4), 20–24.

Kemmis, S. and McTaggart, R. (2005) Participatory action research: communicative action and the public sector. In: Denzin, N.K. and Lincoln Y.S. (eds) *Handbook of Qualitative Research*, 3rd edn. Sage, Thousand Oaks, California, pp. 559–603.

Killion, G.L. (1992) *Understanding Tourism*. Study Guide. Central Queensland University, Rockhampton, Australia.

Kotler, P., Adam, S., Brown, L. and Armstrong, G. (2001) *Principles of Marketing*. Pearson – Prentice-Hall, Frenchs Forest, Australia.

Lincoln, Y.S. and Guba, E.G. (2005) Paradigmatic controversies, contradictions, and emerging confluences. In: Denzin, N.K. and Lincoln, Y.S. (eds) *Handbook of Qualitative Research*, 2nd edn. Sage, Thousand Oaks, California, pp. 163–188.

Loker-Murphy, L. and Pearce, P. (1995) Young budget travelers: backpacking in Australia. *Annals of Tourism Research* 22, 819–843.

MacCannell, D. (1973) Staged authenticity: arrangements of social space in tourist settings. *American Journal of Sociology* 79(3), 589–603.

Mano, H. and Elliot, M.T. (1997) Smart shopping the origins and consequences of price savings. *Advances in Consumer Research*, 24(1), 504–510.

McCrindle, M. (n.d.). *Understanding Generation Y*. The Australian Leadership Foundation. Available at: http://www.learningtolearn.sa.edu.au/Colleagues/files/ links/UnderstandingGenY.pdf

National Quality Assessment Scheme (2008) *What Is a Quality Assessment?* Available at: http://www.qualityintourism.com/asp/letsgetassessed.asp

Nickerson, N.P. (2006) Some reflections on quality tourism experiences. In: Jennings, G.R. and Nickerson, N. (eds) *Quality Tourism Experiences*, Elsevier, Burlington, Massachusetts, pp. 227–235.

Office of National Statistics (2008) *Age Structure of United Kingdom 1971–2081*. Office of National Statistics, Newport, UK.

O'Reilly, B. and Vella-Zarb, K. (2000) Meet the future. *Fortune* 142(3), 144–164.

Parasuraman, A. Zeithaml, V.A. and Berry, L.L. (1985) A conceptual model of service quality and its implications for future research. *Journal of Marketing*, 49, 41–50.

Pearce, P.L. (1990) *The Backpacker Phenomenon: Preliminary Answers to Basic Questions*. James Cook University of North Queensland, Townsville, Australia.

Pine, J. and Gilmore, J. (1998) Welcome to the experience economy. *Harvard Business Review* 76(4), 97–105.

Pine, J. and Gilmore, J. (1999) *The Experience Economy: Work is Theatre and Every Business Is a Stage*. Harvard Business School Press, Boston, Massachusetts.

Quality Tourism (2008) Quality Systems. Available at: http://www.qualitytourism.com.au/default.aspx?page_id=140

Qualmark (2008) New Zealand's Official Quality Tourism Website. Available at: http://www.qualmark.co.nz/

Quelch, J.A. and Kenny, D. (1994) Extend profits not product lines. *Harvard Business Review* 72(5), 153–160.

Rathmell, J.M. (1966) What is meant by services? *Journal of Marketing* 30, 32–36.

Richards, G. and Wilson, J. (eds) (2004) *The Global Nomad: Backpacker Travel in Theory and Practice*. Channel View Publications, Clevedon, UK.

Ritchie, J.R.B. and Hudson, S. (2009) Understanding and meeting the challenges of consumer/tourist experience research. *International Journal of Tourism Research* 11, 111–126.

Roberts, K. (1983) *Youth and Leisure*. Allen & Unwin, London.

Ryan, C. (1997) *The Tourist Experience: An Introduction*. Cassell, London.

Ryan, C. (2002) *The Tourist Experience: An Introduction*, 2nd edn. Thomson Learning, London.

Rynehart, R.L. (2004) Foruming: a theory of influencing organisational change. Unpublished PhD thesis. Central Queensland University, Rockhampton, Australia.

Saactchi and Saatchi (1999) *Landmark Study Discovers Connexity Kids*. Saatchi & Saatchi Press Release, 29 January.

Schewe, C.D. and Noble, S.M. (2000). Market segmentation by cohorts: the value and validity of cohorts in America and abroad. *Journal of Marketing Management*, 16(1–3), 129–142.

The Times (2008) X-factor that marks out Generation Y. *The Times*, 17 September 2008.

Tourism Queensland (2003) Adventure Tourism. Available at: http://www.tq. com.au/fms/tq_corporate/research/fact_sheets /adventure_tourism.pdf

Tourism Queensland (2005) International Backpackers Market. Available at: http:// www.tq.com.au/fms/tq_corporate/research/fact_sheets /international_backpackers_market.pdf

Tourism Research Australia (2005) Niche Market Snapshot on Backpackers in Australia. June 2005, TRA, Canberra. Available at: http://www.tourism.australia.com/Marketing.asp?sub=0413&al=2119

Tourism Research Australia (2007) *Backpacker Accommodation in Australia 2007*. Tourism Research Australia (TRA), Canberra.

Teenage Research Unit (TRU) (1999) Teenage Marketing and Lifestyle Study. Press Release. EMERALD.

Teenage Research Unit (TRU) (2000) Teens Serious Quest for Fun. Press Release, Available at: http:// www.teenresearch.com/ pressrelease.cfm?page_id=74

Trunk, P. (2007) What Gen Y Really Wants. *Time*, Thursday 5 July. Available at: http://www.time.com/time/printout/0,8816,1640395,00. html

Youth Tourism Consortium of Canada (March, 2004) Youth Tourism in Canada: A Situational Analysis of an Overlooked Market. Available at: http:// www.omca.com/resource/document/Youth-Travel-Consortium-of-Canada-Report-FINAL.pdf?category-id=4

United Nations World Tourism Organization (UNWTO) and the World Youth Student & Educational (WYSE) Travel Confederation (2008) Youth Travel Matters: Understanding the Global Phenomenon of Youth Travel. World Tourism Organization, Madrid.

United Nations World Tourism Organization (2006) *Tourism Market Trends 2005 Edition*. UNWTO, Madrid.

Winchester, H. McGuirk, P. and Everett, K. (1999) Schoolies week as a rite of passage. In: Teather, E.K. (ed.) *Embodied Geographies; Spaces Bodies and Rites of Passage*. Routledge, London, pp. 59–77.

World Tourism Organization (1991a) *International Conference on Youth Tourism: Draft of Final Report*. World Tourism Organization International Conference on Youth Tourism, New Delhi, India.

World Tourism Organization (1991b) *International Conference on Youth Tourism: Final Report*. 18–21 November, World Tourism Organization International Conference on Youth Tourism, New Delhi, India.

Zeithaml, V.A. Parasuraman, A. and Malhotra, A. (2002) Service quality delivery through web sites: a critical review of extant knowledge. *Academy of Marketing Science* 30(4), 362–37.

7 Nature-based Tourism in North America: is Generation Y the Major Cause of Increased Participation?

Lori Pennington-Gray and Sandy Blair
University of Florida

Introduction

During the early 1900s, Mannehim (2007) defined a generation as a group of people who share common habitus, nexis and culture or a collective memory that serves to integrate. More recent definitions define a generation as an 'aggregate of all people born over roughly the span of a phase of life who share a common location in history and, hence, a common collective persona' (Strauss and Howe, 1997, p. 61). Some of the important criteria which bind generations together are social events and life experiences that create shared meanings, attitudes, preferences and sometime behavior. Research has suggested that these shared meanings and attitudes may result in predictable purchasing behavior or participation patterns that may be attributed to one's generation (Rentz and Reynolds, 1981; Smith et al., 1982). It is therefore hypothesized that different generations may behave differently with regard to travel due to these differences in perceptions.

Literature on Generation Y

In recent years, attention has moved away from the popular Baby Boomers to their children. These children represent a generation called Generation Y or those born between 1977 and 1994 (Gorman et al., 2004). Howe and Strauss (1997), however, define the birth years for Generation Y between 1982 through 2001. Unfortunately, there is not widespread consensus on the dates attributed to Generation Y; however, demographers typically agree that they represent the children of the Baby Boomer generation.

According to one source, Generation Y encompasses over 70 million people in the USA, more than three times the size of Generation X (NAS Insights, 2006). Generation Y makes up almost 24% of the US population, while the next oldest generation 'Generation X' makes up only 16% of the population. Perhaps this is because the time frame for Generation X is shorter than that for other Generations. There are three major characteristics of Generation Y:

1. They are radically and ethnically diverse.
2. They are independent, due to being children of divorced, day-care and single parents.
3. They feel empowered, due to overindulgent, guilty parents who gave them everything (Strauss and Howe, 1997, 2000).

In addition, Generation Y is generally more technologically aware than any other generations due to having grown up with the evolving technological market. As a result, members are familiar with chatting with friends, downloading music, completing homework, actively participating in gaming and e-mailing all at the same time, as the majority of their time online is for entertainment purposes. They are sometimes also referred to as the Internet Generation (Mitra, 2008). Research by Greenfield (1998) has also found that this generation is brighter than previous generations, scoring 15 points higher in raw intelligence than generations from the late 1950s, and that they have superior communication skills and feel comfortable talking to adults and expressing their thoughts. Finally, Generation Y is said to be the most adventurous generation to have lived. Given that it is independent and used to travelling with mobile parents, this generation is more likely to participate in recreation activities such as rock climbing, bungee jumping, wakeboarding and snowboarding (Bennett and Lachowetz, 2004).

Travel Literature Related to Generations

There is a paucity of research that documents different generations' travel behavior. However, an examination of generational effects on the travel patterns of German residents found that type of travel and destination region preferences were dependent on generational membership (Opperman, 1995). Opperman also found that transportation usage differed by generational groups. He found that younger generations gained different experiences when compared to previous generations and were likely to have different tourism patterns in later life stages. In the early 1990s, Warnick (1993a,b) addressed the domestic travel behavior of various generations. He used *Simmons Market Research* data and found that the Baby Boomer Generation's participation rate in domestic travel declined at the same or a lower rate than the overall population. The Silent Generation (those aged 35–44 in 1979 and then aged 45–54 in 1989) experienced a rise in participation rates; while, all other cohorts showed greater declining rates than the overall population. In conclusion,

Warnick argued that documenting the travel behaviour of generations is useful.

According to McPherson (1990), the preferences and needs of future generations of adults can only be understood by studying particular age cohorts at different stages of their lives. A recent study conducted by Pennington-Gray and Kerstetter (2001) did just that. They focused on the changes over time in preferences for pleasure travel between two cohorts of older Canadian adults. This research found that beaches for sunning and swimming, budget accommodations, shopping, nightlife and entertainment, and theme parks and amusement parks were more important to adults aged 55–64 than to adults 65 years of age and older. Also, all five preferences were more important in 1995 than in 1983, regardless of cohort. More recently, You and O'Leary (2000) addressed generational effects on the travel behavior and travel philosophies of older Japanese tourists. Their results indicated that younger cohorts varied from older cohorts with respect to their level of travel activity as well as their philosophies about travelling for pleasure. Lacking from the scholarly literature is empirical research on the generational preferences for different types of travel. Therefore, the main objective of the study presented in this chapter was to examine changes in nature-based tourism over time. A secondary goal was to determine if Generation Y had influenced increases in participation over time.

Literature Related to Nature-based Recreation

Between 2000 and 2007, the total number of people who participated in one or more outdoor activities grew by 4.4%, from an estimated 208 million to 217 million (Cordell, 2008). In addition, the number of days of participation grew almost 14% (Cordell, 2008). Specific activities such as hiking, camping and wilderness backpacking have recognized substantial increases in recent decades (see Table 7.1). In 1995, 41.5 million Americans participated in developed camping, while primitive camping represented 146.6 million primary

Table 7.1. National trends in nature-based tourism activities: age 16 and older. (From Cordell, 2008.)

Activity	Participants (millions) 1982–1983	Participants (millions) 1994–1995	Change (%)
Bird watching	21.2	54.1	155.2
Hiking	24.7	47.8	93.5
Backpacking	8.8	15.2	72.7
Downhill skiing	10.6	16.8	58.5
Camping – primitive area	17.7	28.0	58.2
Off-road driving	19.4	27.9	43.8
Walking	93.6	133.7	42.8
Sightseeing	81.3	113.4	39.5
Camping – developed area	30.0	41.5	38.3
Snowmobiling	5.3	7.1	34.0
Cross-country skiing	5.3	6.5	22.6
Picnicking	84.8	98.3	15.9
Sledding	17.7	20.5	15.8
Running/jogging	45.9	52.5	14.4
Water skiing	15.9	17.9	12.6
Bicycling	56.5	57.4	1.6
Ice skating	10.6	10.5	−0.9
Horseback riding	15.9	14.3	−10.1
Hunting	21.2	18.6	−12.3

purpose trips annually (Cordell, 2008). Projections of camping expect participation to increase between 50% in the next 50 years for developed camping and 24% over the same time period for primitive camping (Bowker *et al.*, 1999).

The statistics also suggest that hiking is the most popular outdoor activity participated in for the USA and it accounted for 50 million participants in 1995. Hiking is expected to grow slightly faster than the population growth (Bowker *et al.*, 1999). Interestingly, Bowker *et al.* (1999) suggest that hiking is less associated with a rural lifestyle and many urban and suburban inhabitants are participating in hiking outside their area of residence. This finding will have tremendous impacts on future participation rates due to the ease of participation regardless of location of residence. Finally, participation in wilderness backpacking represents approximately 33.3 million people annually. About 12% of the population over the age of 16 participate in this activity in the western regions of the USA. Participation in backpacking is projected to increase by 26% (Bowker *et al.*, 1999). Research suggests that race and income may be

the prime factors driving this projected growth. However, this research does not account for generational differences. Overall, participation in 50 nature-based activities recognized increases by more than 22% from 2000 to 2007 (Cordell, 2008). The top activities involved viewing, identifying, visiting or observing. Researchers in the US Forest Service suggest that interest in nature-based outdoor recreation is growing and will continue to do so until 2050 (Bowker *et al.*, 1999).

Research Related to Nature-based Tourism

Similar to nature-based outdoor recreation, nature-based tourism is the fastest growing segment of the USA's US$584 billion-a-year travel industry (Stein *et al.*, 2002). Unlike outdoor recreationists who may stay close to home to recreate, nature-based tourists must travel 50 m (1 m = 1.609 km) one way or more to be considered a nature-based tourist. Nature-based tourists are defined as 'individuals who are interested in experiencing wilderness and undisturbed nature; seeing lakes, streams and mountains; being physically active; and engaging in outdoor activities' (Pennington-Gray and Kerstetter, 2002, p. 418). As noted, staying overnight is not a precursor to being defined as a nature-based tourist. However, distance travelled and purposes of trip are the mandatory criteria for defining this type of tourist.

Research related to nature-based tourism can be broken into supply-side studies and demand-side studies. With regard to the supply side, much of the research is synonymous with the ecotourism literature. For the purpose of this chapter, this literature will be omitted. On the demand side, scholars have defined nature-based tourists and also examined their psychographic profiles and their behaviors. Various authors have described nature-based tourists as individuals who are interested in experiencing wilderness and undisturbed nature (Eagles, 1992; Fennell and Eagles, 1990; Kretchman and Eagles, 1990; Silverberg et al., 1996; Leones et al., 1998; Meric and Hunt, 1998; Wight, 1996; Sirakaya et al., 1999). Silverberg et al. (1996) completed an investigation into the psychographics of nature-based travellers in south-eastern USA. They found that there were six types or clusters of nature-based travellers based on psychographic dimensions: education/history; camping/tenting; socializing; relaxation; viewing nature; and information. The youngest travellers aged between 35 and 44 accounted for over half of the information group, which was distinguished by items such as 'shopping around' for vacation bargains and being prepared for a trip through planning choices. Finally, in a study conducted by Pennington-Gray and Spreng (2002), the preferences of Canadians for national and provincial parks were examined in relation to age, generation and time period. These authors found that as generations aged, they became less interested in national and provincial parks. This suggests that people in the earlier years of their lives (younger ages) are more interested in visiting national and provincial parks as a part of their pleasure travel. They suggest this may be one of the reasons for the increased trend in nature-based tourism. Thus, the purpose of this chapter is to examine whether Generation Y is responsible for increased participation

in nature-based tourism in the USA. The key research questions which will guide the analysis are:

1. What is the relationship between one's generation and changes in camping/overnight participation over time?
2. What is the relationship between one's generation and changes in hiking/overnight participation over time?
3. What is the relationship between one's generation and changes in wilderness backpacking participation over time?

Methods

Measuring change over time can be accomplished in multiple ways. However, when looking for the influence of one's generation on change over time, cohort analysis is the most widely accepted method of analysis. Although measuring a true effect on change is difficult, cohort analysis allows for examination of three variables simultaneously (age, generation and period). One of the more recognized methods of cohort analysis is called Palmore's triad analysis (Palmore, 1978; Reynolds and Rentz, 1981). Palmore's (1978) triad method emphasizes three levels of analysis in order to prevent conceptual and operational confusion that may arise from lack of ability to partial out the immediate effects of age, period or cohort/ generation (for a more in-depth explanation of Palmore's cohort analysis see Pennington-Gray et al., 2002). Palmore's method is used here to try and determine if Generation Y is affecting North American nature-based tourism participation.

Sample and longitudinal database

Sports Business Research Network (SBRnet) data are the primary source of data for the analysis. The SBRnet has conducted research on various sports and activities since 1996. This data set is appropriate in that data that have been collected over time are critical to using cohort analysis and, more importantly, these data sets need to be comparable. The

SBRnet uses a mail panel resource of more than 300,000 pre-recruited households to collect the data overtime. The panel is balanced on a number of characteristics determined to be key indicators of general purchase behavior, including household size and composition, household income, age of household head, socio-economic status of the household, and region and market size (www.SBRnet. com). In January each year, a self-administered questionnaire is mailed to 20,000 households. The sample is weighted by 'return rate' and region of the country, thereby yielding a return sample which is correctly representative of the continental USA based upon these characteristics.

The age categories were comprised of four generations: Silent, Baby Boomers, Generation X and Generation Y, according to Strauss and Howe's birth-year delineations:

- The Silent Generation 1925–1942.
- The Baby Boomers 1943–1960.
- Generation X 1961–1981.
- Generation Y 1982–2001.

For the purpose of this chapter, only those 18 years of age and older in the Generation Y group will be included. Although age categories are not entirely representative of each generation, they were close enough to represent each category (see Table 7.2).

Operationalization of the variables

Nature-based tourism

Three activities in SBRnet were used to represent nature-based tourism: camping/overnight; hiking/overnight; and wilderness backpacking. These activities were chosen because they were most likely to fit the definition of tourism activities; specifically they included travel of more than 50 m one way and may have even included an overnight stay (as mentioned in camping and hiking). In the case of wilderness backpacking, it is argued that most participants would live more than 50 m one way from a 'wilderness area' and thus qualify as a tourist, even if it was only a day trip. Other potential activities could have been included; however, there was no easy way to discern if they met the criteria.

Generations

The sample data are made up of only an adult population (those 18 years of age and older).

Data analysis

Three levels of analysis were conducted to understand whether Generation Y is responsible for increased nature-based travel in North America:

1. Computing observable differences.
2. Inferring which effects (i.e. age, generation and period) produced the observable differences.
3. Imputing causes.

Observable differences were measured as:

- longitudinal differences – those between early and later measurements on the same generation;
- cross-sectional differences – those between younger and older generations (and age groups) at one point in time; and
- time-lag differences – those between an older generation at an earlier measurement and a younger generation at a later measurement.

Table 7.2. Generational time frame based on Howe and Strauss (1997).

Generations	Start of generation	End of generation	Oldest age	Youngest age	Ages from SBRnet	Range of ages in SBRnet
Silent	1925	1942	83	66	65–75	10
Boomers	1943	1960	65	48	45–64	20
Generation X	1961	1981	47	27	25–44	19
Generation Y	1982	2001	26	7	18–24	6

The second level of analysis is called 'inferred effects'. These are important because researchers can document which effects (i.e. age, generation or period) best explain the differences (i.e. longitudinal, cross-sectional and time-lag) noted in the first level of analysis. Z-tests are used to determine inferred effects. Each observable difference can only be composed of two effects: (i) longitudinal = age + period effects; (ii) cross-sectional = age + generation effects; (iii) time-lag = period + generation effects.

The final level of analysis is the imputing of causes. This is accomplished by running Z-tests on the differences between proportions. Z-tests were used due to the size of the sample. The first step in the Z-tests was calculating the standard error. Next, a triad table was created, providing the basis for the Z-tests among the three effects. Finally, Z-tests were calculated on the differences between the proportions. The magnitude of the effect is the estimated mean of the two significant effects.

Findings

Step 1: observable differences

The data (i.e. participation in camping/vacationing, hiking/overnight and wilderness backpacking) were used to compute observable differences (i.e. longitudinal, cross-sectional and time-lag). More specifically, differences were calculated using a triad method as seen in Table 7.3. For example, the longitudinal difference for triad 2 in camping/overnight (11.2%) was computed by deducting 5.2 from 16.4 (see Table 7.3 for this data). The cross-sectional difference (13.6%) for triad 1, on the

other hand, was computed by deducting 2.8 from 16.4. The final difference for triad 1, time-lag (–2.4%), was computed by deducting 5.2 from 2.8. Tables 7.2–7.5 provide participation rates for overnight travel with regard to camping, hiking and wilderness backpacking, respectively.

Step 2: inferred Effects

In the second stage of analysis, we assessed which of the effects were at work. This was accomplished by referencing the number of significant differences identified through the z-tests. According to Bonnici and Fredenberger (1991), there are three, and only three, basic patterns of observable differences: (i) no significant differences; (ii) two significant differences; and (iii) three significant differences. 'It is impossible to have only one significant difference because each difference is related to the other two: one can predict any thread difference from the other two' (p. 286). If only one effect is noted, there is an error in the data and no effects are inferred. When two significant differences are present, the effects are 'pure'. This pure effect can be interpreted as follows:

Table 7.4. Participation in hiking/overnight travel (%).

Generation	1993	1997	2000	2003	2007
Silent	5.5	2.4	2.6	3.7	3.3
Boomers	14.9	18.3	20.4	20.5	30.5
Generation X	22.4	21.4	21.9	21.3	21.2
Generation Y	35.1	34.7	31.3	32.1	26.9
Total % represented	72.4	76.8	76.2	77.6	81.9

Table 7.5. Participation in wilderness backpacking (%).

Generation	1993	1997	2000	2003	2007
Silent	1.1	0.5	0.8	1	1.3
Boomers	11	10.2	13.6	14.9	22.3
Generation X	22.4	20.6	19.4	20.3	23.5
Generation Y	43.1	44.4	39.1	38.1	30.1
Total % represented	76.5	75.7	72.9	74.3	77.2

Table 7.3. Participation in camping/overnight travel (%).

Generation	1993	1997	2000	2003	2007
Silent	5.2	2.8	2.5	3.3	3.7
Boomers	15.2	16.4	18.5	19.7	23.4
Generation X	20.1	21.3	20.9	19.2	20.9
Generation Y	34.6	31.8	31.6	31.7	28.9
Total % represented	69.9	72.3	73.5	73.9	76.9

(i) longitudinal and cross-sectional differences equal an age effect; (ii) longitudinal and time-lag differences equal a period effect; and (iii) cross-sectional and time-lag differences equal a generational effect. Using the principle of parsimony, Bonnici and Fredenberger (1991) opted to interpret two significant differences as 'pure' effects. In reality there are two possibilities: (i) there are two equal and opposite effects which are reflected in the two significant differences; and (ii) there is the possibility that there are three effects, two equal and opposite and one effect that is reflected by the significant differences. When three effects are significant, the situation is considered ambiguous because it is impossible to separate the three effects. Hence, as with the situation with one signifi-

cant effect, the results are ignored (denoted by a dash). The magnitude of the effects is the estimated mean of the two significant effects (see Tables 7.6–7.9).

Camping/overnight travel

Results of the triad analysis for camping/overnight travellers (Table 7.9) indicated that there was not one effect that explained all differences. This is noted by the presence of multiple effects across all the triads (age, generation and period). Age was present in two triads (triad 1 and triad 7), while generation was present in triad 9, and period was present in triad 10. In general, the greater the number of significant effects, the greater the strength of

Table 7.6. Triads for camping/overnight participation.

	Triad	Longitudinal difference	Cross-sectional difference	Time-lag difference
Group 1: 1993–1997	1	11.20	13.60	−2.40
	2	6.10	4.90	1.20
	3	11.70	10.50	1.20
Group 2: 1997–2000	4	15.70	−0.30	−0.30
	5	4.50	2.10	2.10
	6	10.30	−0.40	−0.40
Group 3: 2000–2003	7	17.20	16.40	0.80
	8	0.70	−0.50	1.20
	9	10.80	12.50	−1.70
Group 4: 2003–2007	10	20.10	0.40	0.40
	11	1.20	3.70	3.70
	12	9.70	1.70	1.70

Table 7.7. Triads for hiking/overnight participation.

	Triad	Longitudinal difference	Cross-sectional difference	Time-lag difference
Group 1: 1993–1997	1	12.80	15.90	−3.10
	2	6.50	3.10	3.40
	3	12.30	13.30	−1.00
Group 2: 1997–2000	4	18.00	0.20	0.20
	5	3.60	2.10	2.10
	6	9.90	0.50	0.50
Group 3: 2000–2003	7	17.90	16.80	1.10
	8	0.90	0.80	0.10
	9	10.20	10.80	−0.60
Group 4: 2003–2007	10	26.80	−0.40	−0.40
	11	0.70	10.00	10.00
	12	5.60	−0.10	−0.10

Table 7.8. Triads for wilderness backpacking participation.

	Triad	Longitudinal difference	Cross-sectional difference	Time-lag difference
Group 1: 1993–1997	1	9.10	9.70	−0.60
	2	9.60	10.40	−0.80
	3	22.00	23.80	−1.80
Group 2: 1997–2000	4	13.10	0.30	0.30
	5	9.20	3.40	3.40
	6	18.50	−1.20	−1.20
Group 3: 2000–2003	7	14.10	13.90	0.20
	8	6.70	5.40	1.30
	9	18.70	17.80	0.90
Group 4: 2003–2007	10	21.30	0.30	0.30
	11	8.60	7.40	7.40
	12	9.80	3.20	3.20

Table 7.9. Z-tests, inferred effects and magnitude of effects for camping/overnight participation.

	T-tests	Longitudinal difference	Cross-sectional difference	Time-lag difference	Effect	Magnitude
Group 1: 1993–1997	1	−9.005	−4.323	−1.261	A	−2.34
	2	−2.911	−2.233	12.164	–	
	3	3.351	3.248	4.636	–	
Group 2: 1997–2000	4	−5.264	0.081	−0.405	–	
	5	1.725	0.859	12.835	–	
	6	9.614	0.107	−0.083	–	
Group 3: 2000–2003	7	−4.735	−8.585	−0.464	A	1.93
	8	0.312	−0.232	13.371	–	
	9	−2.797	−3.417	8.356	G	−7.60
Group 4: 2003–2007	10	−12.185	−0.230	4.442	P	−14.41
	11	0.530	1.849	14.192	–	
	12	−2.214	−0.378	15.353	–	

A, age effect (significant longitudinal and cross-sectional differences); G, generational effect (significant cross-sectional and time-lag differences); P, period effect (significant longitudinal and time-lag differences).

the effects for that time frame. Given the effects varied for camping/overnight, no single effect was attributed to this trend.

The magnitude of the effects (estimated mean of two significant effects) revealed that for camping/overnight travellers, the magnitude was greatest for period effects, suggesting that participation in more recent times is greater than in the past. In addition, for age effects, the magnitude of effects was greater for group 3 (2000–2003) than for group 1 (1993–1997).

The results associated with triad 9 (Table 7.9) suggested that there are generational effects impacting individuals' participation in camping

and overnight travel and that these generational effects are *fairly* large in magnitude (magnitude = 7.6). The presence of this generational effect does not negate the other effects; rather it suggests that the increase in participation in camping/overnight travel can be accounted for by generation during this time period.

Hiking/overnight travel

Results of the triad analysis for hiking/overnight travel indicated that again changes in participation are a result of two influences: age and generation (Table 7.10). Age effects were

Table 7.10. Z-tests, inferred effects and magnitude of effects for hiking/overnight participation.

	T-tests	Longitudinal difference	Cross-sectional difference	Time-lag difference	Effect	Magnitude
Group 1: 1993–1997	1	−17.242	−8.435	−2.713	−	
	2	−4.274	−1.818	18.429	−	
	3	5.284	5.504	11.230	−	
Group 2: 1997–2000	4	−10.109	−0.016	0.019	−	
	5	1.904	1.175	20.107	−	
	6	14.617	−0.171	0.139	−	
Group 3: 2000–2003	7	−1.470	−1.747	−0.430	A	0.14
	8	0.506	0.451	20.477	−	
	9	−3.548	−3.767	71.105	−	
Group 4: 2003–2007	10	−2.920	0.041	−0.745	−	
	11	0.372	6.923	22.750	G	−4.45
	12	−1.616	0.028	−0.902	−	

A, age effect (significant longitudinal and cross-sectional differences); G, generational effect (significant cross-sectional and time-lag differences); P, period effect (significant longitudinal and time-lag differences).

most pronounced between 2000 and 2003 (triads 7–9) while generational effects were most pronounced between 2003 and 2007. It is of interest that for generational effects, younger generations indicated more participation than older generations. For example, with triad 11, the magnitude is −4.45, a slight impact but negative in direction, meaning younger generations participated more frequently. An examination of the differences associated with the seventh triad suggests that age effects are present. Again, the presence of

age effects does not negate generational effects, instead it suggests that the smaller amount of participation hiking/overnight travel (magnitude = −0.44) can be accounted for by age in that particular time frame.

Wilderness backpacking

Finally, results of the triad analysis for wilderness backpacking indicated that changes in participation are mainly a result of age (Table 7.11). This is noted by the overall presence of

Table 7.11. Z-tests, inferred effects and magnitude of effects for wilderness backpacking participation.

	T-tests	Longitudinal difference	Cross-sectional difference	Time-lag difference	Effect	Magnitude
Group 1: 1993–1997	1	−1.77	−34.57	0.12	−	
	2	−10.30	−338.58	0.89	A	164.14
	3	54.16	44.60	14.12	−	
Group 2: 1997–2000	4	−48.02	−4.63	−1.44	A	−21.70
	5	17.97	6.74	434.26	−	
	6	37.10	27.31	−2.21	A	4.89
Group 3: 2000–2003	7	−287.07	−562.63	−8.19	−	
	8	13.07	10.86	82.73	−	
	9	−519.66	−399.06	104.41	−	
Group 4: 2003–2007	10	−4,900.88	−5.51	5.99	−	
	11	13.58	12.07	363.47	−	
	12	−1,708.37	−22.52	23.47	−	

A, age effect (significant longitudinal and cross-sectional differences); G, generational effect (significant cross-sectional and time-lag differences); P, period effect (significant longitudinal and time-lag differences).

age effects across all the triads (1–6). Age effects were most pronounced between 1993 and 1997 (magnitude of 164.14). More specifically, age effects were present in two of the four groups (i.e. 1993–1997, 1997–2000). The number of age effects was greater for the second (i.e. 1997–2000) group of triads. This group had two significant age effects. The greater the number of significant effects, the greater the strength of the period effects for that time frame

The magnitude of the effects (estimated mean of two significant effects) revealed that for wilderness backpacking, age effects were greater for younger age groups. For example, in the first and second group of triads, triad 1 to triad 6, age effects were present. However, in triads 7 to 12, no age effects were present.

Discussion

We set out to use Palmore's cohort analysis to determine if Generation Y was mainly responsible for the increased participation in nature-based tourism. Across the three types of activities used to represent nature-based tourism, generational effects were only present in one triad of camping/overnight and one triad of hiking/overnight. Given this finding, we are unable to confirm that generational effects are responsible for the increased participation in nature-based tourism and more specifically that Generation Y can be attributed to this growth. However, in both cases where generational effects were present, younger generations, or Generation Y, were more likely to participate (e.g. camping/overnight and hiking/overnight) at a higher rate than the other two generations.

With regard to the first research question, the greatest influence on changes in camping/ overnight vacationing has been a combination of all three effects. No one effect dominated the results. Thus, one cannot attribute changes singularly to age, generation or period. In the early time periods, age appeared to play the dominant influence on change; however, in more recent times (2003–2007), period effects were more influential. Through examining the percentage participation, it is evident that

Generation Y actually decreased in its participation in more recent time periods (31.7% in 2003 to 28.9% in 2007). This is offset by Boomer increases in participation over time (15.2% in 1993 to 23.4% in 2007). Thus, participation has been increasing over time.

With regard to changes in hiking/overnight participation, few significant decipherable findings were found. Of the 12 triads, only two indicated significant differences. These were later triads and they were attributed to age and generation. Similar trends were found in hiking/overnight participation, to camping, in that Generation Y tended to decrease its participation levels from 2003 to 2007, whereas Boomers increased their participation. Overall, the increases in participation are notable; however, based on this data, it is still difficult to discern the greatest influence on this change.

Finally, wilderness backpacking also indicates growth over time. However, age effects seem to be the greatest influence on these changes. Generation Y decreases in participation rates from 2003 to 2007 (similar to the other two activities), while increases are seen from Boomers and Generation X-ers. Examining participation patterns reveals a clear trend that the older generations have started to take up backpacking in more recent years, and that younger generations are proportionately staying at the same rate. Perhaps this is because Boomers have more time than they did in the early 1990s, when many of them were at the peak earning years, and are now closer to retirement. These results may refute findings by Pennington-Gray and Spreng (2002) who found that as generations aged, they became less interested in national and provincial parks. Their findings suggest that people in the earlier years of their lives are more interested in visiting national and provincial parks as a part of their pleasure travel, while the findings of this particular study suggest that older generations in this time period are more likely to take up these activities than younger generations in the same time period.

It is interesting to note that age effects were the dominant effect over the three activities. Regardless of the type of nature-based activity, changes in behavior were due primarily to age effects (the combination of longitudinal and cross-sectional differences). This suggests that younger individuals are more likely to participate in these activities than older individuals. This is perhaps good news for nature-based tourism in the short term. Because Generation Y ranges in ages from 7 to 26, forms of nature-based tourism still may experience growth due to new members of this large demographic segment of the population taking up the activity.

In summary, recognizing that generations exhibit distinct patterns of travel behavior is important to the planning and marketing of travel services. However, these particular activities that are associated with nature-based tourism are perhaps changing in participation patterns because of other things; some of these factors may include changes in attitudes by the American population towards nature-based tourism, and changes in population demographics such as race/ethnicity. In the future, if marketers want to predict for travel participation patterns, they should adopt techniques such as Palmore's triad method with various other types of travel activities.

References

Bennett, G. and Lachowetz, T. (2004) Marketing to lifestyles: action sports and Generation Y. *Sport Marketing Quarterly* 13(4), 239–243.

Bonnici, J.L. and Fredenberger, W.B. (1991) Cohort analysis – a forecasting tool. *Journal of Business Forecasting* 10(3), 9–13.

Bowker, J.M., English, D.B.K. and Cordell, H.K. (1999) Projections of outdoor recreation participation to 2050. In: Cordell, H.K., Betz, C., Bowker, J.M., English, D.B.K., Mou, S.H., Bergstrom, J.C., Teasley, R.J., Tarrant, M.A. and Loomis, J. (eds) *Outdoor Recreation in American life: A National Assessment of Demand and Supply Trends.* Sagamore Publishing, Champaign, Illinois, pp. 323–351.

Cordell, H.K. (2008) The latest on trends in nature-based outdoor recreation. *Forest History Today* Spring: 4–10.

Eagles, P. (1992) The travel motivations of Canadian ecotourists. *Journal of Travel Research* 32, 3–7.

Fennell, D. and Eagles, P. (1990) Ecotourism in Costa Rica: a conceptual framework. *Journal of Park and Recreation Administration* 8(1), 23–34.

Gorman, P., Nelson, T. and Glassman, A. (2004) The millennial generation: a strategic opportunity. *Organizational Analysis* 12(3), 255–270.

Greenfield, P.M. (1998) The cultural evolution of IQ. In: Neisser, U. (ed.) *The Rising Curve: Long-term Gains in IQ and Other Measures.* American Psychological Association, Washington, DC, pp. 81–123.

Howe, N. and Strauss, W. (1997) *The Fourth Turning: An American Prophecy.* New York: Broadway Books.

Howe, N. and Strauss, W. (2000) *Millennials Rising: The Next Great Generation.* Random House, New York.

Kretchman, J. and Eagles, P. (1990) An analysis of the motives of ecotourists in comparison to the general Canadian population. *Society and Leisure* 13, 499–508.

Leones, J., Colby, B. and Crandall, K. (1998) Tracking expenditures of the elusive nature tourists of southeastern Arizona. *Journal of Travel Research* 36(3), 56–64.

Mannheim, K. (2007) *Essays on the Sociology of Knowledge V5.* Routledge, Kentucky.

McPherson, B.D. (1990) *Aging as a Social Process: An Introduction to Individual and Population Aging.* Butterworths, Markham, Ontario, Canada.

Meric, H. and Hunt, J. (1998) Ecotourists' motivational and demographic characteristics: a case of North Carolina travelers. *Journal of Travel Research* 36(4), 57–62.

Mitra, S. (2008) Recruiting and retaining Generation Y. Available at: www. http://www.cpa2biz.com/Content/media/PRODUCER_CONTENT/Newsletters/Articles_2008/CorpFin/Y.jsp

NAS Insights (2006) Generation Y: the millennials, ready or not, here they come. Available at: http://www.nasrecruitment.com/talenttips/NASinsights/GenerationY.pdf

Opperman, M. (1995) Family life cycle and cohort effects: a study of travel patterns of German residents. *Journal of Travel and Tourism Marketing* 4(1), 23–45.

Palmore, E. (1978) When can age, period and cohort be separated? *Social Forces* 57(1), 282–295.

Pennington-Gray, L. and Kerstetter, D. (2001) Examining travel preferences of older Canadian adults over time. *Journal of Hospitality and Leisure Marketing* 8(3/4), 131–146.

Pennington-Gray, L. and Kerstetter, D. (2002) Testing a constraints model within the context of nature-based tourism. *Journal of Travel Research* 40(4), 416–423.

Pennington-Gray, L. and Spreng, R. (2002) Analyzing changing preferences for pleasure travel with cohort analysis. *Tourism Analysis: An Interdisciplinary Journal* 6(1), 1–13.

Pennington-Gray, L., Kerstetter, D.L. and Warnick, R. (2002) Forecasting travel patterns using Palmore's cohort analysis. *Journal of Travel and Tourism Marketing* 13(1/2), 127–145.

Rentz, J.O. and Reynolds, F.D. (1981) Separating age, cohort and period effects in consumer behavior. In: Monroe, K.B. (ed.) *Advances in Consumer Research*, Vol. 8, Ann Arbor, Michigan.

Reynolds, F.D. and Rentz, J.O. (1981) Cohort analysis: an aid to strategic planning. *Journal of Marketing* 45, 62–70.

Silverberg, K., Backman, S. and Backman, K. (1996) A preliminary investigation into the psychographics and nature-based travelers to the south-eastern United States. *Journal of Travel Research* 35(2), 19–29.

Sirakaya, E., Sasidharan, V., and Sönmez, S. (1999) Redefining ecotourism: the need for a supply-side view. *Journal of Travel Research* 38(2), 168–172.

Smith, H.L., Mason, W.M. and Fienberg, S.E. (1982) More chimeras of the age-period-cohort accounting framework: comment on Rodgers. *American Sociological Review* 47, 787–793.

Strauss, W. and Howe, N. (1997) *The Fourth Turning: An American Prophecy*. Broadway Books, New York.

Stein, T., Tyree, A. and Flanigan, T. (2002) *University of Florida News*. UF expert: nature-based tourism requires marketing know-how. Available at: http://news.ufl.edu/2002/06/12/ecotourism/

Warnick, R. (1993a) *Back To The Future: US Domestic Travel and Generational Trends, 1979 To 1991*. Paper presented at the Resort and Commercial Recreation Association Annual Congress, Mohonk Mountain House, New Paltz, New York, November.

Warnick, R. (1993b) *US Domestic Travel: Back To The Future. The Impacts of an Aging US Population on Domestic Travel Trends. The Annual Review of Travel* (1993 edn) American Express Travel Related Services, Inc., New York, pp. 75–89.

Wight, P. (1996) North American ecotourism markets: motivations, preferences and destinations. *Journal of Travel Research* 35(1), 3–10.

You, X. and O'Leary, J. (2000) Age and cohort effects: an examination of older Japanese travelers. *Journal of Travel and Tourism Marketing* 9(1/2), 21–42.

8   Tourism and the N Generation in a Dynamically Changing Society: the Case of South Korea

Minkyung Park[1], Hochan Jang[2], Seokho Lee[2] and Russell Brayley[1]
[1]School of Recreation, Health and Tourism, George Mason University; [2]Korea National Open University, South Korea

Introduction

South Korea is one of the many nations with populations that are marked by distinct generations and equally distinct gaps between them. The emerging consumer generation, known as the N Generation (for Net Generation), is comprised of particularly computer-savvy individuals who were born between 1977 and 1997, have grown up surrounded by the digital media and have ready access to World Wide Web technologies (Tapscott, 1998). The N Generation in Korea is also referred to as the Netizen Generation (for Network Citizens) and is further characterized by its propensity to exchange information through computers and shape opinions and have their opinions formed by influences in the cyber world (DongA IlBo, 2007). The N Generation is a regional equivalence of the Y Generation concept.

In Korea, this new generation is vastly different from those that have preceded it in the history of the nation and culture. The N Generation that emerged with the development of web technology and the resulting Internet culture has distinguished itself by its attitude and behaviors, in many aspects of social life, from political participation to patterns of consumption. As their ages reach the 20s and 30s, Korean Netizens are spreading their influence online and offline throughout the entire society. While such growth in the

N Generation's influence may be a familiar phenomenon in other countries, the related social stirring in Korea deserves special attention because such sharp generational differences have not been experienced in the past, and because there is clearly more to explain the wide generational gap than just web technology development.

Since the late 1970s, the political, economic and social environments in South Korea have undergone rapid changes. These changes have created new non-technologically defined conditions (including support for international travel) that could also influence the emergence and characterization of a new, unique generation. These dramatic social, political and economic changes in Korea have made it possible for the N Generation to live in a more prosperous, democratized and open society than previously existed. While web technology and a culture of Internet literacy are key elements in defining the global N Generation, they are insufficient explanations for the Korean situation. Any discussion of the N Generation in Korea must include a thorough treatment of the new conditions or environments in which the Netizens live, especially those that relate to travel experiences and travel's impact on their identity. It may be argued that, if significant social changes can *facilitate* the emergence of a new generational cohort, then rapidly changing societies hold potential for *causing* new generational cohorts to develop. Similarly, it can be expected that the differences observed in a new generation would be more profound in dramatically changing societies, such as Korea.

The purpose of this chapter is to provide a comprehensive discussion of how dramatically changing environments stimulate, influence and interact with the emergence of a new generation in a society, by examining the case of the N Generation in South Korea. The chapter will also explore how dynamic environments contribute to characterization of the emerging generation in relation to its attitudes or identity in general, as well as to its travel experiences and consumption patterns in particular.

The first section of the chapter will examine the socio-economic and political situations and changes that have affected Korean society, with emphasis on the time period during which the N Generation had its genesis, developed to adolescence and on to adulthood. It will also emphasize how other societal transitions during that time interacted with, and influenced, the characteristics of a new generation in Korea. The second section will focus on the main factors (Internet and globalization) that most characterize the N Generation in Korea. This will lead to a discussion of how the N Generation in Korea can be understood in a unique environment, a dynamically changing society and a globalizing modern world. The final section will deal with what the existence of a new generation means to the travel and tourism field in Korea by focusing on the N Generation's online activities, as it pertains to the travel and tourism experience, and on its travel information seeking behaviours.

This chapter will emphasize that the emergence of a new generational cohort and its distinctiveness in one society need to be understood in these unique historical contexts. It will demonstrate that a new generation is not only a product of a changing world, but is also a result of the interaction between unique and local changing environments.

Dynamic Changes in the Socio-economic and Political Domains

Different generations in a global society have been spotlighted at different times throughout history. In modern Korean history, there have been 'Korean Baby Boomers' (born in the post-Korean War era between 1955 and 1963). Then, there is 'Generation X' or '386 Generation' (used to categorize those who were in their 30s, attended college in the 80s and were born in the 60s). 386 Generation was a salient phenomenon during the 1990s and has been the central feature of the Korean social and political history since the late 1980s. The term was first used in the mid-1990s, but became somewhat outdated a decade later, when most of the 386 Generationers are now in their 40s. A better name for this cohort would now be '486ers'. Rising from the increasing social insignificance of Korea's 386 Generation comes a new generation called the 'N Generation'. The influential lifespan of a distinct generation is closely associated with concurrent changes in society. This section will shed the light on the socio-economic and political circumstances associated with the rise and development of the N Generation in Korea.

The N Generation demonstrates different values and attitudes towards established systems, including political, economic, social and even international sport. Like the Y Generation in other countries, the N Generation in Korea is generally individualistic, inclines to values of diversity rather than homogeneity and pursues quality of life more than money and power (Seo, 2003). Members of the N Generation also develop strong cultural alliances and, having grown up in a time of more open, affluent and democratized society, have a more liberal outlook and greater self-confidence than previous generations in Korea (Seo, 2003).

In addition to their characteristics in values and attitudes, those in their 20s and early 30s among the N Generation in Korea have also positioned themselves at the centre of economic trends. Their purchasing activity now accounts for over 50% of business involving the use of credit cards, mobile phones, shopping and leisure (including travel and tourism) (Seo, 2003). The N Generation has already demonstrated the highest recorded propensity to consume. Its influence on the business sector is expected to further increase, as more from the N Generation will be absorbed into the market in coming years.

By the late 1980s, evidence of the emergence of a new generation with diverse and significant implications to Korean society was indisputable. The birth of the new generation coincided with important social and political changes in Korea. Before the late 1980s, Korean society was dominated by authoritarian and regulated systems. Then this society began to change towards open and deregulated economic, social and political systems. The country began the transition to democracy in 1987 (Lee, 2008) with the first substantial democratic presidential election since the end of the Korean War in 1953. During the preceding three decades, the country had been ruled by a civilian dictatorship followed by military dictatorships. The political transition in 1987 was the result of a strong democratic movement in the first half of that decade, which culminated in the military regime's acceptance of the citizens' demand for true democracy through the direct election of South Korea's president by the people. The civil rights movement in 1987 is considered a landmark moment in Korea's quest for democracy (Seo, 2003).

In the wake of 1980s democratic movement, a variety of voluntary organizations and civic groups emerged in Korea (Lee, 2008). According to the *Encyclopedia of Korean Associations*, the number of voluntary associations rose from about 3900 in 1996 to 23,000 in 2005 (Cho, 2000), and their rapid growth has contributed to a high level of political activism (Lee, 2008). The N Generation in Korea was raised and nurtured in the light of such a participatory democratic movement and its social political activism was celebrated with unusual national enthusiasm for the 2002 World Cup soccer team, and a presidential election in the same year. A culture of voluntary and equal participation shared by this generational cohort was demonstrated when, wearing red T-shirts, thousands of young Koreans cheered for the World Cup soccer team and staged spontaneous street festivals (a new cultural scene in Korean society). The 2002 Korean presidential election gave the N Generation several defining moments, but was also important in world political history because of the extensive use of Internet communications in election campaigning. Informed citizens were mobilized,

and especially participatory were the young voters who dubbed the 'N Generation' (Seo, 2003).

While the Korean society was democratized politically in the late 1980s, the society was also experiencing rapid economic growth. The gross domestic product (GDP) reached US$1089 billion in 1986 for the first time. Rising like a phoenix from the ashes of the Korean War in early 1950s, South Korea, once one of the world's biggest borrowers, became a creditor nation in 1986. In three subsequent years, Korea enjoyed a double-digit economic growth of 12% or more (Reuters, 1988). This growing wealth brought about a significant upsurge in South Korea's domestic demand and the changing Korean society was entering a level of growth that was strongly supported by domestic demand (Watanabe, 1989). At the same time, the national income per capita rose to the point where Koreans were considered by a global standard to have achieved an affluent society. Considering the fact that a nation's GDP is one of the strongest indicators for predicting tourism demand, it should be no surprise to observe that the growth of outbound travel by Koreans mirrored the growing trend of the nation's GDP (see Fig. 8.1).

While the strong economic growth facilitated increasing demand for travel and changes in travel patterns, it was still impossible for most Koreans, especially young Koreans, to take a trip to foreign countries until the late 1980s. This was due to tight restrictions on overseas travel. The Korean government imposed restrictions on overseas travel for economic and ideological reasons. During the years of foreign exchange shortages in the nation, the government discouraged unnecessary (referring mostly to leisure purposes) overseas travel by implementing harsh passport laws and restrictions on travel abroad. Until August 1981, no one was able to go abroad for leisure travel purposes. The passport was only issued for business purposes or to study abroad. Between 1981 and 1987, only South Koreans over the age of 50 could go abroad as tourists. To these older travellers, the government issued one-time-use passports that were valid for just 1 year. The overseas travel restrictions also served to secure authoritarian

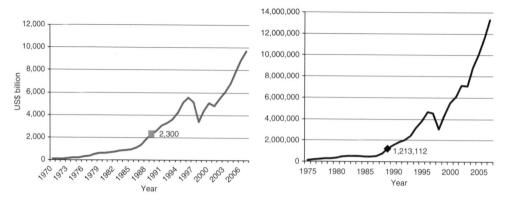

Fig. 8.1. Growth trends of GDP and outbound travel in Korea: 1970–2007.

governance by keeping most Koreans away from contact with the outside world. For example, South Koreans who may have wished to visit communist countries were required to get prior approval from the Foreign Minster.

The rapidly growing economy and the achievement of political democracy brought changes to the travel and tourism environments in Korea. In 1988, the government gradually reduced foreign-travel age restrictions

to 30, and lifted the age ban completely in early 1989 (Reuters, 1989). As South Koreans earned freedom to travel abroad, more than 1.2 million did so in 1989. This was a 68.3% increase from the previous year (Korea Tourism Organization, 2008). However, it was just the prelude to a surge in outbound tourism, especially by young people who had the money and time to travel. As Table 8.1 shows, outbound tourism in Korea has grown considerably every

Table 8.1. GDP and outbound travel volume in Korea: 1970–2007. (From Korea Tourism Organization; Korea National Statistical Office.)

Year	GDP(US$ billion)	Outbound travel	Year	GDP (US$ billion)	Outbound travel
1970	82	NA	1990	2,635	1,560,923
1971	95	NA	1991	3,076	1,856,018
1972	107	NA	1992	3,293	2,043,299
1973	137	NA	1993	3,614	2,419,930
1974	192	NA	1994	4,223	3,154,326
1975	212	129,378	1995	5,155	3,818,740
1976	293	164,727	1996	5,553	4,649,251
1977	377	209,698	1997	5,136	4,542,159
1978	529	259,578	1998	3,404	3,066,926
1979	629	295,546	1999	4,400	4,341,546
1980	627	338,840	2000	5,096	5,508,242
1981	697	436,025	2001	4,811	6,084,476
1982	744	499,707	2002	5,475	7,123,407
1983	828	493,461	2003	6,086	7,086,133
1984	912	493,108	2004	6,824	8,825,585
1985	942	484,155	2005	7,901	10,080,143
1986	1,089	454,974	2006	8,887	11,609,878
1987	1,382	510,538	2007	9,713	13,324,977
1988	1,864	725,176			
1989	2,300	1,213,112			

year, reaching more than 13 million in 2007. The population of South Korea is about 48 million and about one out of four Koreans travelled overseas in 2007. This figure is noteworthy in itself, but even more so when put into the context of travelling for different purposes. Since deregulation of overseas travel, overseas travel for pleasure purposes increased by 940% and 235% in 1988 and 1989, respectively. Outbound travel for pleasure exceeded travel for business purposes in 1989 and has remained a major (over 50% of outbound foreign travel) market segment.

Fundamental changes achieved in the late 1980s have improved the nation's political rights, civil freedom and economic powers, and the N Generation who grew up in these more liberal, affluent environments is the major beneficiary. It could be argued that this new generation who grew up in a fundamentally different system would, in general, reflect distinctive values and attitudes, compared to the previous generations of Koreans. In the same context, it can be suggested that the changes in the social, political and economic domains in the past decades contributed to not only the improvement of travel conditions for the N Generation but also to the travel experiences of the N Generation. These experiences will determine their travel attitudes and preferences as well as their interaction with the travel and tourism industry.

Internet and Globalization

While the dramatic changes in Korean society during the late 1980s are a unique experience for the N Generation, Internet access and globalization are common conditions experienced by its global counterpart, the Y Generation. As discussed earlier, there could be many factors that surround the emergence and formation of a new generation. Among them, however, the Internet and globalization are regarded as the most important factors behind the emergence and unity of the N Generation in Korea (Seo, 2000; Lee, 2004). Having grown up in a time of globalization and benefiting from the use of high technology, especially the Internet, the N Generation is characterized as a technologic-

ally advanced group that easily adopts and adapts to the new technology.

Korea is one of only a few countries that has quickly accommodated information technologies (ITs) and it has provided one of the best IT environments in the world. According to the Korea Statistical Information Service (2008), more than half (53.8%) of all households in Korea had personal computers in 2001. In 2007, eight out of ten Korean households had personal computers, and about 83% of those households had broadband and high-speed access to the Internet (Ministry of Information and Communication, 2008). With respect to Internet usage, 76.3% of the population had used the Internet at least once a month, and it is estimated that 34.8 million Koreans had used the Internet at some time in 2007. Nearly three-quarters (72.5%) of the total population used the Internet in 2007, compared to less than a half (44.7%) of the population that used the Internet in 2001 (Ministry of Information and Communication, 2008). In a 2006 global survey of computer access and Internet use by households, Korea ranked sixth for personal computer access and first for Internet usage out of 32 OECD countries (OECD, 2008). Mobile telephone service is another technological dimension of the N Generation in Korea. The number of people who subscribed to mobile service increased explosively from just 20,353 in 1988 to 40,197,115 in 2006 (Korea Statistical Information Service, 2008). These data point to a high rate of diffusion for Internet service and digital technology and it is only natural to expect that its differential impact on unique generations will be significant.

The data presented in Table 8.2 describe the age-cohort level of computer and Internet usage, the purposes of Internet usage and the comparative use of mobile telephone service by different age groups. The N Generation is represented by those in their 10s and 20s and is clearly more digitally connected (almost 100% Internet usage) than the generation represented by individuals in the 50s and 60s age ranges (18–47% Internet usage). Furthermore, the N Generation uniquely regards Internet as its main leisure activity and uses the Internet to collect information more than by any other conventional communication medium such as

Table 8.2. Computer and Internet usage by age group. (From *2007 Media and Consumer Research in Korea*, Korea Broadcast Advertising Corporation; *2008 Survey on the Computer and Internet Usage*, Ministry of Information and Communication.)

		10s	20s	30s	40s	50s
Main leisure activity		PC game/Internet	PC game/Internet	Watching television	Watching television	Watching television
Media consumption (first/second)		Internet/television	Internet/television	Television/Internet	Television/Internet	Television/newspaper
Internet users (%)		99.8	99.3	96.5	79.2	46.5
Portal service usage other than information search or service		Game, blog, online community, UCC	Shopping, blog, online community, UCC	Game, shopping, blog, online community	E-mail and game	E-mail and game
Purpose of internet use (%, multiple responses)	Getting information	81.0	98.4	95.9	93.3	90.3
	Communication	95.8	97.2	91.4	80.2	76.3
	Leisure (online game, etc.)	98.3	97.8	90.2	73.9	60.8
	Shopping	44.4	82.5	69.0	39.2	25.2
	Homepage	59.4	70.4	40.2	19.6	14.3
	Community	45.1	61.1	41.1	23.3	15.9
Internet shopping	No. of purchases per month	1.9	2.3	1.7	1.3	1.5
	Average costs	US$21.3	US$42.6	US$52.3	US$40.5	US$39.4
Mobile phone use		Calling, receiving, voice mailing, sending message and wireless Internet	Calling, receiving, voice mailing, voice mailing and sending	Calling, receiving and voice mailing message	Calling and receiving	Calling and receiving

television or newspaper. More importantly, the N Generation uses the Internet not only for searching for information, but for social interaction through Internet blogs, cyber communities and personal homepages. Brought up in an age of interactive communications in cyber space, the N Generation naturally creates information through interaction (Heung, 1999). To the N Generation, cyber space is regarded as its main social space and it is an indispensable element of a full social life. Being 'connected' and 'networked' by an electronically mediated communication system is, to the N Generation, as natural as face-to-face communication (Heung, 1999). Making friends in a chat room is as easy as making friends in the classroom. In many situations, the spontaneity and anonymity of online communication liberates the N Generation from the formalities that surround face-to-face communication in Korea (Heung, 1999). As in most other Asian countries, the Korean social order and tradition is based on the Confucian ideal which emphasizes the age hierarchy. Korean society is also characterized by a sense of collectivism that values group's benefits over the interests of the individual. However, these traditional norms and values can be suspended or abandoned in cyber space. In the anonymity of cyber space, there is no hierarchy based on age, and human relationships and social roles are much less stratified than those in real social life. Consequently, the N Generation tends to express its opinions more freely and actively in cyber space (Yu and Kim, 2001). The N Generation is thereby able to reject the traditional rules shaped by previous generations and build its own subcultures (Sung *et al.*, 2000). 'Word-of-mouth' communication over the Internet epitomizes the subculture of the N Generation. Once members of the N Generation have new information or an experience with new products or services, they enthusiastically exchange their information and experiences, and share their opinions with others through their blogs, cyber communities and homepages. The word of mouth quickly and indiscriminately spreads through cyber space. Furthermore, due to the culture of voluntary and active participation by the N Generation (rooted in the political democratization discussed earlier), the process

of cyber-facilitated word-of-mouth communication extends beyond cyber space and leads to the substantial actions offline. Since this new form of word-of-mouth communication and the ability to mobilize people offline is so fast and powerful, the N Generation has an enormous influence in a wide range of social issues from politics to business practices (including travel and tourism).

As noted earlier, the 2002 World Cup and the presidential election illustrated the power of the N Generation's word-of-mouth communication through the Internet and the mobile phone. Initiated on the Internet and spread out via the Internet and cellular phones, the idea of watching a soccer game together and supporting a national soccer team resulted in more than a hundred thousand people gathering at the square in front of Seoul City Hall (now called 'Seoul Plaza'). The Internet and cellular phones also played a vital role in mobilizing the mass turnout of young voters at the polls in the 2002 presidential election. In addition, the idea of candlelight vigils originally suggested by one Netizen on the Internet to honour and remember two middle-school girls killed by a US Army armoured vehicle in June 2002 was realized offline and resulted in thousands of people gathering at the centre of the city of Seoul. Since the first experience of this massive assembly of the public in 2002, the Internet is getting more attention as a means of organizing and mobilizing the public off-line. The N Generation is at the centre of this whole phenomenon.

While the Internet and digital technology provide the N Generation with the cyber space where they can be liberated from the old rules and values, globalization opens the door for the N Generation to connect to contemporary generations around the world. With globalization, there has been greater uniformity among young consumers with respect to clothing styles, music tastes and media habits (Kjeldgaard and Askegaard, 2006). Now, many young Koreans are regular patrons of global brands, which is quite a different picture from the scene where McDonalds opened its first Korean restaurant in 1988 and Coca Cola started Korean sales in 1951 (Suplico, 2008). By consuming global brands such as Nike, Gucci and Starbucks coffee, and by sharing the same intense exposure to MTV, movies, travel and the Internet, they are not only absorbed into the global economy but are engaged in the process of global acculturation (Seo, 2000; Richards, 2007). Given these conditions, the N Generation in Korea may find more similarities with the Y Generation in other parts of the world than with other generations in Korea. In this context, globalization reinforces individualism among the N Generation in Korea as it pursues more individual freedom and social autonomy.

In response to globalization trends, the Korean government adopted a globalization or 'SEGYEHWA' policy in 1994 to strategically develop a competent workforce that is able to think and work globally. The government encouraged greater competition, privatization and deregulation within the Korean economy and society in the process of SEGYEHWA (Suplico, 2008). As a result, international education and experience and the ability to speak foreign languages became a critical component of the formal education of the N Generation. In 1995, 106,458 Koreans left the country to study abroad. The numbers steadily increased to 157,877 in 2001 and 219,875 in 2006 (Ministry of Education, Science and Technology, 2007). Significantly, the proportion of younger students from elementary to high school that studied abroad increased substantially from 5% in 2001 to 13.4% in 2006 (Ministry of Education, Science and Technology, 2007). The younger members of the N Generation show more positive attitudes towards study abroad for younger ages. A recent telephone survey conducted by *JoongAng Daily* newspaper showed that half of the respondents in their 20s had positive attitudes about a study-abroad experience for younger ages (elementary to middle school) while 26.2% of those in 50s and 33.7% of those in their 40s supported a study-abroad experience for younger ages (Seo and Jeong, 2007). Clearly, the N Generation is more interested in first-hand globalized education and has greater opportunities to experience foreign cultures and seek international schooling at their early ages.

Globalization and the increased interest in foreign languages, particularly English, would contribute to reducing the language barrier among the overseas travellers, which may lead

to the changes in travel patterns. In fact, travel agency statistics indicate that the independent travel segment in Korea has grown rapidly since 2004 (Kim, 2007). It has more potential to grow as the N Generation keeps entering into the market.

Paradoxically, however, globalization in Korea does not contradict with the N Generation's emerging sense of nationalism (Shin, 2003). While many members of N Generation regard globalization as a means to achieve a competitive edge for the nation and themselves, their confidence with, and the pride in, the nation is higher than observed in previous generations. The confidence and national pride of the N Generation has been demonstrated in several events mentioned earlier and also has significant implications for the travel and tourism industry.

Travel and Tourism and N Generation

According to the Korea Tourism Organization (2008), travel participation rate is correspondingly high across all age groups (Table 8.3). National tourism survey reports that 93.5% of teenagers and 94% of individuals in their 20s had domestic trip experience in 2007, while 94.1% of 30s, 93% of 40s, 89% of 50s and 81.9% of 60s and older did. Teenagers and those in their 20s tended to have more overnight trips than day trips, whereas individuals in their 50s and 60s were more inclined to day trips. This final section will address what the existence of a new generation means to the travel and tourism field in Korea and how the N Generation's online activities relate to its travel and tourism

Table 8.3. Domestic travel by age group in 2007. (From *National Tourism Survey*, 2008. Korea Tourism Organization.)

Travel experience	10s[a]	20s	30s	40s	50s	60s+
Total trip	93.5	94.0	94.1	93.0	89.0	81.9
Overnight trip	84.3	85.2	85.0	82.7	70.7	57.7
Day trip	69.5	74.7	81.5	79.5	76.9	69.0

[a]This category represents age range 15–19, since the survey includes individuals aged 15 years or older.

experience as well as its travel information seeking behaviors.

The unique characteristics of the N Generation are shaped by the direct and indirect influences of new political and technological environments that have also affected patterns of consumption in travel and tourism. The N Generation is the first generation to live with the universal culture of the Internet and its dependence on the Internet is heavier than any other generation. For the N Generation, the Internet is a significant part of life and the pattern of Internet use heavily influences the shape of its life. The N Generation has more positive perceptions towards the importance of the Internet to its life than the other generations. According to the National Internet Development Agency of Korea (2007a), teenage Internet users (61.1%) and individuals in their 20s (72.1%) showed higher agreement with the statement that 'the Internet is important to my daily life' than did those in their 30s (61.6%), 40s (60.0%), 50s (35.7%) and 60s (24.5%). Consequently, they use the Internet for various purposes in their daily life including information searching, online purchasing and social networking. The N Generation's high dependence upon and usage of the Internet determines its unique behaviors related to travel and tourism.

The Internet is the most important information source for the N Generation. Survey results about computer and Internet usage (National Internet Development Agency, 2007a) showed that 60.1% of teenagers and 63.8% of individuals in their 20s check the Internet first

when they need to know, or are curious, about something, while 52.5% of those in their 30s, 35.5% of those in their 40s, 23.1% of those in their 50s and 13.6% of those in their 60s do so. The survey also revealed that travel and leisure-related information (61.9%) was the most commonly sought information on the Internet behind shopping/product-related information (64.7%) and living-related information (traffic, cooking, etc.) (63.3%). Overall, those in their 20s were most inclined to use the Internet for all types of information. Their travel/leisure information searching on the Internet surpassed that of all other age groups. Likewise, they use the Internet as the main information source when planning their trips. According to the Korea Tourism Organization (2008), most Korean overseas travellers seek their travel information through the Internet. Travel agencies are the next most popular information source, followed by family and friends. Without question, the N Generation shows a clear propensity to become highly dependent on the Internet as a travel information source (Table 8.4). However, travel agencies are still an important information source for older travellers.

As also observed in the global marketplace, another characteristic of the N Generation in Korea is its tendency to purchase travel and tourism products online (Weber and Roehl, 1999). Online shopping markets are growing rapidly in Korea. In 2006, they generated US$13.5 billion (Korea National Statistical Office, 2008) and accounted for 7.4% of the total retail sales of US$181.6 billion (a bigger share than was recorded in the USA (2.9%) and Japan (2.9%))

Table 8.4. Overseas-travel information source by age group. (From *National Tourism Survey*, 2008. Korea Tourism Organization.)

Information source	10s	20s	30s	40s	50s	60s
Internet	46.8	50.6	42.8	29.7	13.8	9.3
Travel agency	18.5	18.9	22.8	29.3	42.5	39.4
Family and friends	26.5	19.6	20.9	25.2	25.2	30.1
Guide book	3.7	4.4	2.0	2.8	2.0	1.1
Television/radio/newspaper/ magazine	1.1	0.5	0.8	0.9	2.8	4.3
Previous experience	0.0	0.3	0.6	0.8	0.3	0.2
Tourism authority/embassy	0.5	0.9	0.5	0.1	0.0	0.2
Airline/hotel	0.0	0.3	0.7	0.2	0.1	0.3
None	2.6	4.3	8.8	11.1	12.9	14.8

(Bank of Korea, 2007). The largest share of transactions was for clothing, footwear and sporting goods, followed by travel-related services, electric/communication goods and computer products. Notably, the online reservation and purchase of the travel products increased significantly from US$370.6 million in 2002 to US$2.42 billion in 2007, accounting for 15.3% of the total Internet sales transactions (Korea National Statistical Office, 2008). The number of Internet mall users is continually increasing as is the concept of online shopping malls. Research about the use of Internet shopping malls (National Internet Development Agency, 2007a) reveals that the N Generation's online shopping rate (54.4% of teenagers and 79.3% of those in their 20s) is substantially higher than for other generations (38.1%, 24.1% and 11.1% of those in 40s, 50s and 60s, respectively). Considering the fact that most of the N Generation is not yet of the age when it has full economic capability, and that travel products are relatively high priced, it is reasonable to expect that travel purchases via online shopping malls is expected to significantly increase as the N Generation enters and becomes the mainstream workforce of the near future.

This Internet-savvy generation created a totally new way of communicating its travel experiences and disseminating travel information. Blogs, travel communities including clubs or cafes in the portal sites and the homepages ('minihompi') on the Internet have played a major role in conveying the N-generation's travel experiences to others. A number of Internet communities associated with travel and tourism opened in the three major portal sites in Korea. In October 2008, a total of 101,716 travel/tourism-related clubs or cafes were identified. As Table 8.5 indicates, many travel and tourism-related activities are taking place in cyber communities. One of the largest online communities has more than 730,000 members, which means that the opinions of one member may reach out to nearly three-quarters of a million potential customers. In fact, one out of two Internet users in Korea is a member of an Internet community (National Internet Development Agency, 2007a).

The N Generation participates in online social-networking activities more actively than any other generation. Significantly, 41.3% of teenagers and 76.4% of those in their 20s are members of online cafes/communities. Older Koreans are also members, but the percentage of each cohort decreases as the defining age increases (58.3%, 41.3%, 27.9% and 13.5% of those in 30s, 40s, 50s and 60s, respectively). According to the National Internet Development Agency (2007b), 40% of the Internet users in Korea have their own blog or 'minihompy' and the greatest number of bloggers is classified as members of the N Generation (Table 8.6). Bloggers produce and share information or knowledge more actively than non-bloggers. Two out of three bloggers (67.9%) are members of online social-networking sites such as online cafes or communities, whereas only 21.3% of the non-bloggers are online community members. One-third of the bloggers upload their UCC at least once a month. These figures emphasize the importance of Internet communities as the major spaces for the N Generation to exchange travel information and share travel experiences.

Table 8.5. Number of travel-related online communities in Korea.

Internet portal sites	Keyword	Number of communities	Number of members
NAVER	Travel	20,636	301,773
	Tourism	2,150	45,654
DAUM	Travel	40,433	733,591
	Tourism	6,246	27,294
CYWORLD	Travel	27,390	646,557
	Tourism	4,861	12,783
Total	Travel and Tourism	101,716	1,767,652

Note: As of October 2008

Table 8.6. Internet users and bloggers by age group. (From *Survey on the Blog Use,* 2007. National Internet Development Agency.)

	10s	20s	30s	40s	50s	60s	All
Internet users	99.7	98.9	94.6	77.8	45.6	17.4	75.5
Bloggers		59.3	67.5	36.5	14.1	6.3	1.4	30.2
Bloggers among Internet users		59.5	68.2	38.6	18.1	13.7	8.1	40.0

As Internet communities allow more people to participate in the production and distribution of information, there is a recognizable shift in the role of a particular class of consumers who are referred to as 'prosumers'. The word 'prosumer' has a dual meaning. One origin of the word is a combination of 'producer' and 'consumer', referring to an active consumer involved in the production process (Quinion, 2008). The other is a blend of 'professional' and 'consumer' which refers to the enthusiastic consumers who pursue their skills and knowledge with certain products, especially technology-related products such as digital cameras, at a level likened to professionals (Quinion, 2008). While traditional consumers passively buy goods or services, prosumers actively express their opinions and preferences to the manufacturers or service producers so that their preferences can be reflected on the products (Sung *et al.*, 2000; Lee, 2004).

Prosumer activity is not limited to the production process but extends to the production and distribution of information about the product. Most Koreans tend to believe that consumer reviews are more reliable and persuasive than advertisements, which are intended to induce purchasing, since consumer reviews deliver personal opinions and feelings based on the experiences with the products without exaggeration. People tend to seriously consider other consumers' opinions and comments when making a purchasing decision. The results of a consumer survey showed that 45% of the online shoppers were influenced by other consumers' evaluations and reviews when making the final purchase decision (National Internet Development Agency, 2007a). Teenagers (41.2%) and those in their 20s (50.4%) were more likely to be influenced by consumer/prosumer product reviews, compared to those in their 40s (36.4%), 50s (28.6%) and 60s (30.3%). Correspondingly, those in their teens (17.4%) and those in their 20s (25.8%) were more active in writing comments/reviews on purchased products and services than those in their 30s (20.6%), 40s (15.2%), 50s (12.2%) and 60s (5.0%). Seong *et al.* (2001) argue that the influence of word of mouth is more powerful in the online shopping realm, and is more powerful in decisions about purchasing intangible products.

Considering the intangible nature of travel services, the multilateral nature of Internet communications and the tendency of the N Generation to heavily use the online shopping mall, the influence of word of mouth on purchase decisions about the travel products will be even more important in the very near future.

Furthermore, the N Generation produces information on the Internet more actively than other generations. The majority of those in their 20s have 'posted comments on news articles or posting by others' (90.3%) or 'posted to the Internet forums, social networking sites such as clubs, communities and blog/minihompy' (86.4%) (National Internet Development Agency, 2007b). In order to identify the volume of information created on the Internet, a search was conducted in 2008 of NAVER, the largest portal site in Korea. The results indicate that, on average, about 2000 new travel comments or contents are posted daily.

It should be noted that the N Generation's online-community activities related to travel and tourism straddle the boundary between the consumer and the mediator. Some travel and tourism businesses quickly respond to this trend and try to capitalize on the power of these online communities and word-of-mouth communication on the Internet. Some online travel communities get sponsorships from travel and tourism businesses including travel, hotel and restaurant discount coupons, sponsorships for the paid banners and useful travel and hospitality information. Some resorts or travel companies even offer free travel to the main members of the communities such as a chairperson and his/her associates. For example, one of the NAVER cafés named 'TAESARANG' (meaning 'love Thailand') provides travel discount coupons and paid banners for a variety of travel and booking agencies, as well as a host of travel information for backpackers who want to travel to Thailand. It was opened in 1999 and more than 9000 people visit the site everyday.

Another example can be found in the other Internet portal DAUM café called 'I love you Hokkaido'. This online cafe generally provides information about ski resorts in Japan including those in the Hokkaido area. It also provides discount prices for various ski resorts in Japan. Since 2007, the café has conducted ski resort familiarization tours which are sponsored by the Furano Tourism Association and the Transportation Department in Japan. Members of the café are eligible to be selected for the tours and six members were selected in 2008. The familiarization tour programme covers most expenses for the selected members, including round-trip airfare, hotel rooms and breakfast, welcome dinner and transportation from the airport to the resorts or ski hills. Some blogs, cafes and communities are rewarded for their influential evaluations in the areas of travel, lodging and food services. They usually receive some valuable offers including free meals or other benefits from related businesses. These anecdotal cases illustrate the recognition given by the travel and tourism industry to the influential power of online travel and tourism communities or cafes.

The situation where nearly every household has Internet access with the fastest connections was one referred to as a 'Broadband Wonderland' (Lewis, 2004). The existence of that situation in Korea, as well as the N Generation's superior ability to find information and identify product options on the Internet, allows the N Generation to assert greater influence on family travel decision making (Belch *et al.*, 2003). Its influence on family decisions related to travel purchase is further enhanced by the information and knowledge that is gained from active online communities where, in Korea, most of the travel information is shared and exchanged.

The N Generation's Internet use is not bound by wires. As the N Generation easily adopts new technology, it is leading in wireless Internet use. Its wireless-Internet use rate is doubled compared to that of other generations (National Internet Development Agency, 2007c). The N Generation's high usage of wireless Internet will stimulate the development of a variety of services. Regarding travel-related services, it is expected to encourage ubiquitous services such as real-time road reports, traffic monitoring, travel information searches, reservation services and audio–video interpretation.

Conclusion

Different generations in society experience unique historical transitions. The N Generation in Korea has grown up in a dynamically changing society. Since the late 1980s, Korea has undergone dramatic evolutions in democratization, deregulation, economic wealth, globalization and technology. Accordingly, the N Generation reflects distinctive views and attitudes that were developed through the transitions. These unique views and attitudes make it distinct from previous generations in Korea.

Because the N Generation has more pronounced differences than previous generations, its impacts on travel and tourism are expected to be much greater. The N Generation has unique travel consumption patterns and practices. First, the Internet is its main source of travel information. It relies less on the conventional information channels and has developed a dependency on the Internet as a way of exchanging and disseminating information. That dependency is increasing. Second, the online shopping mall and business transactions on the Internet will continue to grow as the N Generation enters the workforce and the travel market in the coming years. Third, the direct transaction between the consumer and the producer will increase as the N Generation expands its prosumer role. This will be accomplished largely through its activity in producing and distributing travel and tourism information in online communities or cafes. Fourth, the N Generation's high demand for, and early adoption of, new technologies based on the wireless Internet will require the travel and tourism industry to provide ubiquitous services that make travel and tourism products available at any time and any location.

It is undeniable that the 21st century in Korea opened with the emergence of the N Generation. The N Generation in Korea will strongly influence the social, economic and cultural development of the country until circumstances change significantly and a new generation emerges to reflect those changes. Human history has continuously witnessed the fall of an old generation and the rise of a new generation. As the Baby Boomers and Generation X were defined by their times, the distinctiveness of the N Generation in Korea is the outcome of the ongoing interactions between this new generational cohort and the unique local and global environments. Just as the other generations reflected their times, the N Generation will reflect and change the face of Korea as it enters the mainstream of society.

References

Bank of Korea (2007) *Effects of Structural Changes in Wholesales and Retail Businesses on the Economy of Korea*. Seoul, Korea.
Belch, M.M., Krentler, K. and Willis-Flurry, L. (2003) Teen Internet mavens: influence in family decision making. *Journal of Business Research* 58(5), 569–575.
Cho, H.-Y. (2000) Democratic transition and changes in Korean NGOs. *Korea Journal* 40(2), 274–304.
DongA Ilbo (2007) *DongA Sisa Dictionary*. Available at: http://www.donga.com
Heung, B. (1999) Introducing the 'N' generation. *The Korea Herald*, 20 October 1999.
Kim, M.K. (2007) FIT marketing – there is no distinction between wholesalers and backpacker-agency. *The Travel Post*, Post issue. Available at: http://www.etravelpost.co.kr/news/articleView.html?idxno=2114
Kjeldgaard, D. and Askegaard, G. (2006) The globalization of youth culture: the global youth segment as structures of common difference. *Journal of Consumer Research* 33, 231–247.
Korea Broadcast Advertising Corporation (2007) *2007 Media and Consumer Research in Korea*. Seoul, Korea.
Korea National Statistical Office (2008) Report of e-commerce. Available at: http://www.nso.go.kr
Korean Statistical Information Service (2008) Society statistical index. Available at: http://www.kosis.kr/
Korea Tourism Organization (2008) *2007 National Tourism Survey*. Seoul, Korea.
Lee, J. (2008) Path toward democracy in South Korea: Social capital and democracy embedded in the citizens. *Asian Survey* 48(4), 580–602.
Lee, S. (2004) An ethnographic analysis of the N-generation's consumer culture. *Korean Journal of Advertising* 15(3), 71–90.
Lewis, P. (2004) *Broadband Wonderland*. Fortune, New York.
Ministry of Education, Science and Technology (2007) 2007 Statistics for general study abroad. Available at: http://english.mest.go.kr/
Ministry of Information and Communication (2008) *Survey on the Computer and Internet Usage*. Seoul, Korea.
National Internet Development Agency of Korea (2007a) *Survey on the Computer and Internet Usage*. Seoul, Korea.
National Internet Development Agency of Korea (2007b) *Survey on the Blog Use*. Seoul, Korea.
National Internet Development Agency of Korea (2007c) *Survey on the Wireless Internet Use*. Seoul, Korea.
OECD (2008) OECD factbook 2008: economic, environmental and social statistics. Available at: http://masetto.sourceoecd.org/vl=3922286/cl=24/nw=1/rpsv/factbook/index.htm
Quinion, M. (2008) World wide words. Available at: http://www.worldwidewords.org/turnsofphrase/tp-pro4.htm
Reuters (1988) South Korean debt ending. *The New York Times*, 29 December 1988, Section D, p. 12.
Reuters (1989) Tourist craze hits South Korea as young earn right to travel. *The Financial Post*, 10 January 1989.
Richards, G. (2007) Introduction: global trends in cultural tourism. In: Richards, G. (ed.) *Cultural Tourism: Global and Local Perspectives*. The Haworth Hospitality Press, Binghamton, New York, pp. 1–24.
Seo, C. (2000) N-generation and marketing strategies. *AD Information* 2000(1), 125–130.
Seo, H. (2003) Generation 2030 emerges as catalyst for change in Korean politics, society. *The Korean Herald*, 1 January 2003. Seoul, Korea.
Seo, S.J. and Jeong, H.W. (2007) Study abroad at early age, how much was it dispersed? *EAI Public Opinion Briefing* 16, 7–9.
Seong, Y., Yoo, H. and Jang, I. (2001) Online word-of-mouth for consumption experiences. *Proceedings of Annual Conference on Advertising Society*. 3–12.
Shin, K.-W. (2003) The paradox of Korean globalization. The working paper, Shorenstein. APARC. Stanford University, Stanford, California. Available at: http://fsi.stanford.edu/publications/paradox_of_korean_globalization_the/
Sung, Y.-S., Jang, S.-W. and Kang, J.-S. (2000) Digital networking: psychology of N-generation communications. *Korean Journal of Consumer and Advertising Psychology* 1(2), 1–24.
Suplico, L. (2008) Just how global are South Koreans? *The Korean Herald*, 30 April 2008, Seoul, Korea.
Tapscott, D. (1998) *Growing Up Digital: The Rise of the Net Generation*. McGraw-Hill, New York.
Watanabe, T. (1989) South Korea is entering growth supported by domestic demand. *The Japan Economic Journal*, 13 May 1989, p. 8.
Weber, K. and Roehl, W.S. (1999) Profiling people searching for and purchasing travel products on the world wide web. *Journal of Travel Research* 37(3), 291–298.
Yu, S. and Gim, C. (2001) The study on attribute of net generation's target advertising. *Korean Journal of Consumer and Advertising Psychology*, 2(1), 19–42.

9 Beach Safety and Millennium Youth: Travellers and Sentinels

Jeff Wilks[1] and Donna Pendergast[2]
[1]Tourism Safety; [2]Griffith University, Gold Coast, Australia

Introduction

Sun, sand and surf remain a major attraction for young travellers worldwide. Indeed, beaches are a key competitive feature for many tourist destinations wishing to capture the youth market. Ironically, young people between the ages of 18 and 34 years, which includes the oldest of the Y-Generation cohort, and especially males and international tourists generally, are specifically identified as 'at risk' groups for drowning. This chapter examines the characteristics of Millennium Youth or Gen-Y travellers in relation to beach safety, including issues of language barriers, unfamiliar environments, unfamiliar activities and holiday behaviour, such as alcohol use, that place them at risk. In this chapter, members of Generation Y are identified as those born between 1982 and 2002.

The chapter also describes the best-practice risk-management initiatives in place to safeguard young travellers at the beach. The focus here is on the next generation of surf lifesavers, themselves Millennium Youth, who are highly trained and voluntarily give their time during the summer months to patrol Australian beaches. According to Martin and Tulgan (2001), these young people are part of a generation leading a new wave of volunteerism. However, there are unique challenges in retaining these sentinel volunteers. The chap-

ter describes the role of sporting events and emergency-service training that shape the role of patrolling lifesavers and contribute to the generation's concern for personal and public safety.

Beaches and Tourism

Beaches are a major attraction for many tourism destinations. In their 2007 Country Brand Index, for example, the marketing group FutureBrand (2007) rated the Maldives as the leading beach destination among 54 countries. The top 10, in order, were: Maldives, Tahiti, Bahamas, Australia, Dominican Republic, Jamaica, Aruba, Bermuda, Mexico and Fiji. The criteria for selection were 'pristine beaches, from the remote to the mainstream' and the rating process involved customer surveys as well as expert opinion from travel journalists and industry members. Interest in the physical characteristics of beaches is also evident in the popularity of websites like Coastalwatch.com, which provides real-time monitoring of beaches around Australia using fixed cameras. Winner of the Hitwise National Performance Award for most popular water-sports website in Australia during 2007, Coastalwatch.com, receives approximately 500,000 'hits' or visits each month from people wanting to check on conditions at the beach. Anecdotal evidence indicates that many of the people visiting the coastalwatch website are Gen X and Y surfers assessing conditions for 'a surf' before or after work.

As noted by De Nardi and Wilks (2008a), in addition to their physical characteristics, beaches are social centres that attract people for a number of recreational activities. These can be divided into water- and land-based activities. Land-based activities range from active recreational pursuits such as fishing, ball sports – for example, beach volleyball which is now an Olympic sport – walking, jogging, exploring, metal detecting and fossicking; to passive leisure activities such as sunbathing, sightseeing and socializing. Water-based sports include swimming, surfing, windsurfing, kitesurfing, jet and waterskiing, snorkelling, skin diving, scuba diving, kayaking and boating. The beach is therefore a meeting point for both tourists and local residents, covering a number of different interests. The beach clearly appeals to Gen Y's lifestyle interests and caters to the stimulus junkies among them (Sheahan, 2005).

Recognizing the importance of beaches to the youth market, Australia's five-time World Champion professional surfer, Layne Beachley, was appointed an Australian Tourism Ambassador in 2003 to boost the country's profile as an exciting surf and sun holiday destination for young travellers (Tourism Australia, 2003). Announcing the appointment at the time, the Minister for Small Business and Tourism, the Hon Joe Hockey MP observed:

> Our surf, sun and beaches are famous around the world and play a key role in attracting international travellers. Layne will help to promote our surf and beach culture to an important and emerging tourism market – the youth traveller, including backpackers.

He also noted:

> Surfers travel the world in search of a perfect break – we want this search to end in Australia. Many young travellers who come to Australia take up the opportunity to experience our beaches, from surfing to scuba diving and we are looking to further highlight these experiences in Australia.

Among the key facts supporting this initiative were:

- 29% of international visitors to Australia indicated that Australia's coastline and beaches was the key factor influencing their decision to holiday in Australia.
- Of all travellers to Australia, 20–24 year olds account for 9%, and 25–29 year olds account for 12%.

Beach Settings and Beach Culture for Gen Y

Millennium or Gen-Y youth have embraced beach culture. This is obvious in a number of ways, most notably in the multimillion dollar industry that has developed around surf clothing. Catering to the Gen-Y subgroup of surfer–skateboarder, companies like City Beach in Australia and Pacific Sunwear (Pacsun) in the USA have created mall-based stores that look somewhat like beach shacks, with employees encouraged to wear beach attire. City Beach announces on its website that 'City Beach is more than just somewhere to score the latest clothes; it's a great place to hang out and meet up with your friends'.

Gen Y's interest in the beach is also reflected in the popular media, with a range of surfing movies released in recent years: *Blue Crush* (2002), *Billabong Odyssey* (2003), *Step into Liquid* (2003) and the hugely popular computer-animated mockumentary *Surf's Up* (2007). *The Beach*, starring Leonardo de Caprio in 2000, was another popular movie about young backpackers who were trying to create their own tropical utopia under the cover of an off-limits marine park, where armed drug dealers were growing cannabis (Higgins-Desbiolles, 2008). While the original novel by young British author Alex Garland was written as an anti-travel book, the movie has developed something of a cult following and increased the tourism profile of Thailand among young travellers.

For tech-savvy Gen-Y tourists, the Internet is an excellent source of information and advice for selecting the right beach, whether for romance (Travelchannel.com) or fun and activity (Yahoo! Travel). The number and diversity of beach photos and videos posted on websites such Travelchannel.com is further testimony to the interest Gen Y has in the beach.

Gen Y at Risk

While Gen-Y youth are socially very much at ease with beach clothing and enjoy leisure time at the beach, they are also consistently identified as an 'at risk' group for drowning, especially in the surf. According to the Australian Water Safety Council (2008) young males (18–34 years) are a particular target group for drowning prevention, based on factors such as alcohol use, peer pressure and risk-taking activities. The Council reports that of the 172 drowning deaths in men aged 18–34 years in the 3-year period for 2005–2007, alcohol or drugs were detected in 35% of cases, and with improvements in data collection the true picture of alcohol use is likely to be much higher.

Tourists as a general group have also been identified as being 'at risk' for injuries at the beach due to the unfamiliarity of the environment, participation in unfamiliar activities (such as body surfing), possible language barriers and a general lack of attention to detail that is part of being on holiday (Wilks et al., 2005; Wilks, 2008). While the international lifesaving practice of placing flags on patrolled beaches to mark the safest place to swim under direct supervision is well established, a recent study on drowning and rescues by Wilks et al. (2007) revealed that tourists continue to disregard safety messages and swim outside the flagged areas, believing erroneously that swimming in some close proximity to the flags will provide the same benefits if assistance is required.

In relation to young tourists' understanding of the need to swim between the flags, a study of 176 university students (30% overseas students) by Ballantyne et al. (2005) found that a majority of the Australian students (90%) stated they would swim between the flags or where the lifesavers were located when visiting the beach, compared with only 51% of the international students. Most of the Australian students surveyed (79%) stated they knew what a rip was, while the majority of the international students (77%) did not. Given that a

large number of all rescues conducted by Surf Life Saving Australia (SLSA) occur in rips (a rip being a relatively narrow, seaward moving stream of water), this is critical surf-safety information (Surf Life Saving Australia, 2005). Further confirmation of their inability to recognize a rip emerged when students were asked to indicate where they would swim in a photograph of an Australian beach that pictured two rips. Overall, 61% of the students selected the rips as where they would be most likely to swim.

International students are probably a good barometer of Gen-Y travellers when it comes to beach safety, so the Ballantyne et al. findings raise some serious issues about the level of information available on beach safety and the extent to which it is received, understood and acted upon by Gen-Y travellers. Evidence from coronial inquests suggests that overseas students are not routinely given beach-safety information as part of their orientation to living in Australia (Cocks, 2005; Wilks, 2005) and that static signage at the beach site is 'too little, too late' for most tourists who are very excited about being on holiday and are unlikely to stop and read safety information (Taylor, 2004; Wilks, 2006). This is further compounded if tourists do not speak English or the language in which signs and instructions are presented (De Nardi and Wilks, 2007; Wilks, 2007).

Concerns about young people and water safety are not unique to Australia. In a new report by EuroSafe (2008) the tourism and water-related fact sheet includes the following points:

- Drowning is the second leading cause of injury death to children in Europe.
- Nearly 70% of Europeans spend their holidays by the waterside, mostly visiting other European countries, and 25% of these tourists are travelling with children under 18 years of age.
- It is estimated that each year 50,000 Europeans in the EU 27 are injured while taking part in water sports or boating activities.

While drowning is the most significant safety concern at the beach, De Nardi and Wilks (2008b) identify a range of other hazards that can result in injury, including: marine animals (bites and stings – jellyfish); litter (cuts – broken glass); wave action (broken bones – collarbone from wave dumping); equipment (head injury – hit by surfboard); cliffs (fall – trip on cliff edge); water pollution (infection – gastroenteritis because of faecal contamination); underwater object (spinal cord injury – diving into sandbar); criminal activity (assault – robbery); and sun (sunstroke – sun exposure). SLSA records show that lifesavers and lifeguards are often called to assist with many of these safety issues on the beach. Table 9.1 presents a snapshot of lifesaving actions during the 2006–2007 season.

In one of the few available studies of crime on Australian beaches, Staines *et al.* (2005) found that a total of 1584 reported offences occurred at Victorian beaches or foreshores over a 2-year study period (July 2000 to June 2002). Staines *et al.* note that the majority of crimes were committed against property (67.7%), though there were also a substantial number of crimes committed against people (20.7%), mostly sexually related offences. Of particular relevance to this chapter is the finding that crime against people at beaches appeared to be primarily a problem for adolescents and young adults aged 15–29 years (61.2%). The offences against children in the 0–14-year age group were primarily rape (four females) and non-rape sex, which includes offences such as indecent exposure, indecent assault and carnal knowledge (7 males, 14 females); while for 15–29-year-old victims, assault (36 males, 22 females), rape (15 females) and non-rape sex (1 male, 30 females) predominated.

Many coastal destinations promote the idea that tourists can get away from the crowds and spend time on deserted beaches, being close to nature and experiencing a sense of freedom. This notion appeals to Gen-Y travellers, especially those from Europe where overcrowding and pollution are common on many popular beaches during the summer months. While nude bathing is not permitted at public access beaches in Australia, the idea of sunbathing and swimming in the nude on a deserted beach is also very appealing to many young travellers. Indeed, artificial lagoons have been build on the foreshore in Cairns and Airlie Beach (Whitsundays) to accommodate mainly young overseas backpackers when adverse weather prevents trips out to the Great Barrier Reef. Topless sunbathing is permitted at these lagoons, though full-nude bathing is prohibited. Ironically, Queensland has one of the highest incidences of skin cancer in the world due to intense UV radiation, and lifesavers are frequently called to treat cases of sunburn and heat exhaustion at the beach. Adolescent girls may be at particular risk due to their higher propensity for visiting the beach to tan their skin relative to other groups (Pratt and Borland, 1994).

Risk-management Initiatives in Place for Gen Y

Risk-management initiatives to assist young travellers take several forms. Acknowledging the importance of the Internet to Gen Y, government programmes tend to favour information on websites. For example, Tourism Australia produces brochures and a handbook online through the National Visitor Safety Program (2008). To date there has been no empirical evaluation of the effectiveness of these resources, though the beach-safety information provided, largely sourced from SLSA, is evidence-based and sound. Box 9.1 provides a summary of these points.

Of particular note in Box 9.1 is the advice for travellers to check with a lifesaver if they are unsure of the beach surf conditions. Having volunteer lifesavers and salaried lifeguards on the beach is a proven injury-prevention strategy since it provides an on-site safety net (Wilks *et al.*, 2005). According to a review

Table 9.1. SLSA lifesaving actions during the 2006–2007 season.[a]

Lives saved (rescues)	9,318
Resuscitations	94
Fractures	167
Stings	22,786
Suspected spinal injuries	158
Major wounds	313
Minor cuts/abrasions	5,279
Preventative actions	203,337

[a] Includes both lifesavers and lifeguards.

Box 9.1. National visitor safety tips – beaches.

Surf lifesavers

Surf lifesavers wear distinctive red and yellow caps, and patrol the areas between red and yellow flags on the beach. If you get into trouble in the water, stay calm, raise your arm in the air to signal a lifesaver for help. Surf lifesavers give their time as volunteers in the service of their communities.

Flags for safety
- At the beach always swim inbetween the red and yellow flags – not outside them. The flags mark the safest place to swim and the area where lifesavers and lifeguards patrol.
- Read and obey warning signs on beaches, beach access points and at waterways.
- If you are unsure of the beach surf conditions check with a lifesaver.

F – find the red and yellow flags and swim between them.
L – look at the safety signs.
A – ask a lifeguard or lifesaver for some good advice.
G – grab a friend to swim with you.
S – stick your hand up for help if you get into trouble in the water.

Waves, rips and water dangers
- Always swim with others.
- Children should always be accompanied in the water by an adult who can swim.
- Many surf beaches in Australia have strong currents, called rips. These are powerful currents of water that can drag you along and out to sea. If you find yourself being caught in a rip, do not panic.
- If you get into trouble in the water, stay calm, raise your arm to signal for help. Float with a current or rip – don't try and swim against it.
- Never swim at unpatrolled beaches.
- Never swim at night.
- Never swim under the influence of alcohol.
- Never dive into the water.

---

of lifeguard effectiveness conducted by the US National Centre for Injury Prevention and Control, statistics estimate that the chance of drowning on a beach protected by lifeguards trained under United States Lifeguard Association standards is less than 1 in 18 million per year (Branche and Stewart, 2001).

In Australia, the safety net in place on many beaches consists of Gen-Y lifesavers as sentinels and first responders. As the largest voluntary community-based service organization in the country, SLSA has almost 115,000 members across more than 300 clubs. Approximately 51,000 of these members are 7–18 years of age (Wilks et al., 2006).

Sentinel Gen-Y Lifesavers

Training to become a lifesaver begins at an early age, and SLSA believes this is a lifelong learning process (Pendergast and Wilks, 2007). In order to work effectively as part of a life-

saving team, each member must be physically fit, knowledgeable about water safety and beach conditions, highly skilled in the delivery of first aid and emergency care, and committed to the ideal of community service. There are so many competing interests for young people nowadays, especially in the area of sport, that surf lifesaving needs to offer a comprehensive package in order to engage and retain youth members. Perhaps the two main differences between surf lifesaving and other competing activities for young people are the voluntary commitment to weekends in the summer months, year after year; and the very serious nature of actually saving lives.

SLSA structures its educational and training activities along three broad youth bands. Young people aged 7–12 years are called 'nippers'; those 13–14 are 'cadets'; and the 15–18-year group are referred to as 'juniors'. Educational and training activities are guided by the SLSA Development and Retention Framework (National Youth Development Committee, 2005). Table 9.2 presents the

Table 9.2. SLSA Development and Retention Framework.

Guiding principles	Values
• Retention is a life-cycle concept	• Safety and support
	• Fun and friendship
• Developmental pathways provide ongoing opportunities and challenges	• Teamwork and trust
	• Caring and camaraderie
	• Learning and leadership
• Diversity is a strength and a reality	• Excitement and enjoyment
	• Respect and responsibility
• Outcomes can be delivered through a range of programmes	• Challenge and achievement

Age groups	Outcomes	Programme options
5–10 years	Enjoyment and fun	SLSA age managers programme
	Learning	Surf education
	Skill development	Restricted competition
	Group interaction and participation	Restricted competition rules
		Lifesaving passbook
11–14 years	Enjoyment and fun	SLSA age managers programme
	Personal development	Surf education
	Increased self-confidence	Restricted competition
	Improving skills	Lifesaving passbook
	Demonstration of skills	TROYS (targeted retention of youth scheme)
	Awareness of responsibilities	Development camps
	Social interactions	TOAD (teamwork opportunity and development) camp
		YIPS (youth involvement program scheme)
		CAPS (challenge achievement pathways in sport)
15–17 years	Enjoyment and fun	TROYS and CAPS
	Peer interactions and teamwork	Lifesaving passbook
	Improving performance	Duke of Edinburgh
	Improving personal development	Youth committees/panel
	Leadership skills	Youth leadership camps
	Health and lifestyle awareness	Personal development
	Organizational awareness	Awards – training/assessment
	Life skills	Future leaders programme

guiding principles and values underpinning the programmes, and shows how skills and knowledge are built incrementally. At the top of the list for each age cohort is the importance of enjoyment and fun, recognizing that this is a key issue for engaging and retaining youth in voluntary activities.

At each age level, training to be a surf lifesaver involves personal development, skills and teamwork. The skills required to successfully conduct a real-life rescue on the beach are honed over time through surf sports competitions, carnivals and championships, which challenge young lifesavers both physically and mentally. Among the competition activities are surf swimming, board riding, board paddling, rescue and resuscitation, iron person and first-aid events.

The goal of early training is to earn a Bronze Medallion, which is the core operational award of SLSA. It is available to all teenagers over the age of 15 and is the minimum requirement to actively patrol Australia's beaches (Surf Life Saving Australia, 2003). In addition to a highly physical component, it includes valuable and transferable skills such as first aid and cardiopulmonary resuscitation (CPR), rescue techniques, radio communications and teamwork. The Bronze Medallion is recognized by the International Life Saving

Federation (ILS) and is one of a number of SLSA awards that meet the Australian Public Safety Industry's Units of Competency and Qualifications (Public Safety Industry Training Advisory Body, 2003). The public safety industry is comprised of the police, fire brigade, state and territory emergency services, emergency management sectors and SLSA.

Table 9.3 outlines the units of competency required for the Certificate II in Public Safety (Aquatic Rescue) and their mapping to the Bronze Medallion, highlighting the emphasis placed on the provision of emergency care (De Nardi *et al.*, 2005).

What this means in practical terms is that holders of the SLSA Bronze Medallion are nationally recognized as having the same core skills and high standards of public safety management as adult members of other services such as the fire department and state emergency services. Coupled with additional skills and certificates in the use of defibrillators and spinal management, licences to drive rescue craft and all-terrain vehicles and a radio operator's licence, these Gen-Y teenagers have transferable skills and knowledge that makes them very attractive to employers (Wilks *et al.*,

2006). Perhaps equally attractive is that these qualifications represent years of responsibility and commitment as a club member undertaking patrols and actively participating in community-based activities. At the 15–18-year cohort level, SLSA focuses particularly on leadership, teamwork and personal development to complement the high level of skills and knowledge already in place.

The Next Generation of Surf Lifesavers

Recognizing that retention of members is an active process, SLSA is constantly seeking new opportunities to challenge and reward its lifesavers. Table 9.5 shows that SLSA has achieved a comprehensive coverage by incorporating educational strategies recommended for each of the core traits of the millennial generation. Of special note is the involvement of parents as trained age managers, the development of member-protection policies and an organizational focus on safety for members and beach users addressing the 'special' and 'sheltered' traits in Table 9.4.

Table 9.3. SLSA Bronze Medallion and Units of Competency in the Certificate II in Public Safety (Aquatic Rescue).

Unit of competency	SLSA Manual Module
• Follow defined occupational health and safety policies and procedures (PUA OHS 001B)	Unit 1 – Safety and well-being
• Apply surf survival and self survival skills (PUA SAR 012A)	Unit 2 – Surf-awareness skills
• Provide emergency care (PUA EME 001A)	Unit 3 – Anatomy and physiology
	Unit 4 – Basic first aid
	Unit 5 – First aid
	Unit 6 – Basic resuscitation
	Unit 7 – Resuscitation (CPR)
• Communicate in the workplace (PUA COM 001B)	Unit 8 – Communication
• Operate communications systems and equipment (PUA OPE 002A)	Unit 9 – Radio communications
• Participate in an aquatic rescue operation (PUA SAR 009A)	Unit 10 – Rescue techniques
• Work in a team (PUA TEA 001A)	Unit 11 – Carries and support
• Work effectively in a public safety organization (PUA TEA 004B)	Unit 12 – Patrols
	On-the-job training

Table 9.4. Howe's (2006) seven core traits of the Millennial generation and proposed strategies for educators. (Adapted from Pendergast, 2007.)

Seven core traits of Millennials	Suggested strategies for educators	SLSA engagement
Special	• Encourage parental involvement	√
	• Seek media and public support	√
Sheltered	• Emphasize school safety and accountability	√
	• Consider class sizes – smaller is perceived as better; learning communities are favoured	√
Confident	• Stress-positive outcomes for everyone	√
	• Use contextual and project-based environments	√
	• Craft personal progress plans to guide students' learning and growth	√
Team-oriented	• Teach team skills	√
	• Build community service into the curriculum	√
	• Provide opportunities for students to help other students	√
Hold conventional hopes and dreams	• Create curricula that every student is expected to master	√
	• Celebrate progress	√
	• Continuously monitor, assess and redirect learning	√
Pressured	• Stress long-term planning	√
	• Structure learning around goal mastery	√
	• Reverse engineer curricula – start with where you want students to be at the end of the year	√
Achieving	• Build challenging curricula	√
	• Emphasize achievement over aptitude and effort	√
	• Incorporate cutting-edge computer technology into the curriculum	√
	• Encourage teachers to set themselves as an example of professional achievement and lifelong learning	√

Gen-Y Surf Lifesaving and Tourism: a Case Study

Extract from a letter describing a surf rescue, from Sam's Dad:

Sam Mandeville and his friend were surfing at the groyne at Noosa (on Queensland's Sunshine Coast); conditions were moderate to large waves. There was a large family of Indians from Brisbane swimming in the sea outside the flagged area. A rip opened up and took a father and daughter out to sea. Luckily Sam was there surfing and saw them waving frantically for help and disappearing under water. He immediately paddled over to give help. Sam had only been in Australia for 6 months and had just joined the Sunshine Beach Nippers, so he had no previous experience of the sea or rescues, which makes his effort even more special.

I am also a Patrol Captain at Sunshine Beach Surf Lifesaving Club and the previous week I had been giving a talk to all the nippers in my nipper age group, of which Sam was a member. We told them what to do if they ever saw a person in danger when they were on the beach or if they were in the sea. We made it very clear that due to their age and physical strength they should never attempt the rescue themselves as they could end up drowning. If they were surfing they should go over, give up their board to the person and swim in and get help.

Fortunately that's what Sam did. The very next weekend that situation presented itself to him. Sam saw the people in trouble and frantically waving and screaming for help and disappearing under the waves, he immediately paddled over and got off his board and ensured both the father and daughter were holding on before swimming in to get me.

Phil Hubble, an ex-Olympic silver medallist, and I swam out to them and brought them back to shore, where we began oxygen therapy on them both. Both father and daughter were being violently sick and falling in and out of consciousness, they were both in a very bad way. Both were taken to hospital and spent the next 2 days in ICU, where they made a full recovery.

I have no doubt that they both owe their lives to Sam. Without his quick thinking in firstly going over to help, then giving up his surf board and ensuring they both had grip of it before he swam in for help, they would be dead today, and Phil and I would have been bringing in two dead bodies from the sea. His act enabled us to swim out and bring them back in to shore and then keep them alive until the paramedics arrived, with the help of Scott Braby, a local Lifeguard also on duty at the time.

Sam received an International Life Saving Federation (ILS) Citation of Merit for this rescue. He was 11 years old at the time.

Conclusions

This dual-focus chapter provides a unique perspective on two groups of Y-Generation youth involved in a major activity in international tourism – spending time at the beach. As travellers, some members of Gen Y – particularly males aged 18–34 years – are identified as an 'at risk' group for drowning. Gen-Y females may also be at increased risk from crimes against people in beach settings, while the attraction of sun tanning in high UV conditions poses safety issues of sunburn, dehydration and heat exhaustion. Other beach-safety issues have been identified for tourists generally, but gaps in current data collection mean that Gen-Y members cannot be specifically identified for safety issues such as marine stings, cuts and abrasions, and fractures that occur at the beach:

safety issues that occur more frequently among tourists than among local residents (Schmierer and Jackson, 2006). International studies and anecdotal evidence suggests that alcohol and drug use contribute to drowning and rescue events involving young people, especially where patrons leave nightclubs in the early hours of the morning and go for a swim before sleeping off the effects of alcohol on the beach (see Australian Associated Press, 2008).

While roving dawn-to-dusk patrols by surf lifesavers have proven to be very effective in reducing drowning rates for tourists swimming outside regular daylight patrol hours and outside of patrol areas marked by red and yellow flags (Wilks *et al.*, 2007), the most effective safety net remains the highly visible surf lifesavers on popular tourist beaches during the day, especially during the summer months.

A large number of these volunteer lifesavers or sentinels are Gen Y, characterized by personal confidence and high self-esteem, an upbeat approach to life, education-minded and willing to commit to community service. SLSA recognizes the importance of fully engaging Gen Y and has put developmental programmes in place that emphasize fun and enjoyment, physical fitness, team activities and community engagement for young lifesavers. Wherever possible, transferable skills and career prospect enhancement is built into the core business of saving lives on the nations beaches. Concluding with a real case study, the chapter demonstrates how 'at risk' youth can be protected by their peers, for the benefit of tourism.

Acknowledgement

The authors would like to thank Monica de Nardi for her work at Surf Life Saving Australia (SLSA) on earlier projects related to tourist safety.

References

Australian Associated Press (2008) Drowned after drinking. Available at: http://www.smh.com.au/news/national/drowned-after-drinking/2008/03/23/1206206914747.html

Australian Water Safety Council (2008) *Australian Water Safety Strategy 2008–11*. Australian Water Safety Council, Sydney, Australia.

Ballantyne, R., Carr, N. and Hughes, K. (2005) Between the flags: an assessment of domestic and international university students' knowledge of beach safety in Australia. *Tourism Management* 26, 617–622.

Branche, C.M. and Stewart, S. (2001) *Lifeguard Effectiveness: A Report of the Working Group*. Centers for Disease Control and Prevention, Atlanta, Georgia.

City Beach (2008) Available at: http://www.citybeachsurf.com.au/index.php?option=com_frontpage&Itemid=1

Cocks, G. (2005) *Inquest into the Deaths of Matthew Vesper, John Speakman, Taha Bashar and Sanghun Kim. Coroner's findings*. Coroner's Court, Gosford, New South Wales, Australia.

De Nardi M. and Wilks, J. (2007) Tourist water safety: Surf Life Saving initiatives for the Japanese inbound market. *Journal of Vacation Marketing*, 13(3), 275–283.

De Nardi M. and Wilks, J. (2008a) Beach tourism and recreation. In: Lück, M. (ed.) *Encyclopaedia of Tourism and Recreation in Marine Environments*. CAB International, Wallingford, UK, pp. 58–59.

De Nardi M. and Wilks, J. (2008b) Beach safety. In: Lück, M. (ed.) *Encyclopaedia of Tourism and Recreation in Marine Environments*. CAB International, Wallingford, UK, p. 57.

De Nardi, M, Wilks, J. and Agnew, P. (2005) Developing an effective emergency management partnership: Surf Life Saving Australia and ambulance services. *Australian Journal of Emergency Management* 20(4), 8–16.

EuroSafe (2008) *Protecting Children and Youths in Water Recreation: Safety Guidelines for Service Providers*. EuroSafe, Amsterdam, the Netherlands.

FutureBrand (2007) *Country Brand Index 2007*. FutureBrand, New York.

Higgins-Desbiolles, F. (2008) The beach novel and movie. In: Lück, M. (ed.) *Encyclopaedia of Tourism and Recreation in Marine Environments*. CAB International, Wallingford, UK, p. 56.

Howe, N. (2006) A generation to define a century. Paper presented to the Association for Supervision and Curriculum Development Annual Conference, Worldwide Issues, Chicago April 1–3. Available at: http://ascd.typepad.com/annualconference/2006/04/a_generation_to.html

Martin, C. and Tulgan, C. (2001) *Managing Generation Y*. HRD Press, Massachusetts.

National Visitor Safety Program (2008) *National Visitor Safety Handbook*, Version 08.3. Tourism Australia, Canberra, Australia.

National Youth Development Committee (2005) *SLSA Development and Retention Framework*. Surf Life Saving Australia, Sydney, Australia.

Pendergast, D. (2007) The MilGen and school education. In: Bahr, N. and Pendergast, D. (eds) *The Millennial Adolescent*. Australian Council for Educational Research, Canberra, pp. 268–313.

Pendergast, D. and Wilks, J. (2007) Lifelong learning. In: Bahr, N. and Pendergast, D. (eds) *The Millennial Adolescent*. Australian Council for Educational Research, Canberra, pp. 244–263.

Pratt, K. and Borland, R. (1994) Predictors of sun protection among adolescents at the beach. *Australian Psychologist* 29(2), 135–139.

Public Safety Industry Advisory Body (2003) Public safety training package: police, state and territory emergency service and emergency management sectors. Australian National Training Authority, Melbourne.

Schmierer, C. and Jackson, M. (2006) Local health impacts of tourism. In: Wilks, J., Pendergast, D. and Leggat, P. (eds) *Tourism in Turbulent Times: Towards Safe Experiences for Visitors*. Elsevier, Oxford, pp. 63–75.

Sheahan, P. (2005) Are you ready for the Y Generation? Available at: http://www.ygeneration.com.au

Staines, C., Morgan, D. and Ozanne-Smith, J. (2005) Threats to tourist and visitor safety at beaches in Victoria, Australia. *Tourism in Marine Environments* 1, 97–104.

Surf Life Saving Australia (2003) *Surf Lifesaving Training Manual*, 32nd edn. Mosby, Sydney, Australia.

Surf Life Saving Australia (2005) Rip currents – fact sheet No. 2. Available at: http://www.slsa.com.au/site/_content/resource/00000346-docsource.pdf

Taylor, K.O. (2004) In the matter of an inquest into the cause and circumstances surrounding the death of Chiraag Shandrikiti Shah, Scott Peter Davis, Peter Jansa and Holger Lankes, Coroner's Court, Noosa, Queensland, 16 April.

Tourism Australia (2003) World Surf Champion, Layne Beachley Announced as New Tourism Ambassador, 20 June. Available at: http://www.tourism.australia.com/NewsCentre.asp?lang=EN&sub=0360&al=313

Travelchannel Best Beaches (2008) Available at: http://www.travelchannel.com/Travel_Ideas/Best_Beaches/ci.romance-list.html.beach?vgnextfmt=beach

Travelchannel Beach Videos and Images Posted (2008) Available at: http://yourtrip.travelchannel.com/SearchResult.aspx?tag=beach

Wilks, J. (2005) Surf Life Saving Australia Submission to the Gosford Coroner for the Inquest into the deaths of Matthew Vesper, Sanghun Kim, Taha Bashar and Jonathon Speakman, Magistrates' Chambers, Gosford, New South Wales, 22 August.

Wilks, J. (2006) Coroners' concerns about international visitor deaths in Australia. *International Travel Law Journal* 13, 42–52.

Wilks, J. (2007) Tourists and water safety. *International Travel Law Journal* 14, 35–43.

Wilks, J. (2008) *Happy Holidays! The Real Story About Tourist Health and Safety Abroad.* Professorial Lecture, School of Law, Northumbria University, Newcastle, UK.

Wilks, J., Dawes, P., Pendergast, D. and Williamson, B. (2005) Tourists and beach safety in Queensland, Australia. *Tourism in Marine Environments* 1(2), 121–128.

Wilks, J., De Nardi, M. and Pendergast, D. (2006) The next generation of surf lifesavers: sustaining a community resource – An Australian case study. Paper presented at the *5th International Household and Family Research Conference*, Savonlinna, Finland, 7 June.

Wilks, J., De Nardi, M. and Wodarski, R. (2007) Close is not close enough: drowning and rescues outside flagged beach patrol areas in Australia. *Tourism in Marine Environments* 3, 57–62.

Wilks, J., Pendergast, D. and De Nardi, M. (2006) Engaging millennium youth: Surf Life Saving Australia. *Australian Journal of Middle Schooling* 6(2), 3–8.

Yahoo! Travel (2008) Available at: http://travel.yahoo.com/beaches

10 Personal Travel Safety: a New Generational Perspective

Jeff Wilks[1] and Donna Pendergast[2]

[1]Tourism Safety; [2]Griffith University, Gold Coast, Australia

Introduction

The Millennial Generation, also known as Generation Y, has grown up in a social context where travel is the norm rather than the exception, and consequently they are more likely to travel than any other generation before them. They also have specific characteristics relevant to travel, including being 'aware', 'independently dependent' and 'tech-savvy', particularly with respect to information and communication technologies (ICTs). Furthermore, they are characterized as a generation that places great importance on 'safety' (New Politics Institute, 2006). These combining effects provide a unique opportunity for the tourism industry to address the needs of Gen-Y travellers at a time when the current emphasis placed on safety as a key aspect of quality service has never been more important.

Travel Safety in Context

The terrorist attacks at the New York World Trade Center on 11 September 2001 marked a turning point in global perceptions of safety in general, and in travel particularly (Wilks, 2006). Security at airports changed dramatically. The tourism industry then experienced safety and security threats from a range of dif-ferent sources across the globe, including the 2002 Bali bombings, targeting nightclubs patronized by tourists; the 2003 severe acute respiratory syndrome (SARS) outbreak that vir-tually shut down tourism in key Asian destina-tions; and the 2004 tsunami that devastated popular coastal sites in Indonesia, Sri Lanka, Thailand and India, and claimed the lives of 229,866 people, including expatriate citizens from 43 countries, many of them Gen-Y holidaymakers.

According to the World Tourism Organi-zation (WTO; Wilks, 2006) risks to the safety and security of tourists can originate from four sources:

- the human and institutional environment outside the tourism sector;
- physical or environmental risks (natural, climatic and epidemic);
- the tourism sector and related commercial sectors; and
- individual travellers (personal risks).

The significant events of 11 September, the Bali bombings, SARS and the Boxing Day tsunami fall into the first two WTO categories, where tourism is impacted by external events over which it has no direct control. Also in the exter-nal category are acts of common delinquency (theft, pickpocketing, assault, fraud) and indis-criminate and targeted violence (rape) where young travellers may become victims as much due to their age or being in the wrong place at the wrong time as the fact they are tourists.

At the time of writing this chapter, DNA analysis had just confirmed that a body recovered from a cove near Dubrovnik (Croatia) was that of missing 21-year-old Australian backpacker Britt Lapthorne (National Nine News, 2008a). She had been missing for 3 weeks after last being seen outside a Dubrovnik nightclub. Britt's social networking Facebook profile listed her interests as travelling, reading and movies. Her friends set up a special Facebook group to help the search for her. In the highly publicized search for Britt, there were accusations that authorities in Australia and Croatia were not doing enough to find the missing woman. One news outlet reported that:

> The local police response in Dubrovnik is characterised not only by operational delays but a palpable and clearly exhibited cultural disdain for the lifestyle and drinking patterns of young Australian backpackers, and particularly the young women who visit the ancient walled town.
>
> (Totaro, 2008)

While Britt's mother told the media she believed her daughter was at the wrong place at the wrong time (National Nine News, 2008b), this tragic event highlights the very real risks Gen-Y youth face as independent, free-spirited travellers in unfamiliar foreign lands.

The deaths of young travellers are very emotional and very newsworthy, as was the case of Caroline Stuttle, a 19-year-old British backpacker pushed to her death from a bridge in the Queensland regional city of Bundaberg in a robbery gone bad. Her killer was later convicted and jailed for life (BBC News, 2004). For 6 years there were media stories about Caroline Stuttle, with the tragic facts revisited throughout the court case and subsequent appeal, through to Caroline's mother visiting Bundaberg in 2008.

Tourist destinations can be significantly harmed if they are perceived to be unsafe over time. Reporting on Britt Lapthorne at least one media commentary noted:

> In 2005, Croatian police came under fire for inaction over the case of a British tourist, Peter Rushton, 30, whose naked body was found in

the sea 20 days after he was reported missing. He had been involved in a drunken argument with a group of local youths who robbed him, tied his legs and tied weights on him before throwing him into the sea.... Two men were later jailed over the murder.

> (Totaro, 2008)

On a more positive note, tourism destinations perceived to be safe have a very real competitive advantage in the international marketplace. In their 2007 Country Brand Index, the public relations and marketing company FutureBrand (2007) rated the top ten countries for safety as: New Zealand, Canada, Sweden, Denmark, Switzerland, Australia, Austria, Ireland, the Netherlands and Singapore. The criteria for this list was 'stable and secure' related largely to World Tourism Organization external factors such as crime and government stability.

Considering the WTO's third source, safety and security risks can originate within tourism operations resulting in injuries and deaths of travellers, lawsuits and damage to reputations. A relevant example is the Swiss canyoning disaster, which resulted in the deaths of 21 young adults (the deceased were aged from 19 to 31) while participating in the adventure pursuit 'canyoning', near Interlaken, Switzerland on 27 July 1999. Canyoning is an adventure sport in which participants abseil, swim and float down through canyons and gorges (Perl, 2000). A flash flood in the gorge caused the deaths. Eight members of the organizing company were charged with negligence causing the deaths (CNN.com, 2000).

Safety as an element of quality service extends directly from the activities of individual tourism businesses to the industry in general. A relevant example is the Childers backpacker hostel fire in Queensland during 2000, where 15 young people died (Barnes, 2006). Most of them were from Europe, engaged as fruit pickers during a working holiday. While the Childers fire was deliberately lit by Robert Long, who is now serving a life sentence for murder, the issue of fire safety in backpacker hostels remains an important one, as hostels are a leading type of accommodation for youth travellers (WTO, 2008). Backpacker hostels offer budget accommodation, and to keep costs low may compromise on safety standards, which in turn place young patrons at risk (Backpackers.com, 2008). A state government review of fire safety in budget accommodation following the Childers fire found that many premises did not comply with basic standards. Fire safety is one of the ten core topics covered by the Federation of Tour Operators (2007) in their Health and Safety Preferred Code of Conduct. The others include food hygiene, water safety, natural disasters and communicable diseases. These core areas are discussed in more detail below.

From the tourism industry's perspective, safety and security are high-priority topics (Visa International Asia Pacific & Pacific Asia Travel Association, 2006; Wilks *et al.*, 2006). Edgell (2008), for example, provides a list of the ten most important world tourism issues for 2009, with 'continued concern for safety and security in tourism' ranked second after 'repercussions of the global economic slowdown on tourism' and ahead of the 'impact of fuel costs on tourism'.

The question for this chapter is whether Gen-Y travellers see travel safety as important personally or do they consider themselves largely 'bullet-proof'? The following section provides an insight into Gen-Y safety issues more broadly, drawing on some common school and community experiences, and identifying the generational characteristics that may place them at risk during travel. The chapter then concentrates on the WTO fourth area of risk – that of the individual traveller or personal risk.

Gen Y and General Safety/Security

As noted in Chapter 1, introducing Gen Y, Howe (2006) has identified seven core traits that mark the cohort as unique to preceding generations. The seven core traits are: generational members consider themselves to be special; they are sheltered; confident; team-oriented; conventional; pressured and achieving.

In terms of being 'sheltered', a recent study of teenaged Millennials (13–17 years old) conducted by the New Politics Institute (2006) revealed that these young people are 'particu-

larly concerned with security issues such as crime and terrorism' and they seem to be 'strikingly shaped' by experiencing their formative years in an era that is often regarded as the Age of Terrorism. While time will tell what were the key events shaping Millennials during their formative years, particularly those born in the latter years of the generation, it is likely to include the influence of safety and security concerns, such as war, school violence, crime and terrorism, including specific terrorist events, such as the 11 September 2001 terrorist attacks in America.

Perhaps closer to home for Gen Y is the school-based violence that appears to be occurring more frequently. The Columbine High School massacre, for example, took place in 1999 at Columbine High School in the USA where two teenage students carried out a shooting rampage, killing 12 fellow students and a teacher before committing suicide. Since then there have been many school-based shootings around the world, with the media reporting graphic details in real time as they unfold.

Evidence of a shift in safety and security attitudes and behaviour more generally is apparent in a variety of areas, including the compulsory wearing of car seat belts in many countries; pool-fencing regulations to prevent childhood drowning; criminal background checks and general screening of teachers and adults working with youth; and closer supervision of children in public places, at events and in community occasions such as Halloween.

The response of parents, policy makers and the broader community has been to cocoon this generation in ways that previously were unimaginable. The simple act of walking to school alone is no longer a viable option for many (Pendergast, 2007). But even with such security measures, the unexpected remains the most frustrating to a society keen to minimize risk. Everyday activities such as shopping in the local shopping mall, walking home after dinner, and visiting a tourist site have proven to be potentially risky events. Each of these locations has been a site playing host to massacres that target no one in particular, adding to the complexity of the security dilemma. One example directly related to tourism is the Port Arthur Massacre in 1996, where a lone gunman went on a killing spree that left 35 people dead and 37 injured. Port Arthur is an historical site and a major tourism destination for visitors to Tasmania.

Events such as these have resulted in a strong safety net being thrown around the MilGen. With this sheltered background, the management and policing of the 'risk' society (Beck, 1992) is a prevailing characteristic of the generation. Carrington (2006, p. 15) concurs with this assessment, noting that:

> as individuals and citizens, we are told we are all at individual risk of harm from terrorists as well as from home-grown crime and violence.

So, while Millennials are sheltered and 'watched over', and as they have come to expect this, does any concern for safety translate across into their travel attitudes and behaviours?

Youth Travel

In their definitive review on youth travel, the WTO (2008) reports that people aged 16–29 constitute more than 20% of the estimated 160 million international tourist arrivals each year. Most importantly for this chapter, the 2007 survey of youth travellers found:

> In terms of events and problems which might prevent people from travelling, such as war or natural disasters, young people reveal themselves to be relatively fearless travellers. Only about 3% of travellers indicated that they had delayed their trip abroad because of terrorism, crime, political instability or other problems. The main reason for young travellers to avoid visiting certain destinations was crime, which is often more of a structural issue in the areas visited than is terrorism or war. Even then, perceived levels of crime were more likely to produce a feeling of anxiety rather than an actual change in travel plans.
> (WTO, 2008)

So while they do not necessarily see themselves as 'bullet-proof', Gen-Y travellers appear not to be overly concerned about external threats to their personal safety. The Internet is their most popular way of keeping in touch with home while travelling, with almost 80%

of the WTO survey respondents reporting use of the Internet or e-mail, especially for those contacting home weekly or more frequently, whereas those keeping in touch everyday are more likely to use text messages. More than half of youth travellers still write letters or postcards, but these tend to be sent fairly infrequently.

One interesting finding from the WTO survey was that not every traveller wants to be in constant contact with 'home'. About a third of young travellers who are away for 1 month or more never make contact with people at home. This may reflect a need for independence by young travellers, but it can also present some safety and security problems. At the time of the 2002 Bali bombings, for example, the Australian Department of Foreign Affairs and Trade (DFAT) pursued almost 5000 whereabouts inquiries triggered by families registering concern that their loved ones may have been in Bali at the time of the attack (Roach and Kemish, 2006).

The WTO (2008) youth travel report concluded the section on safety by describing survey respondents as:

> Intrepid Travellers: very few young travellers are deterred by problems such as terrorism, natural disasters or epidemics. For them, travel is a way of life, and a certain level of risk is a part of travel, even though this can be minimised through careful planning.

Careful planning can mean many things. Most national government websites provide excellent up-to-date travel advice for their citizens, including real-time information on health, safety and security risks. The British Foreign and Commonwealth Office (FCO) travel site, for example, recorded almost 9 million visits during 2006–2007, showing that many people do plan before they go (FCO, 2008a). The FCO also offers a new service called LOCATE, which provides online registration and submission of a travel itinerary so that embassy and crisis staff can provide better assistance in an emergency such as a tsunami or terrorist attack (FCO, 2008b).

As tech-savvy Internet users who utilize the web for trip-planning information, these government sites are readily accessible to

Gen-Y travellers. One of the consistent messages from the government travel sites is the need to purchase travel insurance. Ironically, industry reports still show that many young travellers still do not purchase travel insurance (Davies, 2005), therefore not availing them of a critically important safety net.

According to the WTO (2008) young people are travelling more often and exploring destinations further away from their own home region. They are also 'experience hungry', meaning what they want most of all from their travel is a range of different experiences, often involving the everyday life and culture of the places they visit. Contacts with local people are particularly important in this process. Activity is also important, with adventure sports often combining with off the beaten track itineraries. In terms of personal travel safety, the literature clearly shows that participation in unfamiliar activities, in unfamiliar environments, is most likely to result in accidents and injuries, especially for young people (Wilks, 2004; Wilks *et al.*, 2006).

At-risk Activities for Gen Y – Personal Safety

Reviews of the travel medicine literature show that around 75% of tourist deaths occurring during travel are the result of illness, particularly pre-existing illness (Leggat and Wilks, 2009). Injuries account for up to 25% of deaths. Young people's deaths and injuries are most frequently related to 'accidents', with the leading specific causes being motor vehicle crashes and drowning (Wilks and Davis, 2003).

In safe destinations like Australia, youth-travel deaths do not constitute large numbers, however one preventable death is one death too many. Dickson and Hurrell (2008), for example, report that there were 86 international visitor deaths by motor vehicle crash and 46 by drowning in Australia between 2003 and 2005. Of the deaths by accidental causes, the largest group was the 20–29-year-old age group which represented 31.1% of accidental deaths.

A further 6578 international visitors were admitted to hospital during this 3-year period,

more than half of them (57%) being in the Gen-Y age range of 0–29 years. Highlighting again the risks associated with motor vehicle crashes and drowning, hospital data show 20–29 year olds were involved in 47% of transport injuries, while 0–9 year olds were disproportionately represented in 19.2% of drowning and submersion events. In passing, there were 660 hospital admissions involving assaults, of which 20–29 year olds were predominately involved (59.8%).

For young people, learning to drive a motor vehicle is a significant challenge even in the familiar home environment. Driving on the opposite side of the road (and the opposite side of the car) to that which is familiar, driving long distances, fatigue, not wearing a seat belt, language and signage difficulties, and driving unfamiliar types of vehicles have all been identified as contributing to road crashes involving tourists (Wilks, 1999; Wilks *et al.*, 1999). Some road safety authorities also believe that impatience and overconfidence are hallmark traits of Gen Y that make it a significant at-risk group on the roads (Ironside, 2008).

Following motor vehicle crashes, drowning is the next most significant source of overseas visitor injury death worldwide. As reported by Dickson and Hurrell (2008) it is also a main cause of tourist hospital admissions for children aged 0–9. Cornall and his colleagues (2005) report that 68 British children (45 boys, 23 girls) drowned abroad on holidays between 1996 and 2003; 48 (71%) in swimming pools, mostly in hotels. On average, eight British children under 16 years of age drown each year abroad. In comparison, one child dies each year in municipal swimming pools in the UK, where there is adequate lifeguarding. Cornall *et al.* (2005) concluded that parents may have a false sense of security for their children in pools abroad, based on their experiences of higher levels of supervision available at home.

For teenage and young adult members of Gen Y, alcohol and peer pressure are identified as significant factors in drowning and near-drowning events. Indeed, as noted in the previous chapter, the Australian Water Safety Council (2008) has recently adopted a key life-stages approach to drowning prevention targeting young males (18–34 years) and alcohol use.

While there is no legal duty under common law for tourism operators to warn their customers about an 'obvious risk', including the risk of injury from diving into water that turns out to be shallow (see, e.g., the British case of *Evans v. Kosmar Villa Holidays* [2007] EWCA Civ 1003), the courts are coming to appreciate that what is obvious to an adult who is a local resident of the area, may not be obvious to children or tourists (see the Australian case *RTA v. Dederer* [2007] HCA 42; McMurdo, 2008; Wilks, 2008). Some tourism operators are responding to Gen Y's interest in unique and unfamiliar experiences by offering packages like 'learn to surf' with an emphasis on safety built into the programmes. These programmes are particularly popular with young Japanese visitors to the Gold Coast of Australia (De Nardi and Wilks, 2007).

What should be obvious to all travellers, and is heavily emphasized on government travel advisory sites, is that visitors to a destination should abide by local laws. The British Foreign and Commonwealth office website notes that as of 31 December 2007 there were 2419 British nationals detained overseas, just over 40% (978) for drugs-related offences (FCO, 2008c). Studies show that many young people plan to take drugs while they are travelling, some experimenting for the first time and others expanding the range of drugs they use at home (Bellis *et al.*, 2003). The British Foreign and Commonwealth Office makes it clear that there are a range of consequences for those caught using and/or trafficking drugs, including prison sentences, possibly the death penalty in some jurisdictions, a criminal record on return home and restrictions on future travel as a result of the recorded conviction.

As the media report on Britt Lapthorne (above) suggested, some destinations are becoming very negative and intolerant about young people's drinking, drug use and partying. According to a news item on 7 October 2008, the Indian resort state of Goa, for example, is getting tough on drink, drugs and loud music as the new tourist season starts to restore its tarnished reputation after the shock murder of a British teenager (Barretto, 2008).

Titled 'Goa targets drink, drugs as new tourist season starts' the news item explains:

> Scarlett Keeling's death earlier this year cast a long shadow over the party state in western India, with claims that drug abuse and drunken debauchery were taking place with the full knowledge of the police. But the local force is now looking to crack down on the practice as the first foreign visitors arrive in search of fun and winter warmth on Goa's inviting tropical beaches.
>
> 'From this season onwards, shack (beach hut) owners will be held responsible for drug consumption, sale or deals in their premises', police superintendent Bosco George said.
>
> Scarlett, 15, had been on a six-month holiday with her family when she was found dead on a beach in February. At first it was thought she had drowned. But under pressure from her mother, police opened a murder probe after a post-mortem examination revealed the teenager had taken a cocktail of drink and drugs shortly before her death.
>
> A bartender and an alleged drug dealer are currently awaiting trial, accused of plying her with booze and narcotics in one of Goa's many palm-thatched beach huts. One was said to have repeatedly raped her before leaving her for dead.
>
> George said they were now striving to keep Goa's beaches drug-free – to allay fears about the safety of visitors and dispel claims against the state home ministry that they allowed pushers to target tourists.

In a report commissioned by the US Centers for Disease Control and Prevention to understand health issues and ways of communicating health information to Generation Y, consultants Aeffect (2000) found that:

> Despite their optimism and prosperity, members of Generation Y face worries and pressures their parents may have never encountered. They are often concerned about not performing well in school, not having enough money, getting cancer or AIDS, and experiencing violence (e.g. gangs and school shootings) or peer pressure (e.g. such as to engage in alcohol, drugs, and sexual behavior). It is not just older youth who are facing these issues either. The pressures faced by kids today are happening earlier than ever before, which reveals the need for interventions at even younger ages. For example,

about one-quarter of high school students have smoked a cigarette before the age of 13, and about one-third say they tried alcohol before the age of 13. In addition, nearly half of boys and girls in high school have already had sexual intercourse, and 3 million have already been infected with a sexually transmitted disease.

Along with alcohol use, many young people report a willingness or even an intention to have sex on their holidays (Sönmez *et al.*, 2006) and unfortunately a significant proportion still do not use protection, even though they are aware of the risk of contracting sexually transmitted diseases (*Sydney Morning Herald*, 2008). It appears that this combination of genuine interest in meeting new people at a destination, frequenting bars and nightclubs, the availability of alcohol and drugs, and relative freedom away from the social constraints of family and home community poses the greatest travel risk to young people.

Gen Y's interest in authentic experiences and 'off the beaten track' destinations has driven the growth of extreme sports and adventure tourism activities like scuba diving, bungee jumping, white-water rafting, snow skiing, sea kayaking and sky diving. Destinations like New Zealand have established themselves as international centres for outdoor and adventure recreational tourism activities. However, a review by Bentley *et al.* (2001) found that 5863 overseas visitors were admitted to New Zealand public hospitals as a result of injury during the 14-year period, 1982–1996. The highest incidence of injury involved overseas visitors in the 20–30-years age range (29% of all hospital admissions), while a further 10.3% involved those 10–19 years of age. Bentley *et al.* (2001) noted that many of the visitor injuries were sustained through independent adventure activities (skiing, mountaineering) rather than through organized commercial or guided adventure tourism. They suggested:

The independent adventurer should be the major target for safety communications and other interventions to reduce injury risk amongst overseas visitors to New Zealand and other countries. Such information

should target high-risk travelers (i.e. travelers in the 18–35 age range), and should contain messages about the risks of travelling alone or without a guide, the level of experience and skill required to participate safely, and the fast-changing nature of New Zealand's mountain and marine environmental conditions.

One interesting finding from the Bentley *et al.* study was that commercial adventure-tourism activities that are often perceived to be high risk (white-water rafting, jet boating, kayaking) involved proportionately fewer injuries overall, especially considering their large number of participants. For 'independently dependent' and 'aware' Gen-Y travellers, adventure activities with a qualified instructor, a detailed briefing and clear structure that emphasizes safety is likely to produce a more satisfying experience, especially if it involves group socializing in an ecotourism setting.

While meeting new people and experiencing everyday life at a destination is important, many Gen-Y travellers are on limited budgets, hence the popularity of backpacker hostels in recent years. A new online community called the Couch Surfing Project now offers travellers the opportunity to stay for free at the homes of fellow members in a global reciprocal arrangement that facilitates movement of young people.

An analysis of the Couch Surfing Project reveals a great deal about the personal travel safety issues of Gen Y discussed throughout this chapter. Couch Surfing describes itself as 'a worldwide network for making connections between travelers and the local communities they visit'. Table 10.1 shows the engagement of Couch Surfing as at 20 March 2009.

Table 10.1. Profile of Couch Surfing from their website.

Couch Surfers	1,013,963
Successful surf or host experiences	989,269
Friendships created	1,159,965
Positive experiences	1,878,069
Countries represented	232
Cities represented	55,834

Safety is of particular concern to Couch Surfing and they have several mechanisms to screen members. The most basic is 'verification' of the new member's name (via credit card used) and physical address of residential premises. The next level is 'vouching', where three existing members must know the candidate well in the real world in order to vouch for them. Couch Surfers are also encouraged to write references online about their hosts, including:

- Was the information on the member's profile sufficient and accurate?
- Is that couch safe? Is the person trustworthy? What happened?
- Did you feel good or bad? Why?
- Would you want to surf with/host again this person?
- Was the person interesting? Talkative? Respectful?
- Did you enjoy particular activities with that surfer/host?

Couch Surfing seems to capture the new generational perspective on personal travel safety. It involves tech-savvy use of the Internet to connect with other young people throughout the world, with a view to experiencing everyday life at a destination. Couch Surfing goes beyond free accommodation and offers Gen Y a social networking opportunity where they can share travel stories, meet new friends online and in the real world. Safety is a major concern, so mechanisms have been built into the system to screen members. It remains to be seen how effective these fairly rudimentary screening measures are, and how mishaps will be handled legally and in terms of insurance.

Conclusions

Gen-Y travellers are aware of external threats such as terrorism and crime, and physical and environmental risks, but this does not deter them from wanting to explore other cultures. As tech-savvy users of the Internet they can access and make use of the huge amount of timely information available to them, especially warnings about external risks through government travel advisory websites. As a group they should be encouraged to avail themselves of travel insurance, since this will provide a safety net for the more likely problems they will encounter. This chapter identifies motor vehicle crashes and water safety problems as areas where Gen Y are likely to be injured. Also highlighted are the safety issues related to adventure tourism, where New Zealand data show 20–30 year olds are the largest group for hospital admissions. Participating in unfamiliar activities, in unfamiliar environments, appears to be the key here.

Where Gen Y appears to be at most risk, however, is in social situations involving alcohol, drugs, sex and partying. Many overseas destinations actively encourage young people to have fun and overindulge, while peer pressure increases the risks of exposure to sexually transmitted diseases, breaking the law and coming into conflict with local residents. The tourism industry, especially youth hostels, must take a more active role in customer safety, both in terms of their legal obligations (fire, pool and premises safety) and in the face of alternative accommodation arrangements offered by groups like Couch Surfing. As an 'independently dependent' group, Gen Y need to establish their own identity and travel style (WTO, 2008) while also being assisted to remain safe.

References

Aeffect (2000) Review of Literature and Secondary Research on Generation Y –Lessons to Apply in the Development of a Youth-targeted CDC Website. Report prepared for Centers for Disease Control & Prevention. CDC, Atlanta, Georgia.

Australian Water Safety Council (2008) *Australian Water Safety Strategy 2008–11.* Australian Water Safety Council, Sydney, Australia.

Backpackers.com (2008) Fire Awareness Week: Free Backpacker Hostel Fire Safety Guide Released. Available at: http://www.backpackers.com/blog/2007/11/06/fire-awareness-week-free-backpacker-hostel-fire-safety-guide-released/

Barnes, M. (2006) Inquest into the Palace Backpackers Hostel Fire: Findings of the Inquest. Available at: http://www.courts.qld.gov.au/childers070706.pdf

Barretto, L. (2008) Goa Targets Drink, Drugs as New Tourist Season Starts. Available at: http://www.news.com.au/travel/story/0,26058,24458659–5009000,00.html

BBC News (2004) Addict Jailed for Bridge Murder. Available at: http://news.bbc.co.uk/2/hi/uk_news/england/north_yorkshire/3745460.stm

Beck, U. (1992) *Risk Society: Towards a New Modernity*. Sage, London.

Bellis, M.A., Hughes, K., Bennett, A. and Thomson R. (2003) The role of an international nightlife resort in the proliferation of recreational drugs. *Addiction* 98, 1713–1721.

Bentley, T., Meyer, D., Page, S. and Chalmers, D. (2001) Recreational tourism injuries among visitors to New Zealand: an exploratory analysis using hospital discharge data. *Tourism Management* 22, 373–381.

Carrington, V. (2006) *Rethinking Middle Years: Early Adolescents, Schooling and Digital Culture*. Allen & Unwin, Sydney, Australia.

CNN.com (2000) Swiss canyon deaths: Eight charged. Available at: http://archives.cnn.com/2000/WORLD/europe/11/01/switz.canyon/index.html

Cornall, P., Howie, S., Mughal, A., Sumner, V., Dunstan, F., Kemp, A. and Sibert, J. (2005) Drowning of British children abroad. *Child: Care, Health & Development* 31(5), 611–613.

Couch Surfing Project (2009) Available at: http://www.couchsurfing.com/

Davies, P. (2005) Younger travellers 'less likely' to be insured. *Travel Mole News,* 2 August. Available at: http://www.travelmole.com/stories/104665.php?news_cat=&pagename=searchresult

De Nardi, M. and Wilks, J. (2007) Tourist water safety: Surf Life Saving initiatives for the Japanese inbound market. *Journal of Vacation Marketing* 13(3), 275–283.

Dickson, T. and Hurrell, M. (2008) *International Visitors to Australia: Safety Snapshot 2003–2005*. CRC for Sustainable Tourism, Southport, Australia.

Edgell, D. (2008) The ten important world tourism issues for 2009. Available at: http://www.davidedgell.com

Federation of Tour Operators (2007) *Preferred Code of Practice – Health and Safety*. Federation of Tour Operators, Haywards Health, UK.

Foreign and Commonwealth Office (2008a) Supporting British Nationals Abroad. Available at: https://fco-stage.fco.gov.uk/en/departmental-report/part1/british-nationals/

Foreign and Commonwealth Office (2008b) Locate: Register with Us. Available at: http://www.fco.gov.uk/en/travelling-and-living-overseas/Locate/

Foreign and Commonwealth Office (2008c) Drugs. Available at: http://www.fco.gov.uk/en/travelling-and-living-overseas/be-a-responsible-tourist/drugs

FutureBrand (2007) *Country Brand Index 2007*. FutureBrand, New York.

Howe, N. (2006) A Generation to Define a Century. Paper presented to the Association for Supervision and Curriculum Development Annual Conference, Worldwide Issues, Chicago, 1–3 April. Available at: http://ascd.typepad.com/annualconference/2006/04/a_generation_to.html

Ironside, R. (2008) Gen Ys create havoc on roads. *Courier Mail* (Brisbane), 15 October, p. 15.

Leggat, P. and Wilks, J. (2009) Overseas visitor deaths in Australia 2001–2003. *Journal of Travel Medicine* 16, 243–247.

McMurdo, M. (2008) Legal considerations for beach safety: in defence of the reasonableness of the law. In: Wilks, J. (ed.) *Beach Safety and the Law*: Australian Evidence. Surf Life Saving Australia, Sydney, pp. 13–19.

National Nine News (2008a) Britt's Body Identified. Available at: http://news.ninemsn.com.au/slideshow.aspx?sectionid=6573&subsectionid=146896&sectionname=slideshows&subsectionname=britt (accessed 9 October 2008)

National Nine News (2008b) Britt's Mother Offers Emotional Tribute. Available at: http://news.ninemsn.com.au/article.aspx?id=645322

New Politics Institute (2006) *The Politics of the Millennial Generation: A Survey Comparing Political Attitudes Between Generations*. New Politics Institute, Miami, Florida.

Pendergast, D. (2007) The MilGen and school education. In: Bahr, N. and Pendergast, D. (eds) *The Millennial Adolescent*. Australian Council for Educational Research, Canberra, pp. 268–313.

Perl, D. (2000) Swiss Canyoning Disaster, Saxetenbach Gorge, Switzerland. Available at: http://www.docleaf.com/critique/case%20study.doc

Roach, J. and Kemish, I. (2006) Bali bombings: a whole of government response. In: Wilks, J., Pendergast, D. and Leggat, P. (eds) *Tourism in Turbulent Times: Towards Safe Experiences for Visitors*. Elsevier, Oxford, pp. 277–289.

Sonmez, S., Apostolopoulos, Y., Ho, Y.C., Yang, S. and Mattila, A. (2006) Binge drinking and casual sex on spring break. *Annals of Tourism Research* 33(4), 895–917.

Sydney Morning Herald (2008) Sexual Infections Rise Among Gen Y. Available at: http://www.smh.com. au/news/national/sexual-infections-skyrocket-among-gen-y/2008/07/02/1214950851362.html

Totaro, P. (2008). Missing Britt's Father Still in Dark. Bendigo Advertiser. Available at: http://www. bendigoadvertiser.com.au/news/world/world/general/missing-britts-father-still-in-dark/1325789.aspx

Visa International Asia Pacific and Pacific Asia Travel Association (PATA) (2006) *Asia Travel Intentions Survey 2006*. PATA, Bangkok.

Wilks, J. (1999) International tourists, motor vehicles and road safety: a review of the literature leading up to the Sydney 2000 Olympics. *Journal of Travel Medicine* 6, 115–121.

Wilks, J. (2004) Injuries and injury prevention. In: Keystone, J., Kozarsky, P., Nothdurft, H.D., Freedman, D.O. and Connor, B. (eds) *Travel Medicine*. Mosby, London, pp. 453–459.

Wilks, J. (2006) Current issues in tourist health, safety and security. In: Wilks, J., Pendergast, D. and Leggat, P. (eds) *Tourism in Turbulent Times: Towards Safe Experiences for Visitors*. Elsevier, Oxford, pp. 3–18.

Wilks, J. (2008) Considering the standard of care for tourists. *International Travel Law Journal* 15, 135–142.

Wilks, J. and Davis, R. (2003) International tourists and recreational injuries. *Plaintiff* 59, 8–14.

Wilks, J., Pendergast, D. and Leggat, P. (2006) *Tourism in Turbulent Times: Towards Safe Experiences for Visitors*. Elsevier, Oxford.

Wilks, J., Watson, B. and Faulks, I. (1999) International tourists and road safety in Australia: developing a national research and management programme. *Tourism Management* 20, 645–654.

World Tourism Organization (2008) *Youth Travel Matters: Understanding the Global Phenomenon of Youth Travel*. World Tourism Organization, Madrid, Spain.

11 Adjusting Attitudes Using Traditional Media: Magazines Can Still Move Millennials

Marsha D. Loda and Barbara C. Coleman

Hull College of Business, Augusta State University

Introduction

How can tourism, the world's largest service industry, effectively reach one of the most coveted consumer markets: today's teenagers and young adults who are most often referred to either as Generation Y or Millennials? In the light of the size of this market segment, which is approximately 80 million in the USA, the answer has the potential to impact the profitability of airlines, restaurants, hotels and attractions that combine to form the tourism industry. Because it spans a greater number of years, this segment is considerably larger than Generation X, and because it also has greater spending power than its predecessor, it is especially attractive to marketers (Cheng, 1999; Wolburg and Pokrywczynski, 2001). Because there is a paucity of research with respect to Millennials's preferred informational sources, this study investigates the influence of traditional informational sources as well as the value of advertising and editorial messages among 18–24-year-old college students who are a subgroup of Generation Y.

Background

The economic importance of college students to marketers, and the potential difficulty in communicating with them, calls for research to yield new insights. The research summarized in this chapter has two purposes: it examines the media habits and preferences of Millennials, and it considers several hypotheses that investigate how marketers of tourism products can influence attitudes by building belief strength and belief confidence among college-aged members of Generation Y. A discussion of the expectancy-value (EV) model and information integration as conceptual backdrops is followed with a review of media use by Millennials, and concludes by discussing new research findings to improve marketing effectiveness.

Expectancy-value model

How consumers process and integrate various sources of information to guide behaviour is well researched. Researchers examining this issue often use the EV theory of Fishbein and Ajzen (1975). This is a model of reasoned behaviour or central route processing wherein the consumers carefully consider message content (Petty and Cacioppo, 1986). In these cases, the success of persuasive communications, i.e. message acceptance, depends on the degree to which consumers accept message claims (Smith and Vogt, 1995). Factors that influence message acceptance include perceived credibility and argument strength (Fishbein and Ajzen, 1975).

In the EV model, the first step in message processing is the expectation that the product or service being promoted is associated with the attributes mentioned in the promotional message. This expectation is reflected in belief strength and belief confidence (Fishbein and Ajzen, 1975; Smith and Swinyard, 1982; Smith, 1993). Belief strength is the consumer's presumption that the brand and attributes are associated. Belief confidence is the consumer's degree of certainty that the belief strength estimate is accurate.

In the second stage of response, consumers evaluate each attribute associated with the brand as good or bad, producing expected value. The expected values from all salient attributes are combined for an overall evaluation of the brand, or brand attitude. Moreover, advertising studies have shown that attitude towards the brand can also be mediated by attitude towards the message or attitude towards the advertisement during central route processing (MacKenzie and Lutz, 1989).

Information integration

While the EV model identifies the attributes that are salient to attitude formation and an informed response, integration theory focuses on situations where more than one source of information is available and how the contents of each are cognitively combined. For example, Anderson's (1971) information integration theory describes how people integrate or combine different pieces of information when they make evaluations. The theory states that people assign a weight to each piece of information they receive, commensurate with its credibility or reliability. They then average the information from various sources depending on the weight assigned to each piece. Informational weights are also influenced by the order or sequence of each piece of information that is received. In particular, primacy and recency effects can be pronounced. For example, initial opinion often plays a critical role in attitude formation, and as a consequence, confidently held primary beliefs are

difficult to dislodge, whether they are positive or negative.

In looking at how advertising influences an audience, information response models (e.g. Assael and Day, 1968; O'Brian, 1971) find support for the causal linkages of cognition, affect and conation. Cognition consists of two components: belief strength and message acceptance (Fishbein and Ajzen, 1975; Smith and Swinyard, 1982). The researchers posit that belief strength is directly related to information response models because the probability of association is a function of message acceptance. When acceptance is substantial, higher-order beliefs will result. Furthermore, the format in which the information is presented, i.e. advertising or publicity, is a particularly important variable for message acceptance in advertising response models. That publicity is more credible, persuasive or effective than advertising is often cited in marketing literature (Ray, 1992; Ries and Ries, 2002), but with little substantive empirical support. Marketing texts teach that the advantages of publicity over advertising include lower costs and increased visibility, and that the third-party endorsement effect inherent in publicity is assumed to increase its credibility (Kotler, 1993).

In contrast, Smith and Swinyard (1982) found that 'in general, advertising has been found to be rather limited in its ability to form higher order beliefs' (p. 83). Similarly, Eagly et al. (1978) identified biases when message claims are delivered by a source with an obvious vested interest or profit motive. Especially when profit motives are present, these biases limit the strength of readers' beliefs in advertising claims because of low-perceived source credibility. Credible sources, such as word of mouth or direct experience, where no profit motive is apparent, form a much stronger belief base. The research of Loda and Coleman (2005) confirms that publicity is more effective than advertising for three variables: credibility, message strength and purchase intent.

The present study builds on existing research and examines whether traditional media – specifically magazines – influence decisions made by Millennials, and whether advertising or publicity is more effective at building belief strength and belief confidence concerning the choice of a spring-break tourist destination by Millennial travellers.

A Profile of Millennials

Many analysts contend that Generation Y came out of a different history and with a different set of expectations than earlier generations. Labour statistics show that the current 18–24-year-old cohort – the subgroup of Generation Y also known as Millennials – belongs to the best-educated generation in American history. It is also the most culturally diverse with as high as 30% representing ethnic minorities. About 25% grew up in single-family households, and approximately 75% had a working mother (Neuborne and Kerwin, 1999). Many are extremely literate but take a cynical attitude towards government, believing that the system as a whole, including social security, pensions, health care and job security, will not be there for them (Thau, 1996). There is also a general decline in social trust, 'whether that is trust in their fellow citizens, in established institutions, or in elected officials' (Halstead, 1999).

As members of Generation Y, Millennials also possess a number of positive attributes. For example, Strauss and Howe (2000) predicted declines in what they term Generation Y's pathologies: substance abuse, crime, suicide and unwed pregnancy. Similarly, in a summary of current research on younger members of Generation Y, Markiewicz (2007) noted the conclusion of Gallup that more than 90% of the teens report being very close to their parents. She also included the findings of Applied Research and Consulting LLC that today's youth are apt to trust parents (86%), teachers (86%) and police (83%) more than music celebrities (35%) or sports figures (30%).

Media habits and consumer behaviour of millennials

Because many young adults postpone leaving their parents' home, they have money for cars, nice clothing and other items (Koss-Feder, 1998). They are a high-spending group with a large discretionary income for items such as computers, CDs, concerts, electronics and vacations (Cheng, 1999). Furthermore, marketers are aware that the buying habits Millennials establish now will likely have a significant impact in the retail world in the years to come. Industry analysts have also observed that more is at stake for advertisers and marketers when communicating with Generation Y than with Generation X, again principally because of their size. When the younger cohort – 6–17-year-olds – is added to the 18–24-year-olds, they are a group nearly as large as the Boomers. As a consequence, brands that thrived among Boomers but flopped when aimed at Generation X hurt marketers, but the miss was tolerable. Brands that miss the mark with Generation Y, however, may not recover (Neuborne and Kerwin, 1999).

Having grown up in a media-saturated, brand-conscious world, Millennials encounter advertisements in more and different places than their parents did, and they are believed to respond to them differently. Years of intense marketing efforts aimed at Generation Y have taught youthful members to assume the worst about companies and to conclude that they are merely trying to coax them into buying something. Analysts believe that Generation Y responds better to humour, irony and the 'unvarnished' truth (Neuborne and Kerwin, 1999).

In addition to rejecting the older message strategies, Millennials pose a challenge because they do not seek their entertainment and information from traditional media. Estimates of newspaper readership by this age group indicate a serious decline. One suggests that young adults are one-third less likely than Boomers to read newspapers. Another assessment states that young people represent only 7% of the total newspaper readership (Stepp, 1996). In contrast, in light of their requirement for faster, more immediate sources, the Internet is certainly their medium of choice (Luo *et al.*, 2005).

Despite evidence of alienation from some established media, research also shows that other traditional media classes may still influence young adults. Citing the results of a recent study conducted by Deloitte and Touche, in the USA, Steinberg (2007) notes that Generation Y reads magazines as frequently as other age cohorts. In fact approximately three-quarters of all consumers read magazines for the same information that they could find online. Generation Y also shows more interest in new television programmes and new magazines when compared with the general population. In addition, for new product trials, Generation Y rates television and magazine advertising of higher value than does the general population (Reese, 1997).

Comparative Strengths of Advertising Versus Publicity

Research has shown that intangible, expensive service purchases such as travel involve both financial and emotional risk (Fisk *et al.*, 2000). This is certainly true for college students planning spring-break trips. Spring-break ventures now represent a US$1 billion tourism market (Miller, 2004). While information on how spring-break travellers use information sources is available (Butts *et al.*, 1996; Smith and MacKay, 2001; Klenosky, 2002), no research has been located that specifically examines the effectiveness of advertising and publicity. Because these two elements differentially impact message credibility, it is essential that they be investigated vis-à-vis travel and in particular, spring-break trips. A second issue is whether traditional media investments are more or less effective in communicating destination image. Because image 'affects the intentions and decisions of consumers before visiting a destination' (Tasci and Gartner, 2007, p. 422), it is critical that marketers employ media that best captures the image.

Advertising

Consumers and advertising scholars agree that one of the essential duties of advertising is to provide information. In fact, informativeness is the single factor most strongly correlated with overall advertising value (Ducoffe, 1995). The medium in which the message is embedded also influences perceived value. When three media classes were rated on this characteristic, consumers evaluated banner advertising lowest and television next lowest. They rated magazines highest (Choi *et al.*, 2000).

Publicity

In addition to advertising, publicity is a commonly chosen technique employed by tourism marketers. Research suggests that publicity outperforms advertising when measured on the variables of credibility, message strength and purchase intent (Loda and Coleman, 2005). However, in discussions about media use and techniques, marketers may recognize the advantage in credibility of publicity, but they also decry its disadvantages. These include lack of control of the message and lack of control of frequency, which are two distinct attributes of advertising.

Millennials and magazines

Pragmatic issues dictate that marketers embed their messages in the media that their target segments use. As a consequence, because Millennials use the Internet, tourism marketers have dedicated significant portions of their budgets to electronic resources. Current research, however, has concluded that Millennials also regularly read magazines for information as well as for entertainment (Reese, 1997; Choi *et al.*, 2000; Steinberg, 2007). Moreover, research has shown that placing publicity in magazines is an effective promotional technique (Loda *et al.*, 2005). This raises the question whether marketers should allocate funds in their promotional budgets to print media if they plan to target Millennials. To answer this question, marketers require more information about the individual impact of publicity and advertising when each is placed in print. Specifically, they need answers to the following questions among Millennials:

- Do magazines influence purchase intentions?
- Do publicity or advertising create a higher level of belief strength?
- Do publicity or advertising create a higher level of belief confidence?
- Do publicity or advertising create a higher total expectancy of attributes?

A study was designed to examine these issues in depth. A summary of the research design and results follows.

Research Design

The research was conducted as a post-test-only experiment in which respondents were subjected to stimuli, and then asked questions concerning dependent variables. The respondents were 130 students at a south-eastern university who were instructed to assume they had the time and funds (to increase involvement) to travel over spring break. Stimuli were an advertisement and a publicity article about the island of Aruba. Respondents were questioned about their feelings towards Aruba both before and after exposure to the promotional materials.

An island destination was selected as the subject for stimuli because of the popularity of islands for spring-break vacations. Aruba was selected from a survey of 27 college students who were asked about islands they would consider visiting for spring break, and was chosen for the research because it received the fewest mentions. A factual destination was preferred; however, less awareness about Aruba meant fewer preconceived notions about it as a vacation choice.

Stimulus design

The message points for the advertisement and publicity story were the same. Students were asked, in a free elicitation procedure, to list points that were salient to them in selecting an island vacation destination. The five most frequently mentioned salient points comprised the subject matter of both the advertisement and the publicity story. Those points were: activities, white-sand beaches, good weather, inclusive and reasonable prices and interesting or native foods.

Design of the stimulus materials was based on a content analysis of one-page advertisements and one-page publicity stories in *Southern Living* magazine. This magazine was selected because it received the most mentions from the 27 students in a survey about

their magazine reading habits, and where they would look for information about vacation destinations. Both of the stimulus materials were presented in four colours. Based on the content analysis, travel advertisements averaged 70 words of body copy, while publicity stories averaged 415 words.

Three versions of each stimulus were presented and pretested with a student population. Stimulus materials selected for the survey were deemed equally persuasive on a scale (1 = 'not at all persuasive' to 10 = 'extremely persuasive') concerning the answer to this question: 'Put yourself in the place of a person with the time, money and interest to take a vacation. How persuasive is this message in making you want to go to Aruba?' The article produced a mean of 7.80, while the advertisement had a mean of 8.0.

Five groups were randomly selected for the experiment based on the stimulus they received, and the order in which they received it. These groups were: advertising-only; publicity-only; advertising-then-publicity; publicity-then-advertising; and control group (received no stimuli).

Variables and measures

According to the EV model, consumer response to messages includes belief strength that the brand is associated with the attributes in the promotional message, and belief confidence that that association is accurate (Fishbein and Ajzen, 1975; Smith and Swinyard, 1982). Belief strength and belief confidence, two dependent variables proposed for this study, can be multiplied to generate a total expectancy of destination attributes.

Belief strength and belief confidence were each measured with a single-item scale for each salient attribute presented in the message. They were then multiplied to produce a single measure for the total expectancy of attributes. These scales were developed and used by Fishbein and Ajzen (1975), Smith and Swinyard (1982) and Smith (1993). For belief strength, respondents were asked how likely it is that the destination had a specific attribute. A seven-point Likert-type scale recorded responses ranging from 'zero likelihood' (1) to 'certain' (7).

For belief confidence, a similar scale asked respondents how confident they were that the likelihood of the estimate provided for belief strength was accurate. Responses ranged from 'extremely uncertain' (1) to 'extremely certain' (7).

Purchase intent was measured with two seven-point Likert-type scales developed by Smith (1993). The questions asked how likely the respondent was to select the destination (given he or she is taking a vacation), and how likely the respondent would be to recommend the destination to a friend. Responses ranged from 'not at all likely' (1) to 'extremely likely' (7). Mean scores were combined and averaged to generate one statistic estimating purchase intent.

Ajzen and Fishbein's (1980) model of reasoned action states that attitude leads to behavioural intent. Attitude towards the brand and purchase intent are common variables of marketing research projects (Hallahan, 1999). Therefore, the expected values from all salient attributes are combined for an overall evaluation of the brand, or attitude towards the destination.

Profile of respondents

All respondents in the current study were members of the Millennial cohort. They were predominantly college freshmen or sophomores in day classes, aged 18 to 21. The majority of respondents was female (72.7%) and Caucasian (60.0%). Less than one in three respondents was an African-American (30.0%).

Results

Following the experiment, researchers looked for areas of significance using a series of one-way ANOVAs. A standard value of $p = 0.05$ was used to measure significance. Sequencing effects were examined for five participant groups, which were: advertising-only; publicity-only; advertising-then-publicity; publicity-then-advertising; and a control group that saw no message.

Question 1: do magazines influence purchase intentions?

Results of the research confirm that traditional magazine media does influence purchase intent among potential Millennial customers for a tourist destination. There is also sufficient evidence of sequencing effects, namely that advertising is stronger when it is preceded by publicity, as compared to using advertising alone.

Descriptive statistics for each group were:

* advertising-only (mean = 4.30, SD = 1.42);
* publicity-only (mean = 5.55, SD = 0.758);
* advertising-then-publicity (mean = 4.77, SD = 0.999);
* publicity-then-advertising (mean = 5.25, SD = 1.06);
* control group (mean = 3.03, SD = 1.34).

These differences are visually depicted in Fig. 11.1. Next, a one-way ANOVA compared these means and found statistical differences ($p = 0.001$).

As the control group produced the lowest mean, it suggests that any application of publicity or advertising, or a combination, is better than nothing. Among the groups exposed to stimuli, three comparisons were significant. Significant differences resulted between publicity-only and advertising-only, between advertising-only and publicity-then-advertising and between publicity-only and advertising-then-publicity. In general, groups exposed to a message stimulus followed the pattern set by previous variables. When publicity was the only treatment viewed, or was viewed prior to the advertising message, higher purchase intent resulted. When advertising messages were viewed alone or before publicity, purchase intent scores were lower. As with preceding variables, when advertising preceded publicity, there was not much change in the scores compared to advertising-only. The highest purchase intent score was achieved with the publicity-only sequence. All treatment groups exposed to a stimulus scored significantly higher than the control group.

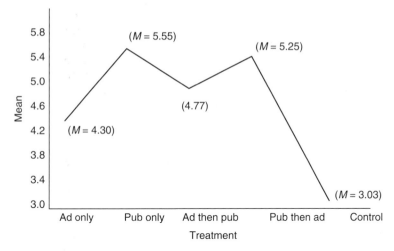

Fig. 11.1. Differences in purchase intent by treatment group. Measured using a seven-point with 1 as 'zero likelihood' and 7 as 'certain'.

Question 2: do publicity or advertising create a higher level of belief strength?

There was insufficient evidence to conclude that publicity creates stronger belief confidence than advertising in tourism communication. Although the results follow a familiar pattern, differences among treatment groups were not statistically significant. When publicity was the only treatment viewed, or was viewed prior to the advertising message, higher perceived belief strength resulted; yet this difference was not significant. When advertising messages were viewed alone or before publicity, belief confidence scores were lower, but not significantly so. As with preceding variables, when advertising preceded publicity, there was little change in belief confidence scores compared to advertising-only. The highest belief confidence score was achieved with the publicity-only stimulus. Descriptive statistics for each treatment group were:

- advertising-only (mean = 5.67, SD = 0.799);
- publicity-only (mean = 6.00, SD = 0.658);
- advertising-then-publicity (mean = 5.64, SD = 0.864);
- publicity-then-advertising (mean = 5.91, SD = 0.744);
- control group (mean = 4.72, SD = 1.17).

These differences are visually depicted in Fig. 11.2. A one-way ANOVA found significant differences ($p = 0.001$). As with belief strength, all multiple comparisons with the control group showed significant differences.

Question 3: do publicity or advertising create a higher level of belief confidence?

Results of the research show that there is insufficient evidence to conclude that publicity creates stronger belief confidence than advertising in tourism communication. Although the results follow a familiar pattern, differences among treatment groups are not statistically significant. Descriptive statistics for each treatment group were:

- advertising-only (mean = 5.10, SD = 0.766);
- publicity-only (mean = 5.57, SD = 0.766);
- advertising-then-publicity (mean = 5.30, SD = 0.657);
- publicity-then-advertising (mean = 5.52, SD = 0.663);
- control group (mean = 4.60, SD = 0.831).

These differences are visually depicted in Fig. 11.3.

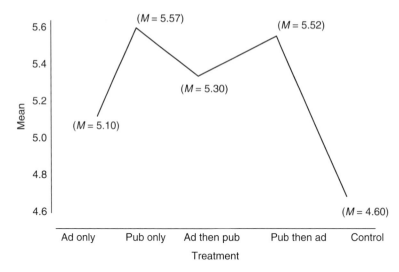

Fig. 11.2. Differences in belief strength by treatment group. Measured using a seven-point scale with 1 as 'zero likelihood' and 7 as 'certain'.

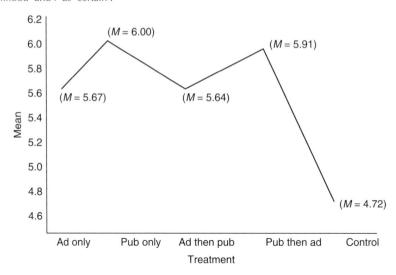

Fig. 11.3. Differences in belief confidence by treatment group. Measured using a seven-point scale with 1 as 'extremely uncertain' and 7 as 'extremly certain'.

When publicity was the only treatment viewed, or was viewed prior to the advertising message, higher perceived belief strength resulted; yet this difference was not significant. When advertising messages were viewed alone or before publicity, belief confidence scores were lower, but not significantly so. As with preceding variables, when advertising preceded publicity, there was little change in belief confidence scores compared to advertising-only. The highest belief confidence score was achieved with the publicity-only stimulus.

Question 4: do publicity or advertising create a higher total expectancy of attributes?

In the EV model (Fishbein and Ajzen, 1975), belief strength and belief confidence are multiplied to generate the total expectancy of attributes. Question 4 explored whether publicity or advertising had a greater impact on total expectancy. Based on the analysis of data, the total expectancy of attributes generated by tourism communication is greater for publicity than for advertising. Descriptive statistics for each treatment group are:

- advertising-only (mean = 28.92, SD = 7.87);
- publicity-only (mean = 33.42, SD = 7.18);
- advertising-then-publicity (mean = 29.89, SD = 6.83);
- publicity-then-advertising (mean = 32.62, SD = 7.19);
- control group (mean = 21.71, SD = 8.80).

These differences are shown in Fig. 11.4. An ANOVA found significance ($p = 0.001$).

Post-hoc tests revealed that all multiple comparisons with the control group showed significant differences. In addition, significant differences were found between the groups exposed to advertising-only and publicity-only. As with the previous variables, this variable follows a similar pattern in that publicity generated higher mean scores than did advertising. The group that viewed publicity-only had significantly higher mean scores than those exposed to advertising-only. However, significant sequencing effects were not evident.

Discussion and Applications

This study replicates the findings of Fishbein and Ajzen (1975) concerning the EV model in which belief strength and belief confidence are associated and combine to produce total expectancy. Respondents to both magazine advertising and magazine publicity generated significantly higher belief strength and belief confidence scores than respondents in the control group. However, belief strength and belief confidence scores for publicity were consistently higher than those for advertising, and they combined to produce a significantly higher total expectancy for those who were exposed to publicity-only versus those exposed to advertising-only. This research shows that these variables also impact purchase intent. The summary of significant findings is presented in the following table (Table 11.1).

Applications

Four practical applications for tourism marketers emerge from this study. First, it shows that traditional magazines are still a viable option for attracting the lucrative Millennial market to a specific tourist destination. Promotion placed in magazines significantly affected belief strength, belief confidence, total expectancy of attributes and purchase intent of Millennials exposed to the stimuli.

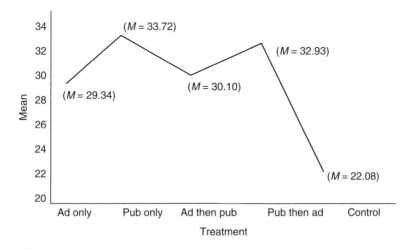

Fig. 11.4. Differences in total expectancy by treatment group.

Table 11.1. Summary of univariate significance.

Dependent variable	Treatment	Mean	Treatment group	Mean	P
Belief strength	Advertisement-only	5.10	Publicity-only	5.57	0.018
	Advertisement-only	5.10	Publicity-then-advertisement	5.52	0.035
	Control	4.60	All	5.37[a]	<0.02
Belief confidence	Control	4.72	All	5.80[a]	<0.02
Total expectancy of attributes	Advertisement-only	29.34	Publicity-only	33.72	0.028
	Control	22.08	All	31.52[a]	0.001
Purchase intent	Advertisement-only	4.30	Publicity-only	5.55	0.001
	Advertisement-only	4.30	Publicity-then-advertisement	5.25	0.046
	Publicity-only	5.55	Advertisement-then-publicity	4.77	0.012
	Control	3.03	All	4.97[a]	0.001

[a] Average mean of all treatment groups.

Second, it shows the strength of traditional advertising in a traditional medium. While publicity outperformed advertising for each dependent variable tested, it is important to note that all multiple comparisons showed significance against the control group. Advertising created significant differences for all variables compared to the control group, which saw no message.

Marketers know that advertising can be expensive, and they employ many means to increase the effectiveness of this investment, from concept and copy testing to readership reports. Third, this research suggests a different technique to improve the effectiveness of advertising: precede it with publicity. For every variable tested, mean scores were higher when respondents were exposed first to publicity, then to the advertising.

Finally, this research underscores the importance of publicity to tourism marketing, especially for the Millennial market. Tourism marketers who do not have a dedicated publicity programme should consider adding one. In addition, publicity should drive the marketing planning effort. Campaigns must be planned well enough in advance to allow for publicity to precede advertising. The research shows that when publicity follows advertising, publicity may not be worth the effort. It is when publicity precedes advertising that marketers can see significant improvements in belief strength, belief confidence, total expectancy and purchase intent.

Conclusion

The Millennial market is large, lucrative and elusive. However, while this age group is the most technologically savvy in history, they still attend to traditional media, such as television and magazines (Reese, 1997; Choi et al., 2000). The tourism industry is arguably the largest in the world. Spring-break travel alone is a US$1 billion tourism market (Miller, 2004). Tourism marketers looking to attract spring-break travellers should, of course, use the Internet aggressively in their media mix. However, the current research suggests that tourism marketers should not abandon the use of traditional magazines. Advertising and publicity can help increase belief strength, belief confidence and purchase intent among the Generation-Y cohort and Millennials in particular. In fact, the most effective traditional media strategy to affect Generation Y seems to be publicity followed by advertising.

References

Ajzen, I. and Fishbein, M. (1980) *Understanding Attitudes and Predicting Social Behaviour*. Prentice-Hall, Englewood Cliffs, New Jersey.

Anderson, N.H. (1971) Integration theory and attitude change. *Psychological Review* 78, 171–206.

Assael, H. and Day, G. (1968) Attitudes and awareness as predictors of marketing share. *Journal of Advertising Research* 8, 3–10.

Butts, F.B., Salazar, J., Sapio, K. and Thomas, D. (1996) The impact of contextual factors on the spring break travel decisions of college students. *Journal of Leisure Marketing* 4(3), 63–70.

Cheng, K. (1999) Setting their sites on generation Y. *Adweek*, August 9, 38–39.

Choi, S., Rifon, N., Trimble, S., Reece, B., Bukovac, J. and Hoic, Y. (2000) Information content in magazine, television and Internet advertising: a comparison and update. Paper presented at the national conference of the *American Academy of Advertising*, April 2000, Newport, Rhode Island.

Ducoffe, R. (1995) How consumers assess the value of advertising. *Journal of Current Issues and Research in Advertising* 17(1), 1–18.

Eagly, A.H., Wood, A. and Chaiken, K. (1978) Causal inferences about communicators and their effect in opinion change. *Journal of Personality and Social Psychology* 36, 424–435.

Fishbein, M. and Ajzen, I. (1975) *Belief, Attitude, Intention, and Behavior*. Addison-Wesley, Reading, Massachusetts.

Fisk, R., Grove, S. and John, J. (2000) *Interactive Services Marketing*. Houghton Mifflin, Boston, Massachusetts.

Hallahan, K. (1999) No, Virginia, it's not true what they say about publicity's 'implied third-party endorsement' effect. *Public Relations Review* 25, 331–349.

Halstead, T. (1999) Politics for generation X. *Atlantic Monthly* 284(2), 33–42.

Klenosky, D.B. (2002) The 'pull' of tourism destinations: a means-end investigation. *Journal of Travel Research* 40(4), 385–395.

Koss-Feder, L. (1998) Want to catch Gen X? Try looking on the web. *Marketing News* June 8, 20.

Kotler, P. (1993) *Marketing Management: Analysis, Planning, Implementation and Control*, 8th edn. Prentice-Hall, Englewood Cliffs, New Jersey.

Loda, M. and Coleman, B. (2005) Sequence matters: a more effective way to use advertising and publicity. *Journal of Advertising Research* 45(4), 362–372.

Loda, M., Norman, W. and Backman, K. (2005) How potential tourists react to mass media marketing: advertising versus publicity. *Journal of Travel and Tourism Marketing* 18(3), 63–70.

Luo, M., Feng, R. and Cai, L. (2005) Information search behavior and tourist characteristics: the Internet vis-à-vis other information sources. *Journal of Travel and Tourism Marketing* 17(2/3), 15–25.

MacKenzie, S.B. and Lutz, R.J. (1989) An empirical examination of the structural antecedents of attitude toward the ad in an advertising pretesting context. *Journal of Marketing* 53(2), 48–65.

Markiewicz, P. (2007) Who's filling Gen-Y's shoes? *Brandchannel*. Available at: http://www.brandchannel.com

Miller, R.K. (2004) *The 2005 Travel and Leisure Market Research Handbook*. Richard K. Miller and Associates, Dublin, Ireland.

Neuborne, E. and Kerwin, K. (1999) Generation Y. *Business Week*, 15 February, 80–86.

O'Brien, T. (1971) Stages of consumer decision making. *Journal of Marketing Research* 8, 283–289.

Petty, R.E. and Cacioppo, J.T. (1986) *Communication and persuasion: Central and Peripheral Routes to Attitude Change*. Springer, New York.

Ray, M.L. (1992) *Advertising and Communication Management*. Prentice-Hall, Englewood Cliffs, New Jersey.

Reese, S. (1997) The lost generation. *American Demographics*, 50–53.

Ries, A. and Ries, L. (2002) *The Fall of Advertising and the Rise of PR*. Harper Business, New York.

Smith, M.C. and MacKay, K. (2001) The organization of information in memory for pictures of tourist destinations: are there age-related differences? *Journal of Travel Research* 39, 261–266.

Smith, R.E. (1993) Integrating information from advertising and trial. *Journal of Marketing Research* 30, 204–219.

Smith, R.E. and Swinyard, W.R. (1982) Information response models: an integrated approach. *Journal of Marketing* 46(1), 81–93.

Smith, R.E. and Vogt, C.A. (1995) The effects of integrating advertising and negative word-of-mouth communications on message processing and response. *Journal of Consumer Psychology* 4(2), 133–151.

Steinberg, Brian (2007) Who still reads magazines? Just about everybody. *Advertising Age*. Available at: http://.adage.com (accessed 26 July 2008).

Stepp, C. (1996) The X factor. *American Journalism Review* 18(9), 34–38.

Strauss, W. and Howe, N. (2000) *Millennials Rising*. LifeCourse Associates, Fairfax County, Virginia.

Tasci, A. and Gartner, W. (2007) Destination image and its functional relationships. *Journal of Travel Research* 45(4), 413–425.

Thau, R. (1996) How do you target a market that wants to be left alone? *Vital Speeches of the Day* 62(21), 664–667.

Wolburg, J. and Pokrywczynski, J. (2001) A psychographic analysis of Generation Y college students. *Journal of Advertising Research* 41(5), 33–53.

12 Understanding Generation Y's Attitudes Towards a Career in the Industry

Scott Richardson

School of Hospitality and Tourism, Taylor's University College

Introduction

The tourism and hospitality industry world-wide, and in Australia in particular, is confronted with the problem of attracting and retaining quality employees. This has led to a shortage of skilled personnel to staff the ever-growing number of tourism and hospitality businesses (Deery and Shaw, 1999; Hinkin and Tracey, 2000; Ferris *et al.*, 2002). This situation is a complex one with many factors contributing to the problem including a young, transient workforce; low pay; comparatively low levels of formal qualifications; high levels of student/part-time and casual workers; a high proportion of low-skilled jobs; a large proportion of hours worked outside normal business hours; a negative industry image in the eyes of potential employees; poor utilization of student labour and high levels of staff turnover (Freeland, 2000; Brien, 2004; Baum, 2006).

The National Tourism Investment Strategy Consultative Group (2006) estimates that the current skills shortage within the Australian tourism industry is nearing 7000 positions with a further year-on-year deficit of up to 15,000 positions. By 2020, more than 130,000 new employees will be needed for the tourism and hospitality workforce. However, if current trends continue, only 45,000 workers are expected to join the industry, increasing the

fears that skills shortages will dramatically increase in the coming years. It has been suggested that due to the fragmented nature of the industry in Australia, it is not well equipped to respond to these future challenges presented by shortages and gaps in needed skills (Service Skills Victoria, 2005).

Studies indicate that the proportion of workers in the tourism and hospitality industry who have tertiary qualifications is much lower than most other industry sectors (Purcell and Quinn, 1996; Australian Bureau of Statistics, 2006). Reports also indicate that many hospitality and tourism management graduates fail to enter the industry upon graduation due to low job satisfaction, poor employment conditions and absence of motivating factors. This results in high staff turnover and wastage of trained and experienced personnel (Zacerelli, 1985; Pavesic and Brymer, 1990; Doherty *et al.*, 2001; Jenkins, 2001).

In the tourism and hospitality industry, having a skilled, enthusiastic and committed workforce is vital to success (Kusluvan and Kusluvan, 2000). As most of the interactions between customers and clients in the industry are in the form of face-to-face exchange with the service being purchased and consumed at the same time, the standard of service provided is of paramount concern. Employee attitudes, performance and behaviour are the key determinants of service quality that have direct linkages to customer satisfaction and loyalty (Heskett *et al.*, 1994). Bettencourt and Brown agree, explaining that:

> contact employees contribute to service excellence by delivering on the promises of the firm, by creating a favourable image for the firm, by going beyond the call of duty for customers, by promoting the firm's products and services and, in general, by providing better service than the competition.
> (Bettencourt and Brown, 1997, p. 39)

The aforementioned factors point to the need to understand the attitudes of the new generation of workers who are now entering the tourism and hospitality industry workforce: Generation Y. Paradoxically, and confirmed by Barron *et al.* (2007), Kusluvan and Kusluvan (2000) and Ross (1994), there is little evidence of research of this type being conducted in this industry.

Characteristics of Generation-Y Employees

The characteristics that Generation-Y employees exhibit towards a career have been much written about. Morton (2002) states that Generation Y employees show a tendency towards valuing equality in the workplace, and they seek positions that offer reasonable wages and good opportunities for training. Morton (2002) also claims that they respect managers who empower workers and who are open and honest with employees. Martin (2005), who terms this generation as 'Y-ers', describes eight main characteristics shown by Y-ers towards their careers. These eight factors can be found in Table 12.1.

Oliver (2006) claims that interest in the Generation-Y worker has intensified in recent years, and while generalizations are plentiful, he claims that the Generation-Y worker is uninterested in a job for life, and instead seeks flexibility and work–life balance. Lloyd (2005) states that in the current economic climate, with skills shortages prevalent, the Generation-Y employees know that they can pick and choose their employer and they use this power to get what they want or else they will find another job. Overall, Generation-Y

workers are seen to have much higher expectations of a job than previous generations, including high expectations of pay and conditions, as well as promotion and advancement (Oliver, 2006). If an employer cannot meet these expectations, the Generation-Y employee will pursue other avenues of employment.

If employers can better understand the psyche of the Generation-Y worker, it can better align with their ideals and expectations. Airey and Frontistis (1997, p. 157) note that perhaps the most important reason for undertaking this type of study is that:

> [T]here are so many questions which still need to be answered about the attitudes of young people to tourism careers. At a time when tourism is held out as one of the world's major industries and sources of employment it would be timely to know more about what potential recruits think about it, in order to provide a basis for attracting the best possible workforce.

Barron *et al.* (2007, p. 122) also claim that:

> Given the implications of this group's features on recruitment to, and retention in, the hospitality industry, in conjunction with management and development needs, it is important for the industry as a whole that this knowledge gap is addressed.

These factors highlight the importance of studying the attitudes and perceptions of Generation Y towards working in the tourism and hospitality industry. One such avenue for undertaking this investigation is to focus on Generation Y students undertaking tertiary study relevant to the industry.

Understanding Generation-Y Tertiary Students

To measure the perceptions, attitudes and career intentions of Generation-Y students who are currently studying tourism or hospitality management at an undergraduate level in Australia, an online survey consisting of elements from two questionnaires used in previous studies was utilized (Kusluvan and Kusluvan, 2000; Kyriacou and Coulthard, 2000). An Internet survey was used as most students use the Internet on a daily basis for e-mail, class

Table 12.1. Characteristics of Generation-Y employees. (Adapted from Martin, 2005.)

Characteristic	Description
Self-reliant and independent	Y-ers were more likely to be brought up in a single-parent family or a family where both parents worked than previous generations. This meant that many Y-ers were forced to 'fend for themselves' from an early age. Many employers see this as a problem whereby Generation Y does not want to be told what to do. This is in fact an incorrect assumption as these workers do want direction and managerial support, but they then want to be left alone to complete the tasks in their own way
Techno-savvy	This is the first generation in which members grew up with computers as an everyday part of their lives. They want to use this technology to complete their work more effectively and efficiently
Have an urgent sense of immediacy	Generation Y has a sense of urgency whereby it does not care about the next month or next year, it wants to know: 'What value can I add today? What can I learn today? What will you offer me today? How will I be rewarded today?' (Martin, 2005, p. 41)
Entrepreneurial	Today's young adults are starting their own businesses in record numbers – from youth employment services to web shows for teens – while they are still in school
Want increasing responsibility	Generation Y sees increasing responsibility not as a burden to be avoided but as a proving ground for its skills and talents. Generation Y requests – even demands – more responsibility
Have a 'get off my back' attitude	Every generation hates micromanagement, so it is no surprise that this is one of Generation Y-ers' pet peeves. The irony, of course, is when Y-ers do have time on their hands, they are easily bored. They have not been taught to manage time for themselves
Seek flexibility	Generation Y-ers seek new experiences. They are looking for careers that offer them the opportunity to move from project to project, move between positions and departments frequently and they are looking for the opportunity to work in different locations
Have adopted the free agency attitude	There has been a paradigm shift from lifetime employment to short-term positions and even changing careers several times during their working life. This will be even stronger with Generation Y-ers as they are learning to negotiate the best deals in ways older generations would never have conceived

registrations, lecture notes, tutorial information and research, and so their skill and familiarity levels are high for this method (Beebe *et al.*, 1997; Sheafor *et al.*, 2000; Sills and Song, 2002). In fact, Sills and Song (2002) claim that for populations that possess technical knowledge – such as students – the cost and ease of conducting this type of survey, as well as the speed and ease of data cleaning and analysis, make this form of survey administration favourable.

An e-mail was sent to approximately 1500 students at eight tertiary institutions in Australia, asking students to complete the online survey. In total 483 students viewed the survey, with 428 of those starting the survey. There were 49 students who did not complete the survey leaving 379 completed, useable surveys. This provided a response rate of 25.27%.

In addition to the online quantitative survey, a qualitative study was also conducted. To ensure that all previous respondents had a chance to participate in this qualitative stage of the research, an online weblog (blog) to record the respondent's views of working in the industry was utilized. In this blog, students were asked to either write comments about specific incidents that had shaped their views of the industry or just their overall views and feelings about working in the industry. A blog is an online diary where writers (bloggers) talk about their lives and share their views and opinions on certain issues. Blogs can be used for short, unofficial announcements, or to share experiences, thoughts and opinions (Ewins, 2005). According to Ewins (2005), blogs are increasingly used by people from all walks of life to create a presence in the web and participate in online debate. Ewins (2005) also claims that in recent years, blogging has increasingly been adopted by academics, both as a teaching tool and to disseminate and discuss their own research interests. For this part of the study, 87 survey respondents who indicated that they would be willing to participate in further research and had experience working in the tourism and hospitality industry were contacted. Eleven of these e-mails did not reach the intended recipient due to problems with the e-mail address, leaving 76 potential respondents who were contacted. Nineteen responded to the request and posted their comments on the blog site, providing a participation rate of 25%.

Characteristics of the survey sample

Demographics

Almost two-thirds of the respondents were females with an average age of 19 – which makes this study very much represented by mainstream Generation Y – with the majority of the respondents aged between 18 and 20. They were from eight tertiary institutions across Queensland, New South Wales, the Australian Capital Territory, Victoria and Western Australia. The largest number of respondents was enrolled at Griffith University, followed by Southern Cross University, the University of Queensland and the University of Technology, Sydney. More than half of the respondents indicated that they were first-year students, having completed 80 credit points (cp) or less. The vast majority of the respondents was enrolled at their institution on a full-time basis and approximately two-thirds identified themselves as being domestic students.

Respondents were asked whether tourism and hospitality was their first choice of study area, with the majority confirming this as the case. Others indicated their first choice included communications, law, physiotherapy, exercise, science, education, psychology and international business. The greatest number of respondents revealed their major was hotel management, followed by tourism management, event management and hospitality management

Work experience

The majority of the respondents reported having some experience working in the industry, the largest number having between 2 and 5 years experience, while almost one-quarter had fewer than 6 months experience. The majority of the respondents worked in the food and beverage departments of the hotels, restaurants or bars. Other areas identified included hotel front office, travel agents and theme parks. Most respondents were working in frontline positions with some working in a supervisory capacity and a small number working as low-level managers.

At the time of the study, almost two-thirds of those with industry experience claimed to be currently working in the industry. The majority of these were employed on a casual basis and worked between 6 and 20 h per week. Possibly the most interesting finding from this section of the survey related to the respondent's perceptions of working in the industry, as well as their intention to pursue a career after graduation. When analysing the data provided by those with work experience, it was found that fewer than half (46.2%) of the respondents claimed that actually working in the industry had positively influenced their perception of working in the industry, while 41.3% of the respondents suggested that working in the industry had negatively influenced their perceptions. Similarly, fewer than half the respondents (47.5%) reported they would definitely or were more than likely to pursue a career in the tourism and hospitality industry when they graduated. The disturbing finding from this question is that a sizeable number (19.6%) of the respondents claimed it was unlikely that they would pursue a career in the industry with a further 18.5% indicating that they would definitely not work in tourism or hospitality after graduation. When asked whether working in the industry had been the main factor in deciding not to pursue a career in the industry, the overwhelming majority (92.6%) stated that it was the main factor in their decision. The remaining 14.4% of the respondents were uncertain about whether or not to pursue a career in the industry. Of these, 53.7% claimed that working in the industry was the main factor contributing to their uncertainty. For those that claimed there were other reasons for their uncertainty, the main reasons given were that the industry required long working hours, the pay rate was low and that they had other interests they wanted to pursue.

Important career factors and the extent to which students believe a career in tourism and hospitality will offer these

This section focuses on the undergraduate's views of tourism and hospitality as a career choice. This section of the survey listed 20 general factors that students may find important when choosing a particular career. Students were asked to rate the 20 factors on the basis of how important they thought each factor was in choosing a career. They were then asked to list whether they thought a career in tourism and hospitality industry offered these factors. In analysing the findings, it was found that respondents rate each item as important, with very few respondents choosing not important for any of the factors. The only factors that received more than 10% of the respondents choosing not important were 'the opportunity to travel abroad' (12.7%), 'a job where I will contribute to society' (14.0%), 'a job where I can care for others' (18.5%), and the factor that was considered the least important, 'a job that can easily be combined with parenthood' (23.2%).

The most important factor identified by respondents was 'a job that I will find enjoyable', which 93.1% of the respondents considered as very important. Based on the number of respondents who chose very important as their response, the next four most important factors in choosing a career were 'pleasant working environment' (73.3%), 'a secure job' (68.3%), 'colleagues that I can get along with' (62.3%) and 'high earnings over length of career' (59.6%).

The notable part of this section is to try to understand the extent to which respondents think a career in the tourism and hospitality industry offers these factors. The first noticeable fact is that while more than 50% of the respondents rate 11 factors as very important – a job that I will find enjoyable, colleagues that I can get along with, pleasant working environment, a secure job, good promotion prospects, a job which gives me responsibility, high earnings over length of career, a job where you gain transferable skills, job mobility (easy to get a job anywhere), good starting salary, and a job that offers opportunities for further training – there are no factors where more than 50% of the respondents claim that the industry definitely offers these factors. For instance, while 93.1% of the respondents claim that finding a job that is enjoyable is very important, only 39.4% believe they will definitely find an enjoyable job in the tourism and hospitality industry.

A paired sample t-test was used to test for significant differences between the importance of each item and the degree to which respondents believed the industry offered these factors. Table 12.2 shows that the majority of the factors were found to be significantly different as their p-value is less than the critical value of 0.05. The only three factors that are not significantly different are 'a job which gives me responsibility', 'the opportunity to travel abroad' and 'a job where I can care for others'. In each of the factors that are significantly different, the importance factor has a lower mean than the extent to which students believe a career in tourism and hospitality offers that factor. This infers that students generally do not believe that a career in tourism and hospitality will offer them the factors that they find important in choosing a future career.

Perceptions and attitudes of undergraduate tourism and hospitality students towards a career in the industry

This following analysis provides an understanding of the perceptions and attitudes of the students to different aspects of working in the industry. The scale consisted of nine dimensions: (i) nature of work; (ii) social status;

Table 12.2. Differences between importance of factors in choosing a career and the extent to which students believe a career in tourism and hospitality will offer these.

Factor	Importance mean[a][b]	T and H offers mean[a][c]	Mean difference	f	p
A job that I will find enjoyable	1.07 (0.268)	1.63 (0.531)	−0.56	−18.537	0.000
Colleagues that I can get along with	1.39 (0.509)	1.76 (0.465)	−0.37	−11.908	0.000
Pleasant working environment	1.27 (0.450)	1.78 (0.492)	−0.51	−16.380	0.000
A secure job	1.34 (0.522)	2.07 (0.643)	−0.73	−17.864	0.000
A career that provides intellectual challenge	1.56 (0.562)	1.82 (0.599)	−0.26	−6.994	0.000
Good promotion prospects	1.44 (0.518)	1.98 (0.789)	−0.54	−12.045	0.000
A job which gives me responsibility	1.52 (0.551)	1.58 (0.583)	−0.06	−1.610	0.108
High earnings over length of career	1.43 (0.546)	2.20 (0.783)	−0.077	−17.218	0.000
A job where I will contribute to society	1.83 (0.649)	1.94 (0.632)	−0.011	−2.832	0.005
A job where I can use my university degree	1.61 (0.622)	1.79 (0.623)	−0.018	−4.806	0.000
A job where you gain transferable skills	1.46 (0.596)	1.58 (0.584)	−0.12	−3.250	0.001
A job that is respected	1.58 (0.618)	1.90 (0.588)	−0.32	−8.257	0.000
Reasonable workload	1.57 (0.542)	2.13 (0.732)	−0.56	−12.736	0.000
A job with high-quality resources and equipment	1.74 (0.586)	1.86 (0.482)	−0.12	−3.652	0.000
The opportunity to travel abroad	1.64 (0.696)	1.61 (0.609)	+0.03	0.771	0.441
Job mobility – easy to get a job anywhere	1.48 (0.593)	1.57 (0.589)	−0.09	−2.316	0.021
A job that can easily be combined with parenthood	1.87 (0.761)	2.32 (0.673)	−0.45	−9.582	0.000
Good starting salary	1.56 (0.620)	2.28 (0.676)	−0.72	−17.389	0.000
A job where I can care for others	1.93 (0.663)	1.87 (0.597)	+0.06	1.382	0.168
A job that offers opportunities for further training	1.44 (0.547)	1.65 (0.525)	−0.21	−6.526	0.000

[a]Values in parentheses are standard deviations.
[b]Importance mean value 1, very important; 2, fairly important; 3, not important.
[c]T and H offers mean value 1, definitely offers; 2, somewhat offers; 3, does not offer.

(iii) industry-person congeniality; (iv) physical working conditions; (v) pay/fringe benefits; (vi) promotion; (vii) co-workers; (viii) managers; and (ix) commitment to the industry. Each of these dimensions will now be considered.

The nature of work

Most respondents find working in the tourism and hospitality industry interesting and believe that there are always new things to learn each day. Yet, the majority of the respondents find working in the industry stressful, believe that the working hours are too long and that the hours worked are unsuitable to lead a normal life. Many respondents believe that family life is negatively affected by the unusual hours worked and feel that finding stable employment in the industry is difficult due to the influence seasonality has on the industry. A number of comments were also made by students in the blog relating to poor working conditions including: being underpaid; working long hours; and working late, as well as being forced to work overtime with no pay. These respondents claimed that the conditions of their employment left them feeling unmotivated, unappreciated and that the morale in the industry is negatively affected by these conditions. One respondent who believed they were asked to work excessive hours claimed:

> I was employed as a casual to work 20–30 hours per week though after several weeks it increased to 50 hours a week. I had to work 6–7 day weeks and was unable to choose which days I could have off.

A second comment regarding the unusual number of hours worked in the industry was:

> [U]nfortunately for us, we are understaffed and overworked. Working 6 days a week, 13 hour days for 3 months over summer does not boost an employee's morale! Under the previous manager staff morale was at an all time low, with many staff leaving, bitching being the most common chat among staff and staff having no reward for their hard work. The staff were forced under a new agreement (apparently a majority vote was for), giving us a base wage increase, but cutting all other penalties – including public holidays. As a high majority of our staff are students this did not go over well as we work the public holidays to make that extra money.

Social status

When investigating the social status dimension, it was found that approximately two-thirds of the respondents claim that their families are proud of their decision to pursue a career in the tourism and hospitality indus-

try and state that they talk to friends and family with pride about their decision to pursue this type of career. More than half of the respondents claim that working in tourism and hospitality is a beneficial and important job, although fewer than half believe that tourism and hospitality workers are valued in society. This is further highlighted by the fact that many respondents believe that the public perception is that tourism and hospitality graduates become waiters.

Industry-person congeniality

The vast majority of the respondents believe that their personality and character fits well with the types of jobs available in the industry and most believe that they will get an opportunity to use their skills and abilities. Most respondents also state that they get pleasure out of seeing satisfied customers. One interesting finding in the industry-person congeniality dimension is that almost three-quarters of the respondents find pleasure working in the industry with only a small percentage claiming not to find pleasure. This seems to contradict the fact that almost one-third of the respondent's claim that they will not work in the industry after graduation. This may indicate that while many respondents may actually enjoy the work that is on offer in the industry, there are other factors affecting the working conditions in the industry that have influenced their decision not to pursue a career in the industry.

Physical working conditions

Physical working conditions in the industry are generally seen as good, with two-thirds of the respondents agreeing with this statement. However, there is some concern among respondents with regard to working conditions, with almost half of the respondents stating that it is a very noisy environment in which to work, while more than one-third claim that the risk of work accidents in the industry is high.

Pay/benefits

The majority of the respondents are unhappy with the pay levels within the industry with more than half of the respondents claiming that pay levels for most jobs in the industry are low, with only a small number stating they are happy with the pay levels in the industry. Half the respondents also state that the level of fringe benefits offered by employers is low, and considering the long hours worked, three-quarters of the respondents believe that pay levels should be increased, with only a very small percentage believing that current wage levels are sufficient. Almost three-quarters of the respondents also agree that the level of penalty rates paid by employers should be increased due to the unusual nature of the hours worked. From the information provided above, it is clear that the pay and benefits offered by tourism and hospitality employers are seen as a major issue for students considering a career in the industry.

Promotion opportunities

The respondent's views of promotions in the industry are quite negative. Fewer than half of all the respondents believe that promotions are based on merit, while one-third claim that promotions are not merit-based. Promotions are also seen as being unsystematic and more than one-third of the respondents are unhappy with the promotion opportunities on offer. Almost half of the respondents claim that the opportunity to be promoted to management level is limited, with a similar number stating that promotions are not handled in a fair manner. More than half also believe that promotions are based on who you know rather than your ability and almost half state that they cannot see a clear career path in the industry. These findings indicate that there is uncertainty among respondents regarding promotion opportunities and paths they need to take to build a career in the industry. On a positive note, many respondents do agree that the number of years worked and academic qualifications are taken into account when applying for promotions.

Co-workers

Respondents are generally happy with their co-workers in the industry. The majority of the respondents believe that team spirit can be found in the industry, it is easy to make friends with co-workers and there is cooperation shown between staff. This good relationship between co-workers was reiterated through the comments made by the students in the online blog. Respondents to the blog claimed that staff communicate and interact well and the people working in the industry are easy-going and friendly. Some comments on this issue include: 'Even though I did not like my job I had good time with my work mates', 'I think that my co-workers are what makes me continue to work in the hospitality industry', 'I actually look forward to going to work because of the great team of people I work with' and 'I know that I love my job at the moment and that is mostly due to the staff'. As can be seen from these comments, respondents claim that one of the main things that motivate them to go to work each day is the relationship they have with their colleagues. These relationships will have a large impact on whether or not the students pursue a career in the industry after graduation.

Managers

While respondents seem to be happy with their relationships with co-workers, this does not appear to be the case when it comes to relationships with their managers, as almost two-thirds of the respondents claim that good relationships did not exist between managers and staff in the industry. More than half of the respondents believed that managers did not act in a fair manner when dealing with staff, and they did not reward staff for doing a good job, while just under half declared that managers do not act respectfully towards employees and they did not put great effort into ensuring employees were satisfied with their jobs. When assessing their manager's level of education, more than half of the respondents state that most managers do not have an academic background in tourism or hospitality, while almost two-thirds state that managers are jealous of graduates with academic qualifications.

This study also found that respondents believe that managers within the tourism and hospitality industry do not empower their employees, with more than half the respondents claiming that managers do not delegate authority in order for employees to perform their jobs in a more effective way, and that managers do not ensure employees participate in decisions affecting their jobs. There has been much written about the importance of empowerment in ensuring a healthy and productive workplace. In recent years, scholars such as Donavan (1994), Lashley (1995) and Chow *et al.* (2006) have written about the benefits to hospitality organizations of empowering employees. Jones and Davies (1991) claim that the idea of empowering employees is to encourage them to be responsible for their own performance and its development. Ripley and Ripley (1993) believe that empowerment will also encourage staff to best utilize their skills and strive to increase their skill set.

When analysing comments made on the blog there were many other responses relating to the poor treatment of staff by managers. Some of these issues included respondents being suspended for taking time off while they were sick, managers constantly screaming at staff leaving them feeling embarrassed and unappreciated, and respondents feeling discriminated against by their manager who was disrespectful and favoured employees of a similar ethnic background to their own. Many other respondents also reflected on their experience with their managers. These included respondents feeling as though they were being undermined by management, managers not trusting employee's judgement to make decisions, managers providing preferential treatment to their favourite staff and management not communicating with staff. One respondent claimed:

> I hated being a supervisor simply for the fact that my manager seemed to be out to get me. She made the rest of my time working there hell. She didn't care much for the staff, had her favourites (who somehow managed to get Christmas off), and preached about how she wanted to help us, yet did nothing.

In contrast to the other findings relating to managers, one area respondents are happy with is the level of vocational training offered by managers. Another area students responding to the blog were happy with managers centred on the rewards offered by their employers.

A number of comments were made in this respect including 'I have added incentives in use of the facilities and meals', 'The hotel really looks after us, giving us free meals and washing our uniforms at the end of every shift', 'Free coffee whenever I wanted and I could take home bags of coffee and boxes of tea once a week if I chose to' and 'The manager made the workplace fun and he would bring in lollies for staff to share'.

Commitment to the industry

The dimension dealing with respondent's commitment to the industry is particularly interesting as it explores the likelihood of students to pursue a career in the industry. From the results gathered in this study, it is difficult to argue that the majority of the respondents are committed to a career in the industry. One of the major findings from this dimension is the fact that almost half the respondents (44.6%) claim that the disadvantages of working in the industry outweigh the advantages, with only one-third claiming that the positives outweigh the negatives.

Other responses to the commitment to industry dimension include 41.4% of the respondents claiming that they are unhappy to have chosen tourism or hospitality as a vocation path, and 37.7% stating that it was a big mistake to choose the tourism and hospitality industry as a career path. Almost one-third of the respondents would not want their child studying or working in the industry, would not recommend a job in the industry to their friends and relatives and claim that they would only work in high-paid jobs in the industry.

The most disturbing findings from this dimension are that one-third (33.3%) of all the respondents claim that they will definitely not work in the industry after graduation. Also, more than half (58.3%) of the respondents claim that they are considering working in other industries with just 18.3% of the respondents claiming that they are not planning to work in any other industry. Finally, 41.7% of the respondents see their professional careers in other industries, while only 36.7% of the respondents see their professional career in the tourism and hospitality industry.

Summary

A number of interesting results have been noted in this study of Generation-Y students undertaking tertiary study in the hospitality and tourism sector. The main findings concur with those of Barron and Maxwell (1993), Getz (1994), Kusluvan and Kusluvan (2000) and Pavesic and Brymer (1990) who all found that having direct experience working in the tourism and hospitality industry may cause students to acquire negative views towards pursuing a career in the industry. An alarming finding is that overall more than one-third of the respondents claim that they will not work in the tourism and hospitality industry after graduation. Even more alarming is that a staggering 42.4% of the respondents with work experience claimed that they would not pursue a career in the industry, with almost all (92.6%) citing the experience of working in the industry as the main reason for this decision. This clearly shows that working in the industry does have a major negative impact on respondents' intentions to pursue careers in the industry.

Since the late 1990s, the growth of employment opportunities in the tourism and hospitality industry in Australia and around the world has been widely reported. If we take the standpoint that students should be encouraged to stay within their trained industry, these findings suggest that industry and educators must work together to solve employment shortfalls by recruiting and retaining qualified graduates. This highlights the need for the industry to adopt tactics and strategies aimed at ensuring that potential employees, i.e. Generation-Y employees, are not leaving the industry or even failing to enter the industry upon graduation. It is clear that there are a number of areas, particularly pay, promotional opportunities and the relationship between respondents and their managers, that the industry must work on to ensure students are receiving positive experiences while they work during their degree. Unless the industry can offer higher wages and improve career paths for its graduating students, the industry will continue to lose these highly skilled and trained employees. It is not being argued that resolving the issues related to salary levels, relationships with managers and career paths are the universal remedy to solve this problem; working hours and job security are also seen as vital elements in ensuring student/graduate satisfaction with the industry. Davidson and Timo (2006) point out that the dilemma facing the industry is that skilled employees are keen to advance. This study has found that Generation-Y employees are also eager for rapid career advancement. Traditionally the tourism and hospitality industry has had limited internal career opportunities, which imposes a ceiling on career growth and is one of the major factors affecting staff exit behaviour.

Similar to the findings of Martin (2005), this study has found that employers need to modify their training and career paths for this new generation of employees. These career structures need to be more clearly defined and Generation-Y employees need to be educated on the paths and training available to them and the time it will take to progress up the ladder. If tourism and hospitality employers do not focus on these issues and try to gain a better understanding of the characteristics displayed by the Generation-Y employee, they will continue to lose these highly motivated and highly skilled employees.

References

Airey, D. and Frontistis, A. (1997) Attitudes to careers in tourism: an Anglo-Greek comparison. *Tourism Management* 18(3), 149–158.

Australian Bureau of Statistics (2006) *Australian Labour Market Statistics* (No. 6105.0). ABS, Canberra.

Barron, P. and Maxwell, G. (1993) Hospitality management student's views of the hospitality industry. *International Journal of Contemporary Hospitality Management* 5(5), V–VIII.

Barron, P., Maxwell, G., Broadbridge, A. and Ogden, S. (2007) Careers in hospitality management: Generation Y's experiences and perceptions. *Journal of Hospitality and Tourism Management* 14(2), 119–128.

Baum, T. (2006) *Human Resource Management for Tourism, Hospitality and Leisure: An International Perspective.* Thomson Learning, London.

Beebe, T.J., Harrison, P.A., Anderson, R.E., Fulkerson, J.A. and Mika, T. (1997) Computerized school surveys. Design and development issues. *Social Science Computer Review* 15(2), 159–169.

Bettencourt, L.A. and Brown, S.W. (1997) Contact employees: relationships among workplace fairness, job satisfaction and prosocial behaviours. *Journal of Retailing* 73(1), 39–61.

Brien, A. (2004) Do I want a job in hospitality? Only till I get a real job! In: Smith, K.A. and Schott, C. (eds) *Proceedings of the New Zealand Tourism and Hospitality Research Conference.* Wellington, New Zealand.

Chow, I.H., Lob, W., Sha, Z. and Hong, J. (2006) The impact of developmental experience, empowerment, and organizational support on catering service staff performance. *International Journal of Hospitality Management* 25(3), 478–495.

Davidson, M. and Timo, N. (2006) *Report on Labour Turnover and Transaction Costs in the Australian Hotel Industry: A Preliminary Survey.* Tourism and Transport Forum/Sustainable Tourism Cooperative Research Centre.

Deery, M. and Shaw, R. (1999) An investigation of the relationship between employee turnover and organisational culture. *Journal of Hospitality and Tourism Research* 23(4), 387–400.

Doherty, L., Guerrier, Y., Jamieson, S., Lashley, C. and Lockwood, A. (2001) *Getting Ahead: Graduate Careers in Hospitality Management.* CHME/HEFCE, London.

Donavan, M. (1994) The empowerment plan. *Journal for Quality and Participation* 17(4), 12–14.

Ewins, R. (2005) Who are you? Weblogs and academic identity. *E–Learning* 2(4), 368–377.

Ferris, G.R., Berkson, H.M. and Harris, M.M. (2002) The recruitment interview process persuasion and organization promotion in competitive labour markets. *Human Resource Management Review* 12, 359–375.

Freeland, B. (2000) *Demands of Training: Australian Tourism and Hospitality.* National Centre for Vocational Education Research, Adelaide, Australia.

Getz, D. (1994) Students' work experiences, perceptions and attitudes towards careers in hospitality and tourism: a longitudinal case study in Spey Valley, Scotland. *International Journal of Hospitality Management* 13(1), 25–37.

Heskett, J.L., Jones, T.O., Loveman, G.W., Sasser, Jr., W.E. and Schlesinger, L.A. (1994) Putting the service-profit chain to work. *Harvard Business Review* 72(March/April), 164–174.

Hinkin, T.R. and Tracey, J.B. (2000) The cost of turnover. *Cornell Hotel and Restaurant Administration Quarterly* 43(1), 14–21.

Jenkins, A.K. (2001) Making a career of it? Hospitality students' future perspectives: an Anglo-Dutch study. *International Journal of Contemporary Hospitality Management* 13(1), 13–20.

Jones, P. and Davies, A. (1991) Empowerment: a study of general managers of four star hotel properties in the UK. *International Journal of Hospitality Management* 10(3), 211–217.

Kusluvan, S. and Kusluvan, Z. (2000) Perceptions and attitudes of undergraduate tourism students towards working in the tourism industry in Turkey. *Tourism Management* 21, 251–269.

Kyriacou, C. and Coulthard, M. (2000) Undergraduates' views of teaching as a career choice. *Journal of Education for Teaching* 26(2), 117–126.

Lashley, C. (1995) Towards an understanding of employee empowerment in hospitality services. *International Journal of Contemporary Hospitality Management* 7(1), 27–32.

Lloyd, S. (2005) Young, smart and hard to find. *Business Review Weekly,* 29 September.

Martin, C. (2005) From high maintenance to high productivity: what managers need to know about Generation Y. *Industrial and Commercial Training* 37(1), 39–44.

Morton, D.L. (2002) Targeting Generation Y. *Public Relations Quarterly* 47(2), 46–48.

National Tourism Investment Strategy Consultative Group (2006) Chapter 10: workforce and training. In: Department of Industry, Tourism and Resources. *National Tourism Investment Strategy: Investing for Our Future.* Canberra, Australia, pp. 63–70.

Oliver, D. (2006) An expectation of continued success: the work attitudes of Generation Y. *Labour and Industry* 17(1), 61–84.

Pavesic, D.V. and Brymer, R.A. (1990) Job satisfaction: what's happening to the young managers. *Cornell Hotel and Restaurant Administration Quarterly* 31(1), 90–96.

Purcell, K. and Quinn, J. (1996) Exploring the education – employment equation in hospitality management: a comparison of graduates and HNDs. *International Journal of Hospitality Management* 15(1), 51–68.

Ripley, R.E. and Ripley, M.J. (1993) Empowering management in innovative organizations in the 1990s. *Empowerment in Organizations* 1(1).

Ross, G.F. (1994) What do Australian school leavers want of the industry? *Tourism Management* 15(1), 62–66.

Service Skills Victoria (2005) *Service Skills Victoria's Response to Victoria's Tourism and Events Industry Discussion Paper*. Melbourne, Australia.

Sheafor, B.W., Horejsi, C.R. and Horejsi, G.A. (2000) *Techniques and Guidelines for Social Work Practice*, 5th edn. Allyn and Bacon, Boston, Massachusetts.

Sills, S.J. and Song, C. (2002) Innovations in survey research: an application of Web surveys. *Social Science Computer Review* 20, 22–30.

Zacerelli, H.E. (1985) Is the hospitality/food service industry turning its employees on or off? *International Journal of Hospitality Management* 4, 123–124.

13 Generation Y and Work in Tourism and Hospitality: Problem? What Problem?

Grant Cairncross and Jeremy Buultjens
Southern Cross University

Introduction

Generation-Y employees currently make up almost 20% of the Australian workforce, a figure which will become increasingly larger as more of them enter the workforce (Australian Center for Retail Studies, 2007). The growing importance of this generation, in terms of the size of the workforce, makes it essential that businesses are able to fully utilize its skills and attributes. The full utilization of Generation Y's skills requires knowledge about its work traits as well as how businesses can effectively utilize its skills.

There are various reports that suggest that, despite their importance to the workforce, the supposed characteristics of Generation-Y employees are often seen as problematic by some employers. Despite being well educated, seekers of an intellectual challenge and being keen to make a difference, Generation Y is viewed negatively by some employers. This perception exists because Generation Y is also seen as lacking deference for authority and as having a desire for immediate satisfaction. This negative view of the cohort could have substantial ramifications for its utilization in the workforce.

This chapter reports on the results from focus groups and interviews that examined tourism and hospitality employers' views of Generation-Y employees and their attempts to

engage and motivate these employees. The focus groups of employers were carried out in Coffs Harbour, Cairns, and Port Douglas in 2006 and a series of interviews was also carried out with human resource (HR) managers in south-east Queensland and Sydney in 2007 and 2008.

The chapter begins by providing an overview of Generation Y and its characteristics. The next section explores the potential of Generation Y as employees in hospitality and tourism. This is followed by the methods section, results and the conclusion to the chapter.

Generation Y, Pop Culture and Work

The members of Generation Y are often the children of the Baby Boomers – those born between 1946 and 1964. Despite staying at home longer and being children of Baby Boomers, Generation Y is said to be more likely to share some of its grandparents' (the Builders Generation) character traits rather than those of its parents (AMP-NATSEM, 2007). The character traits of Generation Y, the Baby Boomers and Builders Generation are set out in Chapter 2. Eisner (2005, p. 6) suggests Generation Y possesses a strong sense of morality, is patriotic, is willing to fight for freedom, values home and family, and is sociable. Additionally, it is said to be extremely brand conscious and brand loyal (Goldgehn, 2004 p. 24); although this latter finding is contested by McCrindle Research, who found it has little brand loyalty (2005). Overall, it is said Generation Y is disposed to being polite, has a generally positive attitude, is inquisitive, energetic and is generally respectful of its parents and grandparents, although its attitude to employers depends on a number of aspects to be analysed later (Goldgehn, 2004; Eisner, 2005). Generation Y also respects different lifestyles, cultures, ethnic groupings and sexuality because of a lifetime immersed in diversity via school, the workplace and popular culture (Bell and Narz, 2007). Generation Y:

> has developed a strong work ethic, with nearly one half of Generation-Y students holding down a job and seven out of every 10 Generation-Y students studying part-time while engaged in full-time work.
>
> (AMP-NATSEM, 2007, p. 1)

Another trait of Generation Y is that it is the most technically knowledgeable cohort in history. A 2003 study found Generation Y devours the equivalent of 31 h of media through multiple mediums within a 24 h period (Weiss, 2003). In addition, an American study (Reynol and Mastrodicasa, 2007) of 7705 American university students indicated:

- Ninety-seven per cent own a computer.
- Ninety-four per cent own a cell phone.
- Seventy-six per cent use instant messaging (IM).
- Fifteen per cent of IM users are logged on 24 h a day/7 days a week.
- Thirty-four per cent use websites as their primary source of news.
- Twenty-eight per cent own a blog and 44% read blogs.
- Forty-nine per cent download music using peer-to-peer file sharing.
- Seventy-five per cent of students have a Facebook account.
- Ninety per cent of college students have a MySpace account and almost all teenagers over the age of 16 have one as well.
- Sixty per cent own some type of expensive portable music and/or video device, such as an iPod.

Australia's Generation Y has very similar usage statistics to those in the American study.

A result of this high level of technology consumption is that Generation Y is comfortable with a high degree of multitasking, having grown up organizing mobile phones, while surfing the Internet and listening to their iPod at the same time. Generation Y is also well read when it comes to new technology and the terminology that surrounds it (Sheahan, 2005). As a result of the relationship between Generation Y and technology, members are used to quick results and would not consider dedicating years developing their career. This generation is not satisfied with starting at the bottom and undertaking such tasks as getting the photocopying or running similar 'menial tasks'. It wants immediate challenges, and with it acknowledgment and respect (Hays Recruitment, 2007).

In addition to being technologically savvy, Generation Y is considered to be one of the most educated and ethnically diverse generations with the highest level of disposable income of any previous generation at the same age. Generation Y wants an intellectual challenge, needs to succeed, seeks those who will further its professional development, strives to make a difference, and wants to assess its own success (Eisner, 2005).

Clearly there are many qualities of Generation Y discussed above that can be seen as strongly positive; however, there are also perceptions of negative work traits held by a surprisingly high number of employers. For example, in a study of 240 Australian business managers, approximately 40% of managers stated Generation Y is awkward to deal with. Supporting this finding, Casben (2007) found 70% of employers in his study were dissatisfied with their Generation-Y employees' performance. A high level of employer dissatisfaction is associated particularly with the poor communication skills of Generation Y, such as inferior spelling and grammar. Another cause of dissatisfaction among employers is that Generation Y does not understand what suitable corporate behaviour is. Approximately 37% of employers complained that Generation Y lacks the professional and technical skills to do their job (Preston, 2007).

Another issue among some employers is the belief Generation Y has less respect for authority than previous generations (Casben, 2007). New technologies and pop cultures are said to have made them impatient with the 'old ways'. Generation Y's higher levels of education and their familiarity with new technology and information may result in them readily questioning how things are done. In addition, Generation-Y workers are perceived as lacking in practical experience, yet are perceived to be overconfident and have unrealistic expectations about their salary. A majority of Generation-Y workers also expect travel opportunities, further training and social events as part of their employment parcels. Employers also believe if they do not like their pay, the work conditions or their managers they will move to another job. Apparently, 1 year in a job is seen to be a long commitment by many in Generation Y (*The Daily Telegraph*, 2007). Casben (2007) suggests some employers believe Generation Y is more challenging than previous generations. Its ability to access instant information via Google, to purchase via eBay and to instantaneously tell the world all about themselves via MySpace has produced an 'immediate gratification generation' (Casben, 2007). Patterson (2007, p. 21) concurs with this appraisal of Generation Y arguing members 'think email is snail mail and want to be chief executive of the company by 25, all in no more than 35 hours a week'.

These alleged qualities of Generation-Y members has resulted in many managers and employers, mostly Baby Boomers, finding them a 'headache' because they do not react to a 'do as you are told' management style (AMP-NATSEM, 2007). In this regard they are said to be the exact opposite of Baby Boomers, in that they appreciate a relaxed, creative, lifestyle-focused workplace (Sheahan, 2005).

The frictions between Baby Boomer managers and Generation Y employees have significant inferences for the workforce in Australia. Generation Y already provides 2.8 million workers for the Australian workforce; compared to the 2.7 million Baby Boomers currently employed (AMP-NATSEM, 2007). These numbers, and the fact that an increasingly larger number of Generation Y will be entering the labour market in the future, suggest a better understanding of how to manage and motivate this generation is needed. Unless Australian managers can understand how to successfully use Generation Y's strengths, workforce productivity is not going to increase in the future.

To ensure productivity among Generation Y, managers need an appreciation of the factors that motivate it. For example, 'To Generation Y, an organisation's reputation or brand, a meaningful profession and a belief in what the company stands for are important elements in their decision to work for an organisation' (Hays Recruitment, 2007, p. 1). A number of organizations have shown that they are aware of this and that they need to become attractive in order to harness Generation Y's strengths. For example, Price-Waterhouse Coopers, St George Bank, Lion Nathan, Sportsgirl, Panasonic, Fairfax, Ford Australia and Harvey World Travel are among a number of organizations who have decided to strategically connect with Generation Y (Sheahan, 2005). These companies have changed their work culture in an attempt to appeal to Generation Y as employees. Lion Nathan, for example, encourage their Generation-Y employees to think of themselves as potential 'leaders'. The word 'leader' is always used instead of manager, and recruitment and training arrangements are put in place so that 'their leaders are equipped with coaching skills, because this is seen as the true way to engage and develop talent in Generation Y' (Sheahan, 2005, p. 215).

Ford Australia is another company that believes that they have paid attention to Generation Y's needs. Ford attributes its high retention rate among its Generation-Y employees to the real work–life balance programmes it offers, making Generation Y's social nature part of the way it does work, while offering an exceptional internal advancement agenda (Sheahan, 2005).

Companies need to be cognizant that their reputation and standing is an important consideration for Generation-Y employees. Hays Recruitment (2007, p. 1) has found that:

> 72% of Generation Y will not apply for a role with an organization if they do not believe in what it stands for. Likewise, nine out of ten Generation Y candidates view the reputation or brand of an organisation as important in their decision to work for a company.

It also appears that managers who are accessible, knowledgeable, ethical, fair and who can be respected are also appreciated by Generation Y (Eisner, 2005). Eisner (2005) also found Generation Y was dismissive of managers who were unable to use technology, did not offer prospects and incentives for achieving high performance, did not provide leadership, and who were unable to think critically and imaginatively.

The aforementioned organizations, in an attempt to attract and retain Generation-Y workers have fostered their talents and expectations over time. They have realized this generation is team- and goal-oriented and can be involved in 'social and community activities' with which an organization is associated (Sheahan, 2005). The AMP-NATSEM survey found Generation-Y workers 'expect social events (68%), further education and training (66%) and travel opportunities (59%) in their employment packages. Many also expected cash bonuses (42%), health insurance (29%) and rostered days off (27%)' (Patterson, 2007, p. 24).

Other research indicates that the provision of benefits is influential for Generation Y. For example, Hays Recruitment (2007, p. 2) found that:

> 42 per cent of Generation-Y respondents said they would not accept a job it if did not provide any perks while 37 per cent would not accept a job if it did not provide parking. In comparison, a lack of benefits would not hold the remainder of the workforce back from accepting a role.

Another feature of Generation-Y members is that they also want 'workmates' or friends at work, and not 'colleagues'. In this regard they are quite communitarian and collectivist, albeit inadvertently. They want to be part of a successful group and team and getting on with their co-workers is very important to them. Industries like tourism and hospitality, that have a high degree of seasonality and are dominated by small businesses, may be problematic for Generation Y, given their liking for community at work. Something that counteracts this is that they are also highly adjustable and are keen on geographical mobility.

Generation Y and Tourism and Hospitality Employment

Generation Y makes up a large proportion of those currently working in the tourism and hospitality industry in Australia. Approximately 30% of the sector's employees are aged between 15 and 24 years of age; the Australian industry average is 22%. Nearly half (45%) of the 15–24 years old in the tourism and hospitality industry are employed as casuals (Australian Bureau of Statistics, 2005, p. 1).

In addition to a young workforce, the tourism and hospitality industry is characterized by a dual work environment. Despite having a somewhat glamorous image involving a high degree of face-to-face personal contact, work in the industry has traditionally been seen as associated with servility (Guerrier, 1999). The industry has been described as having an 'upstairs/downstairs master/servant culture' (Baum, 1995, p. 122). Additionally, the industry can also be 'a picture of drudgery with low pay, antisocial conditions, lack of job security, poor treatment from employers, and contempt from customers despite a very upbeat perspective, which stresses challenge, opportunity, variety, mobility and a strong people dimension' (Baum, 1995, p. 122). An upshot of these negative features of work in the industry has been a high level of labour turnover. This has resulted in the acquiescence of 'a high turnover culture' in the industry, where staff retention has not been taken as seriously as in other industries and sectors (House of Representatives, 2007).

Another feature of Australian tourism and hospitality is that there is very little academic literature pertaining to the industry's strategies for recruiting, retaining and managing Generation Y. The existing literature in terms of the broader tourism and hospitality employment relations notes the industry has been 'tradition-bound'. In addition, management appears to be particularly slow to implement new ideas when it comes to managing staff, a large number of whom are now Generation Y (Buultjens and Cairncross, 2001; Timo and Davidson, 2005; House of Representatives, 2007). The industry appears to be unproductive in dealing with a generation that is 'mature, resilient, fast learners, techno-savvy, practical, enterprising and manipulative' but who also get bored quickly because 'they can be a little too short-term focused' (Sheahan, 2005, pp. 16–17).

The traditional nature of the tourism and hospitality industry has meant largely, although not wholly, the industry has failed to analyse how the work environment needs to change in order to support and maintain brand image, cater for a new customer base in Generation Y itself, yet stimulate a generation and lives by a pop culture ethos that values being smart, connected 24/7, and 'achieving now' (Eisner, 2005, p. 9). Additionally, the industry has found it hard to come to grips with a generation which 'tends to ignore traditional media and advertising channels, plays video games and watches DVDs rather than listed TV programming' (Eisner, 2005, p. 9). This is a generation with more respect for ability and getting things done rather than rank, and which relates job satisfaction to a positive work atmosphere and an expectation of ongoing workplace training and learning (Eisner, 2005). In many ways Australia's tourism and hospitality industry has been slow to offer recognized portable training, while the 'upstairs/downstairs' attitude has not always led to talent being the main reason for promotion (House of Representatives, 2007).

For the tourism and hospitality industry, just like many other industries, Generation Y is a challenge because the technology, mass marketing, political times, and pop culture in which today's youth have grown up has ensured they are significantly different to previous youth cultures. As a result, it has been argued Generation Y will become productive, if a workplace offers multitasking and variety, free access to co-workers, a voice in work, project-centred work and regular company information through information technology (Eisner, 2005). If an organization does this then its Generation-Y employees are likely to be productive.

Special processes and systems tailored to Generation Y's sense of comradeship and office spaces that help promote an exchange of ideas should be encouraged (Sheahan, 2005). Digital training systems are readily accessed by this generation and on-site leadership academies and formal mentoring programmes are also likely to provide effective outcomes for an organization. Additionally, some clear indication that an organization is socially aware and active is considered to be important, particularly in regard to recruiting Generation Y (Eisner, 2005; Sheahan, 2005). These features suggest that different ways of recruitment and selection need to replace the more traditional methods. Career day seminars and stories about people and their success are likely to be more successful in recruitment rather than just using statistics (Eisner, 2005). The implementation of these strategies will not only help recruit and retain Generation-Y employees but, importantly, they can be used to successively address the needs of Generation-Y customers.

Methodology

A series of focus groups and individual interviews involving tourism and hospitality managers were used to examine employee relations in tourism attractions, organized tours, restaurants, cafes and hotels and resorts located between Sydney, New South Wales in the south and Cairns/Port Douglas, Queensland in the north.

The first part of the study consisted of focus groups conducted in mid- to late 2005, in Coffs Harbour, New South Wales and Cairns and Port Douglas in far north Queensland. In this study, 30 managers from attractions, tour companies, restaurants and cafes, hotels and resorts participated in seven focus groups. The managers were identified by the regional tourism organizations and letters were sent out to potential participants inviting them to attend the focus groups.

Three sessions were conducted in the Cairns–Port Douglas region and four in Coffs Harbour, New South Wales. In total, 30 organizations participated in the focus group sessions. Of these, five of the organizations were tour operators and/or attractions, seven were cafes and restaurants while the remaining 18 were hotels or resorts. The five tour operators and four of the cafes and restaurants were small businesses, employing fewer than 20 people. The resorts employed between 50 and 320 people.

The second part of the study, the face-to-face interviews, was undertaken with the HR managers from 17 four-, four-and-a-half-, and five-star hotel and resort chains during the first part of 2007. Follow-up phone interviews were undertaken in 2008. These hotels and resorts were from various geographical locations from near Rockhampton, Queensland in the north to Sydney in the south. The largest organization employed almost 600 people while the smallest had 15 employees. The questions to be used in face-to-face interviews together with a covering letter were then sent by mail or e-mail to the managers who had indicated a willingness to participate in the research. The minimum proportion of employees aged 25 and under was 26% and the maximum amount was 42%.

Synopsis of Results

A number of themes emerged from the focus groups and interviews. Managers believed overwhelmingly the most important requirement for employees in tourism and hospitality was 'people skills' or customer service skills. Employees needed to be well presented and have the confidence to deal with people in a fitting way. It was felt that while technical skills required by employees could be taught, especially 'on the job', people skills were very much more difficult to teach.

The high labour turnover level in the industry was seen as a critical matter by most managers and at the time of the research the problem was exacerbated by the tight labour market. There was a strong feeling that there was a need to change the perception of employment in the industry. A 'career culture', with improved career progression, had to be created to replace the perception of low pay, long hours and boring work. It was felt that many employees, especially the young, saw employment in the industry as an interim measure before getting a 'real' job.

There was also an insight that there was a lack of formal training throughout the sector and this needed to be addressed in order to overcome labour issues in it. In addition, there was also a feeling among managers that there were gaps in training offered by educational institutions, particularly in the area of business and economics. It was also suggested many people who received industry training were inappropriate for the industry. Managers felt

that the unemployed were undertaking training 'often just to get the dole'.

Another particularly strong theme to emerge was in relation to Generation Y employees and their 'work ethic'. A number of employers suggested a number of young employees were impulsive and were unprepared to go through a learning and maturation process and that they wanted promotion straight away. These findings are discussed in greater detail in the next section.

Generation-Y Employees

Twenty-nine of the 30 managers involved in the focus groups indicated they had some issues or problems with Generation-Y employees. Additionally, 13 of the 17 HR managers interviewed in 2006 and 2007 had similar views on Generation-Y employees. These results would seem to support the broader multi-industry view on Generation Y presented by Preston (2007).

Many of the managers explicitly referred to what they considered were Generation Y's reluctance to 'do the hard yards' before seeking promotion. The following statements characterize the opinions of many managers:

> Some of them think that you can come straight out of uni [university] and go straight into a management position. It doesn't work like that.
> (Hotel manager, mid-north coast New South Wales, 2006)

> They don't seem to want to stand still. Trying to keep them focused is the hardest thing. They don't seem to be willing to do what has traditionally been required in a job.
> (Restaurant owner, far north Queensland, 2006)

> They are a hard market. They want everything now but they don't want to work hard for it.
> (HR manager, four-star hotel, south-east Queensland, 2007)

Additionally, a number of the managers interviewed also said they felt Generation Y had naive expectations when it came to promotion and remuneration.

> I told a new staff member who was a Generation-Y graduate not to come to me in 12 months and ask for fifty grand a year because I told her she wasn't going to get it.

So she waited 13 months and then came and asked me for it!

(HR manager, five-star hotel, Sydney, 2007)

Despite most managers having a negative view of Generation-Y employees, four managers were very positive in that they believed that this generation had a number of traits that could be targeted for recruitment and retention and that, if nurtured, could also provide a sustainable competitive advantage. In these four hotels and resorts, employees who were aged 25 years or under constituted between 32 and 45% of their workforce.

Appealing to Generation Y

Despite the managers' generally negative perceptions of Generation-Y employees, most were utilizing strategies that would accommodate this generation. For example, when the managers who were interviewed in 2007 were asked what type of recruitment tools they used, they all stressed the importance they placed on the Internet and the Intranet, understanding that Generation Y is attracted to modern technology. All the hotels and resorts used http://www.seek.com.au, while another eight utilized http://www.mycareer.com.au. In addition, many had spent a lot of time upgrading their own websites so that they were 'attractive and user friendly to Generation Y' (HR manager, five-star hotel, Sydney, 2007). The reasons for the widespread use of the Internet as a recruitment mechanism is summarized by this statement from an HR manager at a four-and-a-half-star hotel in southeast Queensland.

It's our primary tool...both via seek.com and our own homepage, which we set up about 18 months ago. We find we get a lot of younger applicants that way – they [employees] use the internet in the first instance. We get about 60 per cent through our own site, 30 per cent through seek.com and the rest through the others.

In discussing the retention of employees in the industry and strategies that could address the issue, a majority of managers, especially those from larger workplaces, saw training as important to Generation-Y employees. This view

existed despite the wide disparity in the types of formal and informal training offered by the organizations.

Interestingly it was the 'outriders,' or the four organizations that saw Generation-Y employees in a positive light, who offered more in the way of formal transferable training. These four managers from large hotels and resorts, where Generation Y accounted for between 40 and 60% of all staff, had ensured that their training strategies were interactive, portable and could be used and delivered as much as possible via the Internet.

The broad range of employment strategies adopted by these four organizations, who could be considered 'innovators', all took account of the fact that Generation Y is strongly influenced by new information technology and popular culture. The managers' attitude to Generation Y from these four innovative hotels and resorts is summarized by the following comment:

They are the first IT generation and they are switched-on and keen, wanting to be friends with everyone at work and wanting to get ahead fast and achieve. So we have to adjust our recruitment and retention as a part of that. So I've become an instant expert on all things Generation Y. They see training as being very important; it shows to them that you care.

(HR manager, five-star hotel, Sydney, 2007)

Broadly speaking, the four innovators indicated that they had employment strategies focusing on technology, socializing at work, training, social activism and reward and recognition. Their stratagems in relation to each of these themes are now considered.

Technology

The literature suggests Generation Y is the most technologically literate generation in history and enters the workforce with command of a wide variety of information technologies. It often has technological abilities way ahead of the information technology already being used in the workplace (Reynol and Mastrodicasa, 2007). The test for organizations is to utilize the technological skills of their young employees. In the focus-group discussions and interviews it was clear, as stated previously, that a few of the organizations were better in this area than most of the others. The employers who saw this as an opportunity had gone further in using the Internet as a recruitment instrument than the majority of employers. In these cases, the organizations constantly updated their websites and surveyed Generation Y and prospective staff to ensure their sites were user-friendly and attractive. For example, one hotel chain had personalized their websites:

> . . . so prospective employees from Hotel Schools and Universities can see photos of their graduates who have got jobs with us. We find they'll relate to the personal angle far better than dry sums and statistics.
> (HR manager, Sydney, 2007)

> We offer Facebook time now instead of tea and coffee breaks. We find our younger staff appreciate it more than old terms they don't relate to.
> (HR manager, Sydney, 2008)

In addition, all four innovators had staff performing job rotation to various degrees so they could use their technology skills broadly. The four organizations also arranged for staff newsletters to be sent out in hardcopy as well as electronically via staff Intranet thereby catering to the communication abilities of Generation Y in the best possible way.

Socializing at work

As discussed earlier, teamwork, special spaces, processes and systems tailored to Generation Y's sense of comradeship help encourage an exchange of ideas and increase productivity. Sheehan (2005) argues these characteristics should be encouraged in the workplace. The four hotels and resorts who looked on Generation Y's different attitude to work as a positive had grasped this concept eagerly. Teamwork was the norm in all four organizations. In addition, one hotel manager, where 60% of the workforce consisted of Generation-Y employees, understood music was a crucial part of Generation Y's background and make-up and that it could be could be used to obtain happier and more productive employees. The manager stated:

> We spent a lot of time and effort putting piped music into what we call the heart of the hotel, those areas where only staff goes. We have found that piping radio and modern music in has improved their demeanour out of sight. We have an eclectic mix – Nova, Triple M, and Triple J. They are happier. We have bright colours in those areas as well. We are finalizing a new staff canteen. Like McDonalds it will have a minimalist feel. For the first twelve months it is $2.50 a meal then $3.50 a meal thereafter. We have an internet portal in it.
> (HR manager, five-star hotel, Sydney, 2007)

All four innovator hotels and resorts had active social clubs run by volunteers, many of them Generation Y. The activities undertaken in the social clubs were wide-ranging:

> We have a strong social club. Movie nights, canoeing, ten pin bowling, climbing the bridge. Belgian beer restaurant nights. We are even talking about sky-diving. So the sky's the limit – literally!
> (HR manager, five-star hotel, Sydney, 2007)

> We have reef trips and rainforest walks. Diving, sailing, movie nights and restaurant nights as well.
> (HR manager, five-star resort, far-north Queensland, 2006)

One hotel, in response to Generation Y's liking for fitness (AMP-NATSEM Report, 2007), had made a point of catering for this Generation Y characteristic:

> We have introduced an employee gymnasium. I think we are the only five-star hotel that has done that. It has a chill out area with bean bags and flat screen TVs. They can come in during their breaks or before or after work if they want.
> (HR manager, five-star hotel, Sydney, 2007)

In summary, it was evident the four innovative hotels and resorts had implemented approaches to recruiting, retaining and motivating Generation Y that assumed 'if you can't keep Generation Y entertained, you can't keep them' (Sheehan, 2005, p. 63).

Training

Training and development is the key for organizations in their attempts to attract and retain Generation Y. Training can also help members of Generation Y overcome their exaggerated sense of self-importance and impetuosity (Sheehan, 2005), since it helps them mature and learn what they need to do in order to earn promotion with an organization. The four innovator employers understood that members of Generation Y want to continually learn new skills and that it was important to provide an opportunity for them to utilize their old and new skills. Often ongoing learning and development was as simple as setting up an internal mentoring programme or networking sessions, or formal structured courses through external educational providers.

All four innovator organizations understood this and had introduced a series of wide-ranging formal and informal training programmes. Notably their training schemes were more varied in content than the training programmes of the majority of other participating organizations. The importance of ongoing training among innovator managers is indicated by the following comments:

> You've got to keep them stimulated. And that is where training is important. Training keeps them keen and it keeps them around for longer too. It's a great retention tool.
> (HR manager, five-star hotel, Sydney, 2007)

> We realize training is important for our staff, particularly the younger ones. They respond to it well. It's great for motivation.
> (HR manager, five-star resort, south-east Queensland, 2007)

Social activism

Eisner (2005) and Sheehan (2005) argue that Generation Y wants to see some clear sign that an organization is also socially aware and active. One hotel in particular had grasped this concept and was using a pioneering approach in this area:

> We have a hotel environment and social issues team made up of staff volunteers. They have made sure all the light bulbs are eco-friendly. They have also gone further. We have sponsored three staff members from poor families from our hotel in Fiji to work and to play rugby here for a year. When we tell potential

employees about this we get a positive reaction. I've had staff tell me that the environment and social issues team is one of the reasons they came to work for us.
> (HR manager, five-star resort, south-east Queensland, 2007)

Reward and recognition

A number of commentators have noted that employers need to ensure entry-level employees can see there are steps in place to enable them to progress up the career ladder. If jobs are seen as a 'dead end', then organizations will not retain their staff (Eisner, 2005; Sheahan, 2005; Bell and Narz, 2007). These analysts also stress rewards need to be open and provided reasonably frequently where they are deserved. Companies adopting a 'sacrifice now for reward later' policy will suffer, as 'Generation Y won't buy that' (Sheehan, 2005, p. 36). All four managers from the innovator organizations stressed they had widened the type of rewards they provided and, in addition, managers were encouraged to give verbal praise on a frequent basis. Additionally, more novel forms of fiscal reward had also been implemented.

> We have a reward system called cashiers which they can cash in for movie tickets, birthday presents, and that sort of thing. It's very popular. We also have associates of the quarter. We also have team awards. The team award of the year is worth a thousand dollars. They can spend that as they want as a team or split it up among them, they can spend it anywhere in town.
> (HR manager, five-star hotel, Sydney, 2007)

All four innovator employers offered performance assessments at least twice a year, ensured any identified training was performed and any encouragement and rewards were reinforced as part of the process. All four employers paid many of their staff above award wages and shunned individual employment agreements such as Australian Workplace Agreements (AWAs), before they became illegal with the election of the Federal Labor Government, in preference for awards (three) or certified agreements (one). All stated awards and certified agreements tended to be more comfortably accepted by Generation-Y employees. One HR manager stated:

> I use the fact we are on the award and that we pay penalty rates to destroy my competitors in the local labour market.
>
> (HR manager, five-star hotel, Sydney, 2007)

The hotel using certified agreements also offered more permanent employment for staff by reducing the number of casual employees in favour of a flexible part-time arrangement, where part-timers are offered 20 h a week minimum of work at different peak-demand times of the week. Included in the certified agreement was a pay-for-skill-attainment clause where employees got pay rises for achieving competency tests relating to their work. The HR manager said this system 'was very popular with our younger Generation-Y staff.'

Conclusions

Generation Y is the first generation to come to the workplace having mastered new technologies in school and at home. The information technology revolution has been referred to as the 'third industrial revolution' (Greenwood, 1997), but it is different to the previous industrial revolutions in that much of the technology has become available outside of the workplace prior to being accessible in the workplace. Previous generations of employees could only learn new technologies in the workplace, the information technology revolution, on the other hand, has gone beyond the boundaries of the workplace.

As a result, a techno-savvy Generation Y has arrived in the workplace, uniquely prepared like no other, expecting equipment that is up to date. If managers cannot master IT, show they are not competent in it, or are not good mentors, then they will not command the respect from Generation-Y employees. In the words of one manager interviewed in 2007, Generation Y members 'don't respect experience. They expect competency. It highlights some managers who are managers shouldn't be managers' (HR manager, five-star hotel, Sydney, 2007).

Organizations that strategically target their employment policies and practices to address areas of importance to Generation Y will attract and retain Generation-Y employees. Organizations need to provide access to modern IT, an enjoyable and social workplace, offer ongoing training and an awareness of social and ethical responsibility. In addition, they need to reward achievement through the regular use of fiscal and non-fiscal incentives. The four innovator organizations identified in this research had achieved below industry labour turnover rates in the 2007–2008 year with a median rate of 12%. This compares very favourably with an average industry turnover rate of 47% for top-end hotels and resorts (Tourism Transport Federation, 2006).

Admittedly the four innovators were large organizations with substantial resources applying their strategies to a chain of 23 hotels and resorts across Australia. For the smaller operators participating in this study, a number of the initiatives offered in the larger workplaces, such as gymnasiums and piped music, would be beyond their resources. Nevertheless, some of the initiatives implemented require few financial resources and are relatively easy to instigate. Initiatives such as the formation of social groups, the utilization of teamwork, the provision of non-fiscal rewards and Internet access during rest breaks are inexpensive. Yet the impact of such initiatives on morale and staff retention were described as emphatically positive by the managers from the innovative organizations and, as a result, will significantly reduce turnover and its many associated costs among Generation-Y employees.

The need for portable formal training recognition also needs to be strongly and urgently addressed at both a national industry and federal government level, not only because it helps with general staff retention and allows for career paths to be built, but also because it strongly appeals to Generation Y, a mobile generation that nevertheless rewards training with dedication when it is given. The need for a portable recognized national industry scheme has now been identified as an important feature of effective management in the industry (House of Representatives, 2007).

Generation-Y employees have not experienced recessionary economic times and the forces that buffeted the world economy in 2008. This may mean many employers may resort to labour-cutting strategies once again without thinking it is important to consider the initiatives used by the innovators analysed in this chapter. However, organizations that shed staff wantonly without considering part-time work and job-sharing, to name but two options, will find themselves rushing to find good people when the economic cycle turns, as it will.

The innovators have discovered they have benefited from lower staff turnover and higher staff morale from their initiatives addressing the needs of Generation-Y employees. These organizations have realized that Generation Y has moved from the information age to the entertainment age and expects to have fun at work where possible (Sheahan, 2005). This can mean happy staff, and happy staff usually translates into happy customers. Happy customers in turn will ensure word-of-mouth appraisal spreads about Australia's tourism and hospitality industry, and an important export earner will be in a better position to ride out some of the vagaries it needs to regularly confront in today's highly competitive globalized world.

As one human resource manager said 'a lot of employers see Generation Y as a problem. That's not the case here. Problem? What Problem? They are an opportunity' (HR manager, five-star hotel, Sydney, 2007).

References

AMP-NATSEM (2007) *Generation WhY?* Melbourne, Australia.

Australian Bureau of Statistics (2005) *Accommodation Services, Australia, 2003–04. 8695.0* ABS, Canberra.

Australian Center for Retail Studies (2007) *Cross Generational Workforce Report.* Monash University, Melbourne, Australia.

Baum, T. (1995) *Managing Human Resources in the European Tourism and Hospitality Industry: A Strategic Approach.* Thomson International Business Press, London.

Bell, N.S. and Narz, M. (2007) Meeting the challenges of age diversity in the workplace. *The CPA Journal* 77(2), 56–59.

Buultjens, J. and Cairncross, G. (2001) Ten years of enterprise bargaining and the hospitality sector. *Labour and Industry* 12(1), 27–41.

Casben, L. (2007) *Generation Y Disappoints Employers.* Australian Broadcasting Corporation, 8 August 2007.

Eisner, S.P. (2005) Managing Generation Y. *S.A.M. Advanced Management Journal* 70, 4–15.

Goldgehn, L.A. (2004) Generation who, what, Y?: what you need to know about Generation Y. *International Journal of Educational Advancement* 5(1), 24–34.

Greenwood, J. (1997) *The Third Industrial Revolution: Technology, Productivity, and Income Inequality.* The American Institute for Public Policy Research, La Vegne, Tennessee.

Guerrier, Y. (1999) *Organizational Behaviour in Hotels and Restaurants: An International Perspective.* Wiley, Chichester, UK.

Hays Recruitment (2007) Portraying Generation Y. Available at: http://www.hays.com.au/news/ausworkplace/issue4b.aspx

House of Representatives (2007) *Current Vacancies; Workforce Challenges Facing the Australian Tourism Sector.* Standing Committee on Employment, Workplace Relations and Workforce Participation, Canberra.

McCrindle Research (2005) Generation Map Study. Available at: https://campaigns.drake.com.au/cpa/htm/htm_resourcecentre.asp

Patterson, B. (2007) A–Z of Generation Y. *Sunday Herald Sun*, July 08. Available at: http://www.news.com.au/heraldsun/story/0,21985,22034750–5006016,00.html

Preston, M. (2007) Who'd Hire a Gen-Y? 6 August 2007. Available at: http://www.smartcompany.com.au/Premium-Articles/Top-Story/Whod-hire-a-Gen-Y.html

Reynol, J. and Mastrodicasa, J. (2007) *Connecting to the Net.Generation: What Higher Education Professionals Need to Know About Today's College Students.* NASPA, Washington, DC.

Sheahan, P. (2005) *Generation Y; Thriving and Surviving with Generation Y at Work*. Hardy Grant Books, Melbourne, Australia.

The Daily Telegraph (2007) Overconfident and Overpaid. 15 May. Available at: http://www.news.com.au/story/0,23599,21733545–2,00.html?from=public_rss?CMP=KNC-google

Timo, N. and Davidson, M. (2005) A survey of employee relations practices and demographics of MNC chain and domestic luxury hotels in Australia. *Employee Relations* 27(2), 175–92.

Tourism Transport Federation (2006) *Labour Turnover and Costs in the Australian Accommodation Industry*. Tourism Transport Federation (TTF), Royal Exchange, New South Wales, Australia.

Weiss, M.J. (2003) To be about to be – Generation Y. *American Demographics* 25(7), 28–36.

14 Generation Y's Future Tourism Demand: Some Opportunities and Challenges

Petra Glover

School of Tourism, The University of Queensland and University of East London

Introduction

In recent years, a growing interest in generations and their behavioural characteristics has emerged. While the focus was initially on Baby Boomers (Cornman and Kingson, 1996; Muller, 1997; Cleaver *et al*., 2000; Cleaver and Muller, 2002) an increasing number of studies have started investigating the younger generations, especially Generation Y, by focusing on two aspects: workplace expectations and behaviour (Eisner, 2005; Sheahan, 2005; Broadbridge *et al*., 2007; Kim *et al*., 2009); and consumption preferences and patterns, including those for tourism products (e.g. Ateljevic and Harris, 2004; Treloar *et al*., 2004; Ma and Niehm, 2006; Noble *et al*., 2009). The interest in Generation Y seems to stem (similarly to the interest in the Baby Boomers) from its size and purchasing power, but it is also linked to its value system, which is considered to lead to behaviour that is perceived to be significantly different from the earlier Generation X and the Baby Boomers. Such studies address current behaviour and preferences among Generation Y, thus aiming to present product and service providers as well as employers with information and strategies that may assist them in dealing with the current needs of Generation Y.

This chapter, in contrast, focuses on future behaviour, specifically on tourism demand preferences that may be expected from the older members of Generation Y by 2020. For the purpose of this chapter, Generation Y includes everyone born between 1977 and 1998. According to this classification, the size of Generation Y in Australia in June 2007 was almost 6.3 million people, representing approximately 30% of the total population (Australian Bureau of Statistics, 2007). At the time of data collection, the older half of this generation was 18 years old and above (born between 1977 and 1988) and they will be in their 30s and early 40s in 2020. At this time they are expected to comprise a wide range of household structures, including singles, childless couples, single parents and couples with children in different age brackets.

Given the controversy that surrounds the analysis of generation-based behaviour, the chapter starts with a discussion of the value of understanding generational differences between consumer groups. This is followed by providing some insight into the older Generation Y's future tourism demand characteristics and the opportunities and challenges that may arise in the medium- to long-term from generation-related demand changes.

The Value of Generations for Tourism Research

A generation is understood to be a group of people born during the same period of time, and who experience the influence of the same cultural, economic, social, intellectual and political environment (Mackay, 1997; MacManus, 1997). Due to external influences prevalent in their formative years, each generation is expected to display behavioural and consumption patterns that differentiate it from the previous and subsequent generation (Rentz et al., 1983; Rentz and Reynolds, 1991; Meredith and Schewe, 1994; Schewe and Noble, 2000). As the boundaries between external influences are often hard to pinpoint, definitions of specific generations vary between authors and countries (Edmondson, 1995; Tapscott, 1998; Hicks and Hicks, 1999; Tulgan, 2000; Marconi, 2001). It can be argued that the exact delimitation of a generation is not that critical since the values, attitudes and beliefs that define each generation do not change abruptly from one year to the next. Instead, a transition period exists in which values of the older generation subside and those of the younger generation emerge. In addition, Generation Y is a very recent generation, still in the process of defining itself, which causes difficulties in setting a distinct end date.

For tourism purposes, travel-related events may add to defining a generation (Pennington-Gray et al., 2003). As a result of the increasing freedom to travel, growing range of tourism opportunities and greater choice of tourist destinations and activities, each generation, and in particular Generation Y, has been able to accumulate a distinctive set of tourism experiences in the past to which they will add new experiences in the future. Due to their specific set of travel experiences, each generation displays tourism demand characteristics at a given age that is different from the previous or following generation at the same age. If destinations are unable to identify and adapt to these changing demand patterns, they risk decline (Glover and Prideaux, 2009).

However, not all behaviour can be attributed to generational membership because the tourist's age and family life-cycle stage also have a role to play. While some of Generation Y's future tourism demand characteristics may resemble those of older generations at the same age, others reveal distinct differences. Although leisure behaviour (including tourism demand) may be heavily influenced by an individual's family composition and the corresponding stage in their family life cycle (Cosenza and Davis, 1981; Godbey, 2003; Hong et al., 2005), it may be more useful to employ the concept of generations to explain tourism behaviour (Oppermann, 1995). One reason for this may lie in changing family values. The younger generations' reluctance to have children, their delay of marriage, the rise of divorce rates, and the increase of single-parent households result in fewer people progressing through the traditional life-cycle stages, which reduces the value of the family life cycle as a predictive tool. Although family holidays undertaken by future Generation-Y parents may be similar to those taken by Baby-Boomer parents in the past, overall tourism demand may differ due to the growing importance of the demand patterns displayed by a higher number of travelling singles, single parents and childless singles and couples.

The benefits of using generations to identify consumption patterns has been questioned (Marconi, 2001) because it ignores the wide range of personal values, attitudes and beliefs that shape individual preferences and behaviour, thus leading to a variety of demand patterns and market segments within each generation. However, it can be argued that in this respect, generations are similar to cultures. Research into cultures shows that it may be useful for tourism operators to understand the common values, beliefs and attitudes that are shared among people from a specific cultural background, in order to provide adequate products and services and to communicate effectively with international tourists (Reisinger and Turner, 1998, 2002a,b; MacKay and Fesenmaier, 2000; Weiermair, 2000). Nevertheless, despite a shared culture, not all individuals have exactly the same product preferences, as they may not necessarily embrace common cultural values and may instead hold their own values, beliefs and attitudes (Tuleja, 2005). Similarly, members of a generation have a shared value system which may enable tourism providers to gain an idea of general consumption preferences. As each generation grows older, it maintains generation-specific values that influence its current and future consumption patterns, thus providing some indication for future tourism demand (Born *et al.*, 2000; Lohmann and Danielsson, 2001).

In a tourism context, construction, investment and profitability timelines, as well as the consideration of sustainability issues, imply that a long-term view to planning is useful. This long-term view should incorporate potential shifts in broad tourism demand patterns that may be due to the different values held by subsequent generations. Yet, marketing activities, including the design of products, pricing, the selection of distribution channels and the choice of promotional activities (Kotler *et al.*, 1998) need to be more specific to individual market segments in order to be successful. Targeting an entire generation is unlikely to be suitable for specific marketing and promotion purposes, as this approach would fail to acknowledge the vast differences that may exist within a generation (Marconi, 2001). Nevertheless, an understanding of generational consumption preferences may be useful as a broad frame of reference when addressing a particular generation's needs and wants, especially when a long-term view is adopted.

Aspects of Generation Y's Future Tourism Demand

To obtain an understanding of Generation Y's future tourism demand expectations, two studies were undertaken in Queensland, Australia. In 2004, 14 members of Generation Y were consulted during two focus group interviews to share their views on the type of tourism activities that they anticipated undertaking in the future. This exploratory study was followed up by a self-administered survey among 253 members of Generation Y over the Christmas school holiday period in 2005–2006. It contained 28 Likert-scale questions asking for their level of agreement with statements on their future tourism preferences. Since respondents had to be at least 18 years of age at the time of the research, only the older members of this generation were included in the study. The year 2020 was stated as the projection date, when respondents will be between 32 and 43 years old. If they have children, they are most likely to represent a wide range of family structures with many having young or school-age children.

As mentioned earlier, each generation is influenced by the social and economic opportunities prevalent when they are growing up, including the developments in tourism and travel. Generation Y is raised in an environment with a wide and increasing range of tourism and travel opportunities. In recent years, the introduction of low-cost carriers has made travel more accessible not only within Australia, but also to overseas destinations. Many members of Generation Y are experienced travellers and have a strong awareness of travel opportunities. Having accompanied their parents on domestic and international holidays from a young age, they have a strong interest in visiting domestic and overseas destinations by themselves. This becomes evident in the rise of the number of backpackers travelling to an increasing number of destinations that has resulted in the growth of accommodation, tours and activities specifically targeted at this market segment. The survey revealed a continuing interest in tourism activities as the majority of respondents expressed an expectation to travel more frequently in the future. This may provide opportunities for the Australian tourism industry if they are able to offer products and destinations that suit Generation Y's needs. Nevertheless, the expectation of more frequent holiday travel does not guarantee higher visitation for domestic destinations if overseas destinations are considered to be more attractive.

In fact, Generation Y's attitude towards overseas travel was very positive, to the point where it was almost seen as an obligation or a rite of passage. One participant in the focus group interviews suggested that her own and subsequent generations have 'got to go to London and they have to do this experience, they've got to go work overseas'. Although this reflects current behaviour, it is likely that the positive attitude towards overseas travel will continue. At the same time, new destinations have emerged, including in Eastern Europe, Asia, South America and the Pacific Islands. The experiences gained in their teens and early 20s are likely to shape Generation Y's future travel patterns so that foreign countries, including those with emerging tourism industries, remain attractive and desirable destinations. The survey results confirmed the fascination with international destinations and interest in international travel was more pronounced among Generation Y than among older generations. This finding may pose a challenge for the Australian tourism industry as it suggests an increasing level of competition from overseas destinations, particular with regards to targeting the Generation-Y market. By 2020, new destinations would have emerged and new access options would have been established to accommodate Generation Y's desire to travel overseas, which is most likely to challenge domestic tourism destinations. It is likely that similar tendencies apply to other countries as well since tourism opportunities present themselves for Generation Y worldwide.

Nevertheless, at the same time, opportunities may exist for the domestic tourism industry, as strong interest in visiting Australian destinations was also expressed by survey respondents. This may relate to the current practice of taking frequent short breaks by car in the surrounding areas or by plane around Australia, which was conveyed by a number of focus group participants. One respondents described his current traveller patterns as 'I sort of class even going away for a weekend as a holiday. And I do that pretty much every weekend'. Similarly, a female respondent stated that 'at the moment, I'm into short-breaking, because this is what we do really. Go away for three or four nights. Or we do long weekends'. Since this practice seems to be common among an increasing number of Generation-Y tourists today, it is likely to continue into the future. Unless advances in transport technology make an international weekend trip feasible from Australia, the 'weekend away' mindset will provide opportunities for domestic destinations to attract the weekender market as long as they are easily accessible and provide the features expected by Generation Y for its short getaways.

In addition to short breaks, some opportunities may also exist in the market of longer domestic holidays. The interest in taking longer holidays in Australia was clearly related to respondents' expectations regarding their future family composition. Some focus group participants believed that they would take more domestic drive holidays if they had children in the future for reasons of both cost and prac-

ticality. One respondent stated that she enjoyed travelling internationally and would like to continue doing so but she also asked the question: 'If you've got three kids from 1 to 5 are you going to be wanting to take them [overseas] with you?' Another respondent confirmed 'if I do have children I'd probably holiday here, but if I don't I'd probably travel overseas'. The importance of family composition was confirmed by the survey result and demonstrates the family life-cycle component of future tourism demand. Despite the projections that the proportion of families with children is likely to decline (Australian Bureau of Statistics, 2004), demand for the traditional family holiday will continue to exist as the total number of couple families with children may remain stable or even grow. Nevertheless, facilities need to be updated to suit the demands of Generation-Y parents and their children. In addition, as mentioned earlier, the growing number of singles and childless couples as projected by the Australian Bureau of Statistics (2004) results in a larger proportion of Generation-Y members to whom the life-cycle stages and their associated tourism and leisure behaviour do not apply. Demand preferences among childless tourists are most likely to vary significantly from those who travel with children. At the same time, single parents may have different demands and expectations from couple families with children. An increasing diversity of demand is likely to ensue, which may challenge the domestic tourism industry. A division between different types of accommodation, for example, is already noticeable today. The promotion of child-free resorts that offer quiet and relaxing holidays for couples are becoming as common as child-friendly resorts that advertise their wide range of facilities for children of all ages. While the traditional family life cycle may still apply to couple families with children, individual stages may be delayed due to later marriage and childbearing. At the same time, the provision of products and services that cater to a growing population of tourists that do not follow the life-cycle stages is also necessary and becomes an increasingly viable segment as they no longer represent a niche market.

The challenges regarding the provision of tourism facilities become even more paramount as a result of the uncertainty associated with identifying the future population composition and structure. In Australia, three scenarios of population projections suggest that the share of traditional families with children among all family types may fall from 47% (2001) to between 33 and 42% in 2021. The future development of their actual number is less clear as it may either increase or decline by up to 16% between 2001 and 2021. Over the same period, one-parent families, couples without children and lone-person households are projected to increase both in terms of actual number and with regard to their share of total families in Australia, but the level of growth differs between the three projection series (Australian Bureau of Statistics, 2004). As a result of this uncertainty, tourism destinations and providers need to keep a close eye on the actual development of family structures in order to ensure that they offer the appropriate level of family-oriented tourism products and services.

Besides the significance of family values held by Generation Y, the influence of the economic environment in which it is growing up and entering adulthood was evident in both the focus groups and the survey. Focus group participants anticipated cheaper airfares for both domestic and international travel, an expectation that is governed by the increasing number of low-cost carriers that service a growing number of domestic and international destinations. One respondent stated that 'I can see that we are going to be encouraged to travel more and more because of these great airfares' and that she could 'go to New Zealand for like seven days. It's an international destination, . . . they speak the same language, [and] it's cheaper [than domestic travel]'. Furthermore, they believed that they would continue using current and emerging electronic media to ensure that they get the best deal for each product component of their tourism experience. Both aspects were addressed in the survey by asking respondents about their expectations regarding the importance of value for money. Although the vast majority of respondents expected to have more financial resources available for travel in the future, the majority also revealed that getting value for money would become increasingly important for them. These results are compatible as the

concept of value for money sets the price that is paid for a product or service in relation to the quality of service and the ability to meet the customer's expectations. This results in another challenge for tourism destinations as it suggests a highly demanding consumer group which assesses not only the price and affordability of a tourism product but also its quality. As a result of their travel experience, Generation Y will be aware of what it should be able to expect at any given price. Thus, members are likely to seek high quality of product and service delivery but are only willing to pay a premium price for it if they believe that the product, service or experience is worth it.

Generation Y's travel experience was demonstrated by its evident curiosity in exploring destinations not previously visited, which was expressed in the focus group interviews and confirmed by the survey results. The importance of experiencing new destinations was conveyed by one participant stating that 'every year . . . I go somewhere different in Australia where I've never been to before'. Another respondent said that she was 'not really an Asia-person, I don't particularly do Asia' but that she had booked a holiday to Bali 'because it is experimental for me'. This attitude implies confidence in travelling to destinations that they are unfamiliar with. The challenge for tourism destinations is evident as it is likely to be extremely difficult for destinations to establish long-term relationships with Gen-Y customers, as repeat visitation is not a significant component of their mindset. This is consistent with the recent findings by a hospitality research organization that found Gen Y to be the least brand-loyal of all current generations (Barsky and Nash, 2006). This attitude may suggest that Generation Y is not very interested in using a particular hotel chain during its travels around the world or in participating in a frequent-flyer or other loyalty programme. Instead, it may be more likely to seek out independently owned and operated facilities with the aim of gaining a new and unique experience each time it travels.

The importance of uniqueness was underpinned by concerns expressed in the focus group interviews that globalization would make it more difficult to find destinations that are different. One respondent stated that 'we're seeing the start of cultures losing their cultural [significance] because...cultures are becoming too westernized'. Although this comment was related to Asian destinations, it clearly demonstrates the belief that it may become difficult to find different and new tourism experiences. As a result, destinations need to ensure that they offer a unique selling proposition (USP) that differentiates them from others both domestically and overseas. Given the number of emerging destinations worldwide, this objective is becoming increasingly difficult to achieve. This challenge may present itself not only with regards to future local Generation-Y tourists, but may also relate to overseas source markets. Since Australia is already an established destination among young travellers, they may not be very interested in returning to visit at an older age unless the country's future tourist attractions are perceived as providing a new experience. At the same time, opportunities may present themselves for established and

emerging destinations that are able to offer a distinctly different and unique experience.

The discussion of the travel and tourism expectations among today's older members of Generation Y has assisted in identifying some of the potential opportunities and challenges that arise for the future provision of tourism products and services. These are summarized in Table 14.1. However, it has to be acknowledged that the actual future tourism demand will also be subject to a wide range of other external influences. The global economic environment is only one example of an external factor that is likely to affect travel behaviour and the immediate purchase process at any time. For instance, while Generation Y may have a strong desire to travel overseas, cost, affordability and accessibility will need to be assessed to turn the potential into actual demand. The global economic crisis in 2008, which threatened the existence of some international airlines (Done, 2008; Sreenivasan, 2008), illustrates that external drivers may

Table 14.1. Opportunities and challenges derived from the study.

Gen-Y characteristics	Opportunities	Challenges
Previous travel experience	• More frequent travel may ease stagnant domestic market	• High expectations and demanding customers
Interest in overseas travel	• Continuing interest in destinations already visited by Gen Y (e.g. Australia) • Overseas travel as a 'rite of passage'	• Increasing competition from overseas markets • Pressure on domestic destinations
Interest in domestic destinations	• Short breaks to destinations that are accessible by car and air • Longer holidays among singles and couples with children	• Providing the tourism products and services that Gen Y demand • Catering for an increasingly diverse market
Greater diversity of family structures	• Marketing becomes viable for a higher number of market segments, e.g. specific facilities for childless singles and couples	• Difficulty in selecting individual or complementary target markets • Difficulty in anticipating future family structures due to the uncertainties involved
Familiarity with e-media	• Marketing value for money offers	• Providers require knowledge of and access to e-media • Need to provide value for money due to increasingly transparent marketing
Curiosity for new and unique destinations	• Market opportunities for emerging destinations and product innovation	• Difficulty in achieving repeat visitation • Need to provide 'fresh' and unique experiences to attract domestic and international Gen-Y tourists

represent barriers that could impede on realizing intended and desired tourism demand. Unfortunately, the discussion of all potential factors that are likely to influence future tourism behaviour is too complex and far-reaching to be included in this chapter.

Conclusion

This chapter has provided an overview of some of the opportunities and challenges that may arise in the future when the older members of Generation Y are in their 30s and early 40s and encompass a range of household and family structures. The findings from the two studies conducted in 2004 and 2005–2006 highlight that tourism providers, destination planners and policy makers face a number of challenges in trying to meet the future demands of Generation Y. While some aspects of tourism demand can be expected to remain unchanged, others are expected to differ from previous generations, or they are likely to be more diverse. Although a range of personal and external factors will affect the actual choice of destinations and activities or the affordability of travelling overseas, family composition is most likely to have an important role to play in making those decisions. Changing family values lead to a greater variety in family and household structures that is likely to increase the diversity of tourism demand among Generation Y. In addition, Generation Y's existing travel experience is reflected in a strong interest in travelling overseas, in the desire to explore a new destination on each holiday and in high service expectations. Although the discussion in this chapter is derived from two Australian-based studies, it is likely that similar behavioural patterns may emerge in other countries. For tourism providers, this signifies more intense competition from emerging and established international destinations, the need to offer tourism products and services that afford value for money and an increasing difficulty to develop lasting relationships with Generation-Y customers and to encourage repeat visitation.

Such challenges need to be addressed by tourism decision makers to take advantage of the opportunities that arise simultaneously. Innovative and forward-thinking destinations that embrace these challenges are likely to turn them into opportunities. Tourism providers that can successfully implement strategies that identify and promote distinctive and unique destination features, and that assess the cost-efficiency of operations without compromising the quality of service delivery are likely to be competitive in the global marketplace. Furthermore, the greater diversity of demand is likely to produce a critical mass of tourist numbers that turns current niche markets into more mainstream market segments.

An understanding of the demand patterns displayed by Generation Y will provide a broad knowledge base of significant demand changes that may be expected to occur, as the large group of Generation Y continues to graduate from school and university and enters the workforce. It provides opportunities to anticipate changing demand patterns and to put actions in place that address these medium- to long-term changes, thus increasing the probability of providing competitive tourism experiences and destinations. Nevertheless, generational values, attitudes and beliefs and the ensuing demand characteristics need to be evaluated carefully, since the exclusive consideration of generations may lead to misjudgement of the range and diversity of market segments within each generation. Furthermore, they cannot be assessed in isolation but need to be evaluated within the complex system of macro-environmental drivers that affect tourism supply and demand.

References

Ateljevic, I. and Harris, C. (2004) Being cool: Generation Y and tourism. In: Cooper, C., Arcodia, C., Solnet, D. and Whitford, M. (eds) *Creating Tourism Knowledge: Proceedings of the CAUTHE Conference 2004, Brisbane (CD-Rom)*. The University of Queensland, Brisbane, Australia.

Australian Bureau of Statistics (2004) *Household and Family Projections, Australia, 2001 to 2026*, Cat. No. 3236.0. Australian Bureau of Statistics, Canberra.

Australian Bureau of Statistics (2007) *Population by Age and Sex – Australian States and Territories, June 2007*, Cat. No. 3201.0. Australian Bureau of Statistics, Canberra.

Barsky, J. and Nash, L. (2006) Bridge generation gap by knowing guests' wants, needs. *Hotel & Motel Management* 221(21), 8–24.

Born, A., Middendorf, A.S., Perl, W., Bach, J., Weigel, R. and Wiemes, R. (2000) *Tourism in Einer Alternden Gesellschaft [Tourism in an Ageing Society]*. Europäische Gemeinschaft, Europäischer Sozialfond, Gemeinschaftsinitiative ADAPT, Gelsenkirchen, Germany.

Broadbridge, A.M., Maxwell, G.A. and Ogden, S.M. (2007) Students' views of retail employment: key findings from Generation Ys. *International Journal of Retail & Distribution Management* 35(12), 982–992.

Cleaver, M., Green, B.C. and Muller, T.E. (2000) Using consumer behavior research to understand the Baby Boomer tourist. *Journal of Hospitality & Tourism Research* 24(2), 274–287.

Cleaver, M. and Muller, T.E. (2002) The socially aware Baby Boomer: gaining a lifestyle-based understanding of the new wave of ecotourists. *Journal of Sustainable Tourism* 10(3), 173–190.

Cornman, J.M. and Kingson, E.R. (1996) Trends, issues, perspectives, and values for the aging of the baby boom cohorts. *The Gerontologist* 36(1), 15.

Cosenza, R.M. and Davis, D.L. (1981) Family vacation decision making over the family life cycle: a decision and influence structure analysis. *Journal of Travel Research* 20(2), 17–23.

Done, K. (2008) Air traffic growth at five-year low. *The Financial Times*, 30 September 2008.

Edmondson, B. (1995) The next baby boom. *American Demographics* 17(9), 2.

Eisner, S.P. (2005) Managing Generation Y. *S.A.M. Advanced Management Journal* 70(4), 4–15.

Glover, P. and Prideaux, B. (2009) Implications of population ageing for the development of tourism products and destinations. *Journal of Vacation Marketing* 15(1), 25–37.

Godbey, G. (2003) *Leisure in your Life: An Exploration*, 6th edn. Venture Publishing, State College, Pennsylvania.

Hicks, R. and Hicks, K. (1999) *Boomers, Xers and Other Strangers*. Tyndale House Publishers, Wheaton, Illinois.

Hong, G.-S., Fan, J.X., Palmer, L. and Bhargava, V. (2005) Leisure travel expenditure patterns by family life cycle stages. *Journal of Travel & Tourism Marketing* 18(2), 15–30.

Kim, H., Knight, D.K. and Crutsinger, C. (2009) Generation Y employees' retail work experience: the mediating effect of job characteristics. *Journal of Business Research* 62(5), 548–556.

Kotler, P., Armstrong, G., Brown, L. and Adam, S. (1998) *Marketing*, 4th edn. Prentice-Hall, Sydney, New York, Toronto.

Lohmann, M. and Danielsson, J. (2001) Predicting travel patterns of senior citizens: how the past may provide a key to the future. *Journal of Vacation Marketing* 7(4), 357–366.

Ma, Y.J. and Niehm, L.S. (2006) Service expectations of older generation Y customers: an examination of apparel retail settings. *Managing Service Quality* 16(6), 620–640.

Mackay, H. (1997) *Generations*. Pan Macmillan, Sydney, Australia.

MacKay, K.J. and Fesenmaier, D.R. (2000) An exploration of cross-cultural destination image assessment. *Journal of Travel Research* 38(4), 417–423.

MacManus, S.A. (1997) The Nation's changing age profile: what does it mean? In: Thau, R.D. and Heflin, J.S. (eds) *Generations Apart: Xers vs. Boomers vs. The Elderly*. Prometheus Books, Amherst, New York, pp. 110–139.

Marconi, J. (2001) *Future Marketing: Targeting Seniors, Boomers, and Generations X and Y*. NTC Business Books: in conjunction with The American Marketing Association, Lincolnwood, Illinois.

Meredith, G. and Schewe, C. (1994) The power of cohorts. *American Demographics* 16(12), 22–31.

Muller, T.E. (1997) The benevolent society: value and lifestyle changes among middle-aged baby boomers. In: Kahle, L.R. and Chiagouris, L. (eds) *Values, Lifestyles and Psychographics*. Lawrence Erlbaum Associates, Mahwah, New Jersey, pp. 299–316.

Noble, S.M., Haytko, D.L. and Phillips, J. (2009) What drives college-age Generation Y consumers? *Journal of Business Research* 62(6), 617–628.

Oppermann, M. (1995) Travel life cycle. *Annals of Tourism Research* 22(3), 535–552.

Pennington-Gray, L., Fridgen, J.D. and Stynes, D. (2003) Cohort segmentation: an application to tourism. *Leisure Sciences* 25(4), 341–361.

Reisinger, Y. and Turner, L.W. (1998) Asian and western cultural differences: the new challenge for tourism marketplaces. *Journal of International Hospitality, Leisure and Tourism Management* 1(3), 21–35.

Reisinger, Y. and Turner, L.W. (2002a) Cultural differences between Asian tourist markets and Australian hosts: part 1. *Journal of Travel Research* 40(3), 295–315.

Reisinger, Y. and Turner, L.W. (2002b) Cultural differences between Asian tourist markets and Australian hosts: part 2. *Journal of Travel Research* 40(4), 374–384.

Rentz, J.O. and Reynolds, F.D. (1991) Forecasting the effects of an aging population on product consumption: an age-period-cohort framework. *Journal of Marketing Research* 28(3), 355–360.

Rentz, J.O., Reynolds, F.D. and Stout, R.G. (1983) Analyzing changing consumption patterns with cohort analysis. *Journal of Marketing Research* 20(1), 12–20.

Schewe, C.D. and Noble, S.M. (2000) Market segmentation by cohorts: the value and validity of cohorts in America and abroad. *Journal of Marketing Management* 16(1–3), 129–142.

Sheahan, P. (2005) *Generation Y: Thriving and Surviving with Generation Y at Work*. Hardie Grant Books, Prahran, Victoria, Australia.

Sreenivasan, V. (2008) Financial crisis hurting Asia-Pac airlines. *Business Times Singapore*, 2 October 2008.

Tapscott, D. (1998) *Growing up Digital: The Rise of the Net Generation*. McGraw-Hill, New York.

Treloar, P., Hall, C.M. and Mitchell, R. (2004) Wine tourism and the generation Y market: any possibilities? In: Cooper, C., Arcodia, C., Solnet, D. and Whitmore, M. (eds) *Creating Tourism Knowledge: Proceedings of the CAUTHE Conference 2004, Brisbane (CD-Rom)*. The University of Queensland, Brisbane, Australia.

Tuleja, E.A. (2005) *Intercultural Communication for Business*. Managerial communication series. Thomson South-Western, Mason, Ohio.

Tulgan, B. (2000) *Managing Generation X: How to Bring Out the Best in Young Talent*. Revised and updated edn, W.W. Norton, New York.

Weiermair, K. (2000) Tourists' perceptions towards and satisfaction with service quality in the cross-cultural service encounter: implications for hospitality and tourism management. *Managing Service Quality* 10(6), 397–409.

Index